The Social Psychology of Health

The Claremont Symposium on Applied Social Psychology

This series of volumes highlights important new developments on the leading edge of applied social psychology. Each volume concentrates on one area where social psychological knowledge is being applied to the resolution of social problems. Within that area, a distinguished group of authorities present chapters summarizing recent theoretical views and empirical findings, including the results of their own research and applied activities. An introductory chapter integrates this material, pointing out common themes and varied areas of practical applications. Thus each volume brings together trenchant new social psychological ideas, research results, and fruitful applications bearing on an area of current social interest. The volumes will be of value not only to practitioners and researchers, but also to students and lay people interested in this vital and expanding area of psychology.

Books in the Series

Interpersonal Processes, *Stuart Oskamp and Shirlynn Spacapan, Editors*

The Social Psychology of Health, *Shirlynn Spacapan and Stuart Oskamp, Editors*

The Social Psychology of Aging, *Shirlynn Spacapan and Stuart Oskamp, Editors*

The Social Psychology of Health

Shirlynn Spacapan
Stuart Oskamp
Editors

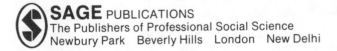

**The Claremont Symposium on
Applied Social Psychology**

SAGE PUBLICATIONS
The Publishers of Professional Social Science
Newbury Park   Beverly Hills   London   New Delhi

For information address:

SAGE Publications, Inc.
2111 West Hillcrest Drive
Newbury Park, California 91320

SAGE Publications Inc.
275 South Beverly Drive
Beverly Hills
California 90212

SAGE Publications Ltd.
28 Banner Street
London EC1Y 8QE
England

SAGE PUBLICATIONS India Pvt. Ltd.
M-32 Market
Greater Kailash I
New Delhi 110 048 India

Printed in the United States of America

Library of Congress Cataloging-in-Publication Data

Claremont Symposium on Applied Social Psychology (4th : 1987)
    The social psychology of health / the Claremont Symposium on
Applied Social Psychology ; edited by Shirlynn Spacapan, Stuart
Oskamp.
        p.   cm.
    Bibliography: p.
    Includes indexes.
    ISBN 0-8039-3162-X   ISBN 0-8039-3163-8 (pbk.)
    1. Clinical health psychology—Congresses.   2. Social psychology—
Congresses.   3. Stress (Psychology)—Congresses.   4. Health
promotion—Congresses.   I. Spacapan, Shirlynn.   II. Oskamp, Stuart.
III. Title.
R726.7.C58 1987
362.1'042—dc19   87-35339
                                                        CIP

FIRST PRINTING 1988

Contents

Preface

The chapters in this volume are based on presentations given at the Claremont Symposium on Applied Social Psychology, held on February 14, 1987. This was the fourth annual conference held at the Claremont Graduate School, bringing outstanding psychologists from various sections of the country to join in discussion and analysis of important topics and issues in the field of applied social psychology. We are grateful for financial support for the past conferences from all six Claremont Colleges (Claremont Graduate School, Claremont McKenna College, Harvey Mudd College, Pitzer College, Pomona College, and Scripps College). This year, we are also indebted to the Haynes Foundation and Harvey Mudd College for fellowships, which enabled the first editor to work on this volume.

To reflect the conference panel discussions and to provide a fuller integration of the several chapters, we have included introductory chapters of background material for each of the two parts of this volume: Psychosocial Mediators of Health Status and Health Promotion. We also encouraged each of the contributing authors to incorporate material addressing some of the questions raised by the audience.

These papers make valuable contributions to the burgeoning field of health psychology. We hope this volume will be interesting and useful to researchers and practitioners in the areas of both social psychology and health psychology, as well as to scholars who want to know more about applied aspects of the field.

Shirlynn Spacapan
Stuart Oskamp
Claremont, California

1

Social Psychology
and Health

SHIRLYNN SPACAPAN

When one mentions psychology and health in the same breath, the most typical connection is the one with mental health. Recently, however, psychologists have studied such varied aspects of physical health as hypertension, coronary artery disease, cancer, gastrointestinal disorders, upper respiratory ailments, and obesity. These new "health psychologists" are interested in illnesses that are not explained by the biological model, and in the behavioral responses (including cognitive and emotional responses) that can contribute to any illness. Essential hypertension, for example, does not fit well in the traditional biological model—it is not caused by microorganisms, nor by physiological dysfunction—but it develops over a person's lifetime and may be related to behaviors like eating and smoking, or responses to stress. Some of the early research in health psychology focused on the role of stress in the relationship between behavior and health; today, health psychologists are interested in "any aspect of psychology that is relevant to understanding health behavior and experiences that people have in relation to health and illness" (Stone, quoted in Krupat, 1982, p. 381).

What do social psychologists have to contribute to psychology's rediscovery of the body as well as the mind? Some of the classic areas of study for social psychology include attitudes, attributions, conformity, influence, group behavior, and interpersonal relations. For each of these areas, there is a variety of potential applications to the health care field. A social psychologist might study, for example, whether people who typically attribute their outcomes to internal factors are more likely to take preventive measures to insure their good health, and whether those who typically make external attributions are more likely to rely on an outside "expert" to prescribe some cure for their poor health. With respect to conformity, a social psychologist might explore the role of peer pressure in leading individuals into diseases of lifestyle (e.g., ones involving smoking, drinking, overeating). As another example, a social psychologist might study the potentially beneficial effects of good interpersonal relations in recovery from illness and surgery. In summary, social psychological research can be very helpful in understanding the relationship between behaviors and health.

In fact, a number of social psychologists have begun to orient their work on traditional psychosocial topics toward application to health-related issues. Two major examples of this approach involve the study of doctor-patient relationships and examinations of the "patient role" in hospital settings. In the first case, social psychological work on conformity and obedience to authority (e.g., Milgram, 1974) has provided a background for exploring patients' reluctance to adhere to regimens specified by their doctors (see Harrison, Caplan, French, & Wellons, 1982). Research in this field is sometimes termed "noncompliance" and reveals that anywhere from 15% to 93% of patients do not cooperate with their doctors' recommendations (DiMatteo, 1979). Attempts to illuminate the causes of this phenomenon (with the goal of avoiding potentially harmful consequences of this lack of cooperation) are not facilitated by labeling the problem as one of "noncompliance." Noncompliance implies that the problem is the patient's, and that there is some failure on the part of the patient. Social psychological study, however, underscores the importance and complexity of the doctor-patient relationship: "compliance" increases dramatically with increases in patient satisfaction with a physician's friendliness/warmth (Francis, Korsch, & Morris, 1969), informative consultations (Stone, 1979), and feedback to the patient (Davis, 1968), among other things.

A second example of a social psychological approach to health involves study of the "patient role" in hospital settings. Applying the social psychological concepts of roles and norms, Taylor (1979) has identified and examined the consequences of two general types of patient roles. According to her analysis, some hospitalized individuals take on a "good patient" role: they are passive, unquestioning, and behave "properly." The positive consequences of this role include being well-liked by the staff, who in turn respond quickly to the "good patient's" emergencies. Like many roles, that of the "good patient" is somewhat superficial and Taylor suggests that, behind the facade, the patient may begin to feel helpless, powerless, anxious, and depressed. The eventual consequences of these thoughts and feelings can include a variety of negative health outcomes, such as possible norepinephrine depletion and a gradual erosion of health; the phenomenon of helplessness has also been found to be related to sudden death. In contrast, other people take on a "bad-patient" role characterized by complaining to the staff, demanding attention, disobeying staff orders, and generally "misbehaving." This refusal to become helpless, and the accompanying anger, may paradoxically have the positive consequences of actually helping these "bad" patients to recover, for they are taking a role in their own health care. The negative side of "bad" patient behavior, however, can involve possible aggravation of conditions like hypertension or angina, as well as staff responses of ignoring, over-medicating, or prematurely discharging "bad" patients (Taylor, 1979).

How can the stressfulness of hospitalization be alleviated? A rapidly developing body of knowledge suggests that there are a number of cognitive and social factors that may ameliorate the negative effects of institutionalization. Some of these factors—predictability of events, feelings of perceived control, realistic prior expectations—have been studied in relation to lessening the negative impact of environmental stressors (e.g., noise, crowding, cold, pollution). Health psychologists have found that these same factors are effective in improving the health of patients in institutional settings (see Langer & Rodin, 1976). One factor that is particularly important from a social psychological perspective is that of "social support"—belonging to a network of people who care about and value us as individuals. According to recent research, social support is a potentially powerful moderator of a variety of stressful life events; it not only can facilitate recovery from illness but also may serve to "buffer" individuals from stress and thus inhibit the onset of illness (see Taylor, 1986, p. 208). Several of these social and cognitive variables are now being listed, along with immune responses and disease states, as critical mediators of health status (Kaplan, 1984).

An understanding of the factors that may reduce or prevent the stress associated with illness is a crucial component of various efforts at health promotion. In general, "health promotion" refers to community and individual programs that encourage life-styles that enhance health (Califano, 1979). In addition to applying the knowledge we have of psychosocial mediators of health status, the field of health promotion draws on other traditional areas of social psychology: the study of attitudes, persuasive messages, social influence, and behavior change. While the cost-effectiveness of some health promotion programs has been questioned (see Kaplan, 1984, for examples), the potential benefits of promoting healthy life-styles are great. Harris (1980) has suggested that life-style accounts for about 50% of mortality from the 10 leading causes of death, with environmental factors contributing about 20% (20% is also attributed to heredity and 10% to inadequate medical services). Similarly, other proponents of health promotion efforts have noted that life-style is a major factor in 7 of the 10 leading causes of death (Terborg, 1986).

Many of the ideas behind the research just discussed are not original to social psychology: The idea that the relationship between physician and patient was important for the recovery of the patient was noted by Hippocrates in the fourth century B.C., and philosophers discussed the importance of people's social needs long before social psychologists coined the term *social support.* What is new is the involvement of concerned social scientists, applying their special skills and empirical findings to facilitate more humane health care services.

Overview of the Volume

The two sections of this volume focus on these two major aspects of health psychology—psychosocial mediators of health status, and health promotion. Both parts begin with brief overviews of the topic, which provide useful background information. Following each introduction are three substantive chapters by distinguished authorities in the field, offering fresh ideas, theory, and/or new research findings.

Part I, Psychosocial Mediators of Health Status, focuses on those social, cognitive, and contextual factors that may reduce or prevent the stress associated with illness. In the first contributed chapter, Sheldon Cohen and Gail Williamson present normative data for Cohen's Perceived Stress Scale, collected as part of a nationwide Harris poll. Their chapter describes in detail the psychometric characteristics of the Perceived Stress Scale, and provides information on the relationship between perceived stress and health behaviors, such as the utilization of health services. Next, Suzanne Thompson, Paul Cheek, and Melody Graham discuss the cognitive factor of "perceived control." To counterbalance the conventional wisdom that perceived control can alleviate some of the stressfulness of an event, they take a careful look at "the other side of the coin," that is, the possible negative consequences to an individual who perceives or exercises control in a situation. Practitioners aiming to design interventions to enhance control in health settings will find a helpful section of this chapter devoted to the practical implications of such interventions. In Chapter 5, Shelley Taylor and Gayle Dakof provide an overview of the literature on the role of social support in reducing the impact of stressful events. They focus on the particularly stressful event of cancer and present empirical evidence about the levels of social support given cancer patients by their significant others, as well as information on problems in social support experienced by cancer patients.

Health promotion efforts are the topic of the second half of this volume. In the first contributed chapter of Part II, James Terborg discusses the corporation, or work setting, as a context for health promotion, and he gives examples of health promotion programs in two very different companies. Applied social psychologists will be particularly intrigued by a section of this chapter in which Terborg suggests that the very things that a careful researcher would avoid in a field study (e.g., threats to validity, as noted by Cook & Campbell, 1979) can be used as "leverage points" to enhance the success of interventions in an organizational setting. In Chapter 8, Nathan Maccoby discusses the noteworthy Stanford Heart Disease Prevention Program, which relies on a multimedia approach combined with community/neighborhood organization efforts. An overview of results from the famous Three-Community Study and the rationale and theory behind the ongoing Five-City Project are provided by Maccoby. In the final chapter, Robert M. Kaplan provides a broad overview of health promotion, emphasizing the issue of promoting people's quality of life. Noting that it is difficult to estimate the costs and benefits of many health promotion efforts, Kaplan argues that public policy on health promotion and medical care should be guided by a consideration of the relative costs of competing alternatives for enhancing health. Kaplan's message provides a fitting conclusion for the volume: Applied social psychology can play an important role in shaping public policy in the effective, efficient use of health care resources.

References

Califano, J. A. (1979). *Healthy people: The Surgeon General's report on health promotion and disease prevention.* Washington, DC: U.S. Government Printing Office.

Cook, T. D., & Campbell, D. T. (1979). *Quasi-experimentation: Design and analysis issues for field settings.* Chicago: Rand McNally.

Davis, M. S. (1968). Variations in patients' compliance with doctor's advice: An empirical analysis of patterns of communication. *American Journal of Public Health, 58,* 274-288.

DiMatteo, M. R. (1979). A social psychological analysis of patient-physician rapport: Toward a science of the art of medicine. *Journal of Social Issues, 35*(1), 34-59.

Francis, V., Korsch, B. M., & Morris, M. J. (1969). Gaps in doctor-patient communication. *New England Journal of Medicine, 280,* 535-540.

Harris, P. R. (1980). *Promoting health—preventing disease: Objectives for the nation.* Washington, DC: U.S. Government Printing Office.

Harrison, R. V., Caplan, R. D., French, J.R.P., Jr., & Wellons, R. V. (1982). Combining field experiments with longitudinal surveys: Social research on patient adherence. In L. Bickman (Ed.), *Applied social psychology annual* (Vol. 3). Beverly Hills, CA: Sage.

Kaplan, R. M. (1984). Connection between clinical health promotion and health status: A critical overview. *American Psychologist, 39,* 755-765.

Krupat, E. (1982). *Psychology is social.* Glenview, IL: Scott, Foresman.

Langer, E., & Rodin, J. (1976). The effects of choice and enhanced personal responsibility for the aged: A field experiment in an institutional setting. *Journal of Personality and Social Psychology, 34,* 191-198.

Milgram, S. (1974). *Obedience to authority.* New York: Harper & Row.

Stone, G. C. (1979). Patient compliance and the role of the expert. *Journal of Social Issues, 35*(1), 34-59.

Taylor, S. E. (1979). Hospital patient behavior: Reactance, helplessness, or control? *Journal of Social Issues, 35*(1), 156-184.

Taylor, S. E. (1986). *Health psychology.* New York: Random House.

Terborg, J. R. (1986). Health promotion at the worksite. In K. H. Rowland & G. R. Ferris (Eds.), *Research in personnel and human management* (Vol. 4). Greenwich, CT: JAI.

PART I

PSYCHOSOCIAL MEDIATORS OF HEALTH STATUS

2

Psychosocial Mediators of Health Status: An Introduction

SHIRLYNN SPACAPAN

Some of the earliest research that falls within the general rubric of "health psychology" focused on the role of stress in the development of illness. Hans Selye (1956), one of the pioneers in stress research (see also, Cannon, 1914), proposed the now-famous "general adaptation syndrome," involving a three-phase, biological model of the relationship between stress and illness. When confronted with a stressor, an organism mobilizes its resources to meet the demand, according to Selye. This "alarm stage" is followed by a stage of "resistance" in which the organism attempts to cope with, or confront, the stressor. If stress is prolonged, "exhaustion" sets in and the organism is vulnerable to disease, tissue damage, and even death.

Subsequent theorists have proposed a variety of other models of the stress-illness relationship (for overviews, see DiMatteo & Friedman, 1982, chap. 7; Taylor, 1986, chap. 6). In each alternative model, the intermediate steps from stress to illness vary. For instance, stress may alter one's normal behavior patterns to the extent that an individual actually adopts unhealthy behaviors—for example, consuming alcohol, sleeping too little—that result in poor health (Conway, Vickers, Ward, & Rahe, 1981). As a second example, the physiological symptoms of stress may be misinterpreted as illness symptoms by an individual who, in the process of dealing with the supposed illness, is reinforced for playing a "sick role" by escaping the otherwise stressful situation of work, a bad relationship, and so on. (Mechanic, 1976, 1978). In this latter model, stress does not necessarily lead to illness per se, but to "illness behavior."

What evidence do we have that stress leads to illness? Selye viewed stress as the "nonspecific response" of the body to any demand made upon it, and one line of research on the stress-illness link has examined a host of "life events" as possible predictors of the onset of disease. In the best-known scales for measuring stressful life events, the Social Readjustment Rating Scale (SRRS) (Holmes & Rahe, 1967b) and the subsequent Schedule of Recent Experiences (SRE) (Holmes & Rahe, 1967a), individuals are asked to indicate which of 43 events they have experienced in the recent past. Each event has a corresponding point value (e.g., death of a spouse has the highest point value of 100, and a minor traffic violation has the lowest of 12), and the sum of an individual's points has been used as a predictor of possible illness. A large number of prospective and retrospective studies have indicated that there is a positive correlation between the total score on these life events and the possibility of illness, but the relationship is only a modest one. More recently, researchers have noted that the minor trials and tribulations of our daily lives may also take their toll on our health. To this end, scales of daily "hassles" (Kanner, Coyne, Schaefer, & Lazarus, 1981) have been developed, and research has indicated that hassles may be a better predictor of health than are major life events (DeLongis, Coyne, Dakof, Folkman, & Lazarus, 1982).

There are a variety of reasons for the lack of a strong relationship between these objective measures of stressful events and health outcomes (Kasl, 1983). In addition to methodological problems and criticisms of the instruments themselves, there are a number of moderators in the chain of events that runs from the initial exposure to a stressor through potentially negative health consequences. Each of the three subsequent chapters in this volume addresses different aspects of psychosocial mediators of health status. In the remainder of this chapter, we introduce relevant background material on several important moderators of the stress-illness relationship and provide overviews of the content of this half of the volume.

Perceived Stress

In contrast to Selye's rather direct physiological route from stress to illness, Lazarus (1966) has developed a more psychological emphasis in his work on stress. In recent years, in fact, cognitive models of the stress process have virtually dominated the field. Sells (1970), for example, argues that stress arises when (a) an individual does not have an appropriate response for a given situation, and (b) the consequences of failure to respond are important to the individual. Lazarus has suggested a two-step process by which an objective event is appraised (Lazarus & Launier, 1978). In "primary appraisal," individuals first appraise an event as to whether it presents a *threat* of some future danger, a *challenge* to overcome, or *harm* or loss that has already occurred. If the event presents one of these possibilities, it is still not "stressful" unless, through a "secondary appraisal," individuals take stock of their resources and realize that they have no means to cope with the event. This, then, suggests a model of the stress-illness relationship as: (potentially stressful) event → primary appraisal → secondary appraisal → event appraised as stressful → stress reaction, involving physiological, cognitive, emotional, or behavioral responses → illness.

Subsequent research has demonstrated that there are a variety of cognitive and contextual factors that may ameliorate the potentially stressful effects of an event (see Cohen, 1980b). The belief that one can exercise some control over the event, or that one has friends who can help one cope with the event, may result in a secondary appraisal that the event is not, in fact, a stressor. Similarly, if one's attitude toward the event is positive, or if the event is seen as part of some larger, worthy project and little personal risk is perceived, "stress" effects will not occur. In short, the likelihood that an event will lead to stress, let alone illness, can be reduced by a number of factors. Moreover, considerable research has made it apparent that an individual's *perception* of an event—that is, a potential stressor—is more important than the objective event itself.

As Cohen, Kamarck, and Mermelstein (1983) have pointed out, it is rather surprising that this current, dominant view of stress has not been complemented by the development of measures of *perceived* stress. Using objective measures of life events, such as the SRE, in order to explore the link between stress and illness runs counter to cognitive models of the stress process, for it suggests that the events themselves are the cause of illness. Cohen and his colleagues note that there are advantages to using the objective scales, as these measures are easy to administer and one can derive estimates of health risks as a result of an identifiable event. However, the gains that may be realized by measuring perceived stress are many, including the possibility of comparing objective and subjective measures of events for the role each may play in precipitating illness.

A "perceived stress scale" has been developed by Cohen and his colleagues in order to measure respondents' cognitive evaluation of stressors—that is, the degree to which individuals feel that the events of their lives are "unpredictable, uncontrollable, and overloading" (Cohen et al., 1983, p. 387). The instrument is a global one (i.e., not tied to specific events) and taps ongoing stress, anticipation of future stressors, and stress that one may be experiencing vicariously through a friend's or family member's life. It also differs from life-event scales in that it is directed at perceptions in the recent past (one month, in comparison to 6-12 months for life-event scales), and it is intended to be predictive of health outcomes in the near future (1-2 months, in comparison to several years for some life-event scales). Finally, there is evidence that the Perceived Stress Scale is a better predictor of health than are some life-event scales (Cohen, 1986; Cohen et al., 1983).

Chapter by Cohen and Williamson

In the following chapter, Sheldon Cohen and Gail Williamson provide new data on the Perceived Stress Scale (PSS) from a probability sample of the United States. As part of a larger survey conducted by Louis Harris and Associates in 1983, the PSS was administered to almost 2,400 individuals along with other measures of stress, life satisfaction, and health. Cohen and Williamson present analyses of these data with the goals of examining the psychometric qualities of the PSS, providing PSS norms, comparing the PSS to other measures of stress, and exploring the relationships between stress and health behaviors, including utilization of health services.

Readers who are not experts on perceived stress will appreciate the background information that Cohen and Williamson supply in the first section of their chapter. In reviewing early approaches to assessing stressful life events, they discuss the advantage of using a scale measuring generalized perceptions of stress, and they present the PSS in its entirety.

They also review the design of the PSS, along with earlier evidence of its validity. The authors address the controversy over the distinction between perceived stress and psychological distress, and they marshal convincing evidence that the PSS does not measure just psychological symptomatology.

Researchers who are familiar with this field and who may wish to use the PSS in their work welcome this full discussion of its psychometric characteristics. The chapter compares the usefulness of the full 14-item PSS to its two shorter versions, and it recommends the 10-item scale (PSS10) for future research use. PSS norms for major subgroups of the U.S. population are provided, enabling future comparisons of research samples. Examination of these data lends further support to the notion that those who are in more demanding environments with fewer resources (e.g., those with less status, wealth, and power in our society—the very young, females, racial/ethnic minorities) are experiencing greater stress.

Health practitioners, as well as researchers, can benefit from this chapter. In addition to revealing which groups experience more stress, Cohen and Williamson present evidence regarding the general belief that increased stress is related to negative health outcomes. Professionals who design interventions aimed at specific health behaviors or services will find data on the relationships between perceived stress and health behaviors, and between perceived stress and the use of various health services. While Cohen and Williamson remind us that these data are cross-sectional, and thus one cannot safely infer causation, their findings may serve as helpful guidelines in real-world applications.

Perceived Control

Laboratory research by Glass and Singer (1972) and others suggests that environmental stressors, at least when they are unpredictable and uncontrollable, have deleterious effects on tasks that are administered relatively soon after termination of the stressor. That is, although individuals may be capable of adapting and maintaining performance during stressor exposure, negative effects have been observed after the stressor is terminated (see Cohen, 1980a, for a review). What are some of these effects? Examples include increased blood pressure, decreased tolerance for frustration, impaired task performance, increased aggression, and decreased sensitivity to the need for help on the part of another person. These "aftereffects" of stressor exposure are well-established and accepted parts of the environmental stress literature. Over the past 15 years, these aftereffects have been found as a result of exposure to a wide variety of stressors including noise, social and spatial density, electric shock, pollution, and cold pressor.

In the prototypical laboratory experiment in this field, subjects are asked to perform a number of simple tasks—for example, comparing pairs of multiple digits and indicating whether the members of the pair are the same or different, adding many series of three-digit numbers, crossing out the letter "a" every time it occurs in long lists of words. One group of subjects performs these tasks in a quiet room. Another group of subjects is exposed to a stressor—for example, 110 decibels (A scale) of noise (about the level of a jackhammer in operation). After 24 minutes of the appropriate exposure (either quiet or noise), a subject is introduced to the poststimulation tasks, and all subjects work in a quiet room on new tasks. The most commonly used poststimulation task is a "tolerance for frustration" puzzle task (Feather, 1961). The usual results are that there are no differences between the noise and quiet groups in task performance during stressor exposure (performance on the simple tasks of comparing numbers, canceling "a" in words, and so on). There are, however, significant differences on poststimulation tasks. In comparison to subjects who had worked in a quiet room, subjects who had been exposed to noise have reduced tolerance for frustration and other impairments.

As noted in Chapter 1 and earlier in this chapter, subsequent research has indicated that there are a variety of cognitive and contextual factors that may ameliorate the negative aftereffects of stressor exposure (Cohen, 1980b). In particular, feelings of control over one's environment appear to be central in determining the effects of a stressor on behavior and health (see Averill, 1973; Cohen, Glass, & Phillips, 1979). Thus, the typical design of aftereffects research now involves three conditions: a condition in which subjects are exposed to a stressor, a nonstressful comparison condition, and a third condition in which subjects are exposed to a stressor but told that they can, if they so desire, terminate the stressor. This latter condition has been labeled a "perceived control" condition since subjects do *not* exercise their option to terminate the experiment. For example, in noise studies, perceived control has been manipulated by providing subjects with a button that, if pressed, would stop the noise; in crowding studies, perceived control is provided by explicitly pointing out the exit and reassuring subjects that they may leave, if necessary.

Substantial research demonstrates that this perception of control over the stressor decreases, and often eliminates, the previously noted aftereffects of stressor exposure (Glass & Singer, 1972; Cohen, 1980a). In addition, perception of control can also reduce the negative effects and aftereffects of anticipating exposure to a stressor (Spacapan & Cohen, 1983).

Chapter by Thompson, Cheek, and Graham

In Chapter 4, Suzanne Thompson, Paul Cheek, and Melody Graham explore the possibility that there are also negative consequences for the individual who perceives and/or exercises control in a given situation. At the outset, these authors define "perceptions of control" in terms of specific characteristics: the *perception* is not necessarily veridical, the control available is *probabilistic,* the desired outcome is *multidimensional,* and the control is only an often-costly *potential* to affect an outcome. Given this broad conceptualization of control, Thompson and her colleagues review empirical work such as that by Glass and Singer (1972) described previously, as well as research in which "control" involves escaping an aversive outcome through good performance, choosing among alternatives, being informed about what to expect in a given situation, and using cognitive techniques to reduce pain or stress. From a variety of evidence, these authors conclude that there are some circumstances in which the perception of control may actually be maladaptive—for instance, when exercising control involves effort, time, and attention, or when a more effective agent is available to exercise control.

Two reports of previously unpublished studies highlight this chapter. In the first set of studies, Thompson and Janigian (1987) concluded that it may be maladaptive to hold oneself responsible for negative events that are tied to one's abilities. Thus having control may not be beneficial in a situation in which the effort to exert control proves unsuccessful in an achievement setting (i.e., a setting that arouses concern about one's enduring abilities or dispositions), for then the tendency to blame oneself can result in negative emotional outcomes. In a second study, Thompson, Cheek, and Graham found that individuals frequently prefer *not* to have or exercise control in a variety of situations. Furthermore, many of the reasons that people gave for preferring no control were ones that previous research had identified as being situations in which exercising control could be maladaptive—for example, a more effective agent of control *was* available, or there *was* a substantial chance of failure.

In this chapter, Thompson and her colleagues also suggest ways to design interventions in health care settings that balance the benefits of perceived control against the possible negative consequences of having such control. Health practitioners, who must actually apply the findings of social psychological research, will profit from this careful consideration of the implications of "giving away" control in the real world.

Social Support

Unlike perceived control, social support was not among the early factors that psychologists studied for its possible role in ameliorating the negative effects of laboratory stressors. For several years, however, epidemiological work in a variety of communities has suggested that social relations have a positive effect on health. For example, work by Berkman and Syme (1979), as well as by House, Robbins, and Metzner (1982), indicated that people (particularly males) with a larger number of social "connections" live longer than people with fewer social contacts. In these studies, "social support" was essentially what sociologists call "social integration" and was measured by simply counting the number of people with whom the respondent interacted on a regular basis, or the number of social roles of the respondent (e.g., roles of spouse, parent, son/daughter, neighbor, friend, church member).

Subsequent conceptualizations of social support are somewhat broader: The idea that an individual is part of a social network of mutual obligations is retained, but social support also connotes the feelings that one has of being cared for and valued by the network (see Cobb, 1976). Furthermore, various types of social support have been specified in terms of the functions served by each type: *Emotional*, or esteem, support confirms that one is accepted and valued as a person; *Informational*, or appraisal, support provides advice in understanding and coping with a stressful event; assistance in the form of money, materials, or services has been called *instrumental*, or tangible, support. Some researchers have also included a fourth type of support, *belongingness* or companionship, to refer to the sharing of leisure pursuits (see Cohen & Hoberman, 1983).

As the definition of social support became broader, the list of beneficial effects of social support began to lengthen. In addition to a positive relationship between social support and longevity, social support is believed to reduce the stress of battle and nuclear accidents, lower the likelihood of becoming ill, and speed recovery of those who are already ill (for overviews, see Gatchel & Baum, 1983, pp. 63-64; Taylor, 1986, pp. 207-211). However, becoming more specific, subsequent theorists have suggested that, in order for the beneficial effects of social support to be realized, there must be a "match" between the specific type of support available and the support needed in the situation (Cohen & McKay, 1984). Thus if one's illness can be attributed to the recent death of a spouse, emotional or esteem support may be beneficial, while offers of information or financial support might be irrelevant.

In answer to the question of why social support could have such far-reaching implications for our health and well-being, two explanations have been offered. The oldest notion, termed the "buffering hypothesis," suggests that one's social environment may buffer—that is, protect—an individual from the potentially pathogenic effects of high levels of stress (see Cassel, 1976). In another model, by contrast, stressors do not play a role. This "main (or, direct) effect model" simply predicts that the more social support one has, the healthier one will be. Statistically speaking, the latter explanation predicts a main effect for social support, while the former suggests an interaction between stress and support, which could take either of two forms—support could either reduce or totally eliminate the deleterious effects of stress. The two models also diverge in specifying the mechanisms through which social support mediates health. In the main effect model, for example, one possible explanation of deleterious effects is that social isolation is stressful in and of itself; alternatively, the presence of a support network could enhance positive affect, which in turn could affect neuroendocrine response or immune system function; or it is possible that the support network would facilitate health-promoting behaviors. On the other hand, in the buffering model, there are two possible points where social support could intervene in the sequence that runs from the potentially stressful life event through illness. First, as noted earlier, unless an event is appraised as stressful, negative consequences are not likely for the individual. Thus support may prevent an event from being appraised as stressful because either the person involved does not find the situation threatening given his or her support network, or the existence of support may assure the person that he or she can cope in the face of this event. The second point where support may buffer the individual is between the physiological stress response and eventual illness. Here again, the support network could facilitate healthy behaviors, or increase positive affect, or suggest a reappraisal, or provide solutions in terms of adaptive responses. (For a fuller discussion of these issues, see Cohen & Wills, 1985.)

Which model of social support is correct? Although a detailed answer to this question is beyond the scope of this chapter, a recent review of the literature by Cohen and Wills (1985) suggests that there is evidence for both models. When social support is conceptualized as social integration—that is, the number of roles one performs—there is a main effect in that people who are socially integrated have lower levels of psychological disorder. Evidence for the buffering model is found when *functional* support is examined: Appraisal and self-esteem support, in particular, appear to buffer individuals from the negative effects of a variety of stressors. In concluding their review, Cohen and Wills (1985) outline a number of specific questions that remain to be answered by future researchers. Among these questions are the issues of individual or group differences in support needs, the relationship of social support to serious health outcomes, and the way perceptions of support are developed through specific social transactions. Each of these issues is addressed in the final chapter of this section.

Chapter by Taylor and Dakof

Shelley Taylor and Gayle Dakof review the results of an eight-year program of research on social support and positive adjustment in the face of the particularly stressful life event of cancer. Their chapter squarely addresses the issue of whether cancer patients experience a lack of support following the cancer incident, and it explores the specific nature of problems in social support for these patients.

In two studies—one involving interviews with 78 breast cancer patients and the other based on a survey of almost 700 individuals with various cancers—positive correlations were found between social support and adjustment across a variety of measures. Moreover, respondents in both studies reported a high level of positive, socially supportive experiences following cancer. Nevertheless, about 40% of the respondents in the first study reported at least one surprising rejection by a friend and indicated a number of strange responses to their cancer—ranging from being treated as if they were contagious, to acquaintances and family members acting as if merely talking about the cancer would lead to its recurrence. Similarly, over half the respondents in the second study desired more open communication with others, and a sizable minority felt misunderstood by their families.

Given these findings, as well as the recent emphasis by social support researchers on specific *types* of social support, Taylor and Dakof moved from investigating global reports of social support to focusing on specific social support transactions. In this chapter, they describe the results of previously unpublished work in which they interviewed 55 cancer patients as to the support provided by each of seven sources (e.g., spouse, friends, other cancer patients, physicians). While concern and empathy were perceived as helpful regardless of the source, the authors confirmed that not all kinds of support were equally helpful across providers. Their data also suggest that different kinds of support may be valued by different individuals in the same stressful situation.

Taylor and Dakof illustrate this review with excerpts from their interviews with cancer patients, thus providing a first-hand feel about many of the aspects of social support. Their chapter will also suggest to researchers numerous opportunities for further work on uncovering the patterns of different *types* of social support needed *by* different individuals *from* different providers. Finally, service providers interested in interventions to support victims of stressful life events can benefit from the authors' detailed account of specific behaviors that were perceived as helpful and unhelpful by cancer patients.

These three substantive chapters provide multidimensional and complementary views of different psychosocial mediators of health status.

References

Averill, J. R. (1973). Personal control over aversive stimuli and its relationship to stress. *Psychological Bulletin, 80,* 286-303.

Berkman, L. F., & Syme, S. L. (1979). Social networks, host resistance, and mortality: A nine-year follow-up study of Alameda County residents. *American Journal of Epidemiology, 109,* 186-204.

Cannon, W. B. (1914). The emergency function of the adrenal medulla in pain and the major emotions. *American Journal of Physiology, 33,* 356-372.

Cassel, J. C. (1976). The contribution of the social environment to host resistance. *American Journal of Epidemiology, 104,* 107-123.

Cobb, S. (1976). Social support as a moderator of life stress. *Psychosomatic Medicine, 38,* 300-314.

Cohen, S. (1980a). Aftereffects of stress on human performance and social behavior: A review of research and theory. *Psychological Bulletin, 88,* 82-108.

Cohen, S. (1980b). Cognitive processes as determinants of environmental stress. In I. Sarason

& C. Speilberger (Eds.), *Stress and anxiety* (Vol. 8, pp. 171-183). Washington, DC: Hemisphere.

Cohen, S. (1986). Contrasting the Hassles Scale with the Perceived Stress Scale: Who's really measuring appraised stress? *American Psychologist, 41,* 716-718.

Cohen, S., & Hoberman, H. (1983). Positive events and social supports as buffers of life change stress. *Journal of Applied Social Psychology, 13,* 99-125.

Cohen, S., & McKay, G. (1984). Social support, stress, and the buffering hypothesis: A theoretical analysis. In A. Baum, J. E. Singer, & S. E. Taylor (Eds.), *Handbook of psychology and health* (Vol. 4, pp. 253-267). Hillsdale, NJ: Lawrence Erlbaum.

Cohen, S., & Wills, T. A. (1985). Stress, social support, and the buffering hypothesis. *Psychological Bulletin, 98,* 310-357.

Cohen, S., Glass, D. C., & Phillips, S. (1979). Environment and health. In H. E. Freeman, S. Levine, & L. G. Reeder (Eds.), *Handbook of medical sociology* (pp. 134-149). Englewood Cliffs, NJ: Prentice-Hall.

Cohen, S., Kamarck, T., & Mermelstein, R. (1983). A global measure of perceived stress. *Journal of Health and Social Behavior, 24,* 385-396.

Conway, T. L., Vickers, R. R., Ward, H. W., & Rahe, R. H. (1981). Occupational stress and variation in cigarette, coffee, and alcohol consumption. *Journal of Health and Social Behavior, 22,* 155-165.

DeLongis, A., Coyne, J. C., Dakof, G., Folkman, S., & Lazarus, R. S. (1982). Relationship of daily hassles, uplifts, and major life events to health status. *Health Psychology, 1,* 119-136.

DiMatteo, M. R., & Friedman, H. S. (1982). *Social psychology and medicine.* Cambridge, WA: Oelgeschlager, Gunn, & Hain.

Feather, N. T. (1961). The relationship of persistence at a task to expectations of success and achievement-related motives. *Journal of Abnormal and Social Psychology, 63,* 552-561.

Gatchel, R. J., & Baum, A. (1983). *An introduction to health psychology.* Reading, MA: Addison-Wesley.

Glass, D. C., & Singer, J. E. (1972). *Urban stress.* New York: Academic Press.

Holmes, T. H., & Rahe, R. H. (1967a). *Schedule of recent experiences.* Seattle: University of Washington, School of Medicine.

Holmes, T. H., & Rahe, R. H. (1967b). The social readjustment rating scale. *Journal of Psychosomatic Research, 11,* 213-218.

House, J. S., Robbins, C., & Metzner, H. L. (1982). The association of social relationships and activities with mortality: Prospective evidence from the Tecumseh Community Health Study. *American Journal of Epidemiology, 116,* 123-140.

Kanner, A. D., Coyne, J. C., Schaefer, C., & Lazarus, R. S. (1981). Comparisons of two modes of stress measurement: Daily hassles and uplifts versus major life events. *Journal of Behavioral Medicine, 4,* 1-39.

Kasl, S. V. (1983). Pursuing the link between stressful life experiences and disease: A time for reappraisal. In C. L. Cooper (Ed.), *Stress research.* New York: John Wiley.

Lazarus, R. S. (1966). *Psychological stress and the coping process.* New York: McGraw-Hill.

Lazarus, R. S., & Launier, R. (1978). Stress-related transactions between person and environment. In L. A. Pervin & M. Lewis (Eds.), *Internal and external determinants of behavior* (pp. 287-327). New York: Plenum.

Mechanic, D. (1976). Stress, illness, and illness behavior. *Journal of Human Stress, 2,* 2-6.

Mechanic, D. (1978). Effects of psychological distress on perceptions of physical health and use of medical and psychiatric facilities. *Journal of Human Stress, 4,* 26-32.

Sells, S. B. (1970). On the nature of stress. In J. E. McGrath (Ed.), *Social and psychological factors in stress* (pp. 134-139). New York: Holt, Rinehart, & Winston.

Selye, H. (1956). *The stress of life*. New York: McGraw-Hill.

Spacapan, S., & Cohen, S. (1983). Effects and aftereffects of stressor expectations. *Journal of Personality and Social Psychology, 45*, 1243-1254.

Taylor, S. E. (1986). *Health psychology*. New York: Random House.

Thompson, S. C., & Janigian, A. S. (1987). *Attributing responsibility to the self for negative events*. Unpublished manuscript. Pomona College, Claremont, CA.

3

Perceived Stress in a Probability Sample of the United States

SHELDON COHEN
GAIL M. WILLIAMSON

I t is a common assumption among health researchers that stressful life events are *not,* in and of themselves, sufficient causes of pathology and illness behavior. Instead, the potential for event-elicited health risk depends on a transaction between the person and the environment (Lazarus, 1966; Lazarus & Folkman, 1984). This perspective assumes that persons actively interact with their environments, appraising potentially threatening or challenging events in the light of available coping resources. Stressful events are assumed to increase risk of disease when they are appraised as threatening or otherwise demanding, and when coping resources are judged as insufficient to address that threat or demand. An important part of this view is that event-elicited disorders are not based solely on the intensity or any other inherent quality of an

AUTHORS' NOTE: The data set used in this chapter was generated by Louis Harris and Associates, Inc., under contract DHHS 282-81-0098 from the Office of Disease Prevention and Health Promotion. The authors are especially thankful to Paul Brounstein for helping us obtain a copy of the data tape. Preparation of this chapter was supported in part by a NIMH Research Scientist Development Award (K02 MH00721) to the first author.

event, but are dependent on personal and contextual factors as well. Although this perspective is widely accepted, it has not been accompanied by the development of psychometrically valid measures of perceived (appraised) stress to test its validity.

The purpose of this chapter is to present psychometric and descriptive data on a scale designed to measure stress perceptions, and to establish that such a scale can predict the range of health-related outcomes presumed to be associated with appraised stress. In the first section, we discuss the advantages of a scale measuring generalized perceptions of stress, describe the Perceived Stress Scale (PSS), and address the controversy surrounding the use of a scale assessing stress perceptions. In the later sections, we report new and exciting PSS data from a large (2,387 respondents) probability sample of the United States collected by Louis Harris and Associates, Inc. in 1983. Data are presented on the psychometric qualities of the scale, and on the relation of the PSS to other stress, health, and satisfaction measures. Mean stress scores (norms) are also provided for breakdowns of the sample on a variety of demographic characteristics.

In an earlier article, we argued that a scale assessing global perceptions of stress can serve a variety of valuable functions (Cohen, Kamarck, & Mermelstein, 1983). First, it can provide information about the processes through which stressful events influence pathology. For example, it can be used in conjunction with an objective scale in an effort to determine whether appraised stress mediates the relation between objective stress and illness. It can similarly be used to assess whether a factor known to moderate stress-illness relations, for example, social support, operates through its influence on stress appraisal or through some other pathway. Second, a perceived stress scale can be used to investigate the pathogenic role of overall stress appraisal in situations in which the objective sources of stress are diffuse or difficult to measure. Similarly, it can be used when the primary issue under study is the role of appraised stress, as opposed to objective stress level. Finally, perceived stress can be viewed as an outcome variable—measuring the experienced level of stress as a function of objective stressful events, coping processes, personality factors, and so on.

Early Approaches to Assessing Perceived Stress

Previous work has employed a number of approaches to assess both global and event-specific levels of perceived stress. For example, several investigators have modified stressful life-event scales in an attempt to measure global perceived stress. The modification involved asking respondents to rate the stressfulness or impact of each experienced event. In general, life-stress scores based on self-ratings of event stressfulness are better predictors of health-related outcomes than are scores derived from either a simple counting of events (i.e., unit weighting) or event scores based on weights assigned by external judges (e.g., Sarason, Johnson, & Siegel, 1978; Vinokur & Selzer, 1975). However, increases in predictability provided by these ratings are small. A major reason that any increase in predictability of a weighted event score over a simple count of events is likely to be small is that alternative weighting schemes yield composite scores that are substantially correlated with the event count (Lei & Skinner, 1980). Consequently, this measurement technique does not allow for a single event to have the impact of four or five less significant ones. Other weaknesses of global perceived stress scales that are based on a specific list of events include insensitivity to chronic stress from ongoing life circumstances, to stress from events occurring in the lives of close friends and family, from expectations concerning future events, and from events not listed on the scale.

Subjective measures of response to specific stressors have also been widely used, e.g., measures of perceived occupational stress (Kahn, Wolfe, Quinn, Snoek, & Rosenthal, 1964). There are, however, some practical and theoretical limitations of measures of specific stressors. Practically, it is difficult and time-consuming to develop and psychometrically validate an individual measure every time a new stressor is studied. Theoretically, there is an issue of whether measures of perceived response to a specific stressor really assess evaluations of that stressor. There is, in fact, evidence that people often misattribute their feelings of stress to a particularly salient source when that stress is actually due to another source (Keating, 1979; Worchel, 1978; Worchel & Teddlie, 1976). Another problem with measures of response to specific stressors is that such measures imply the independence of that event in the precipitation of disease. However, it is likely that the illness process is affected by global stress level, not just by the response to a particular event.

The Perceived Stress Scale

The PSS is a measure of the degree to which situations in one's life are appraised as stressful (Cohen et al., 1983). Items were designed to tap how unpredictable, uncontrollable, and overloaded respondents find their lives. These three issues repeatedly have been found to be central components of the experience of stress (Averill, 1973; Cohen, 1978; Glass & Singer, 1972; Lazarus, 1966, 1977; Seligman, 1975). The scale also includes a number of direct queries about current levels of experienced stress. The PSS was designed for use in community samples with at least a junior high school education. The items are easy to understand, and the response alternatives are simple to grasp. Moreover, the questions are of a general nature and hence are relatively free of content specific to any subpopulation group.

The original scale contained 14 items. Four-item (PSS4), and 10-item (PSS10) versions of the scale have also been validated. We present data on the psychometrics of each version of the scale in this chapter. We will argue later that the PSS10 allows the assessment of perceived stress without any loss of psychometric quality (actually a slight gain) over the longer PSS14.

All 14 items used in the original scale are presented in Appendix A.[1] The PSS10 includes items 1-3, 6-11, and 14, and the PSS4 includes items 2, 6, 7, and 14. The questions in the PSS ask about feelings and thoughts during the last month. In each case, respondents are asked how often they felt a certain way. PSS scores are obtained by reversing responses (e.g., 0 = 4, 1 = 3, 2 = 2) to the seven positively stated items (items 4, 5, 6, 7, 9, 10, and 13) and then summing across all scale items.

The PSS does not tie appraisal to particular situations; it is sensitive to the nonoccurrence of events as well as to ongoing life circumstances, to stress resulting from events occurring in the lives of friends and relatives, and to expectations concerning future events. It is an economical scale that can be administered in only a few minutes and is easy to score. Because levels of appraised stress should be influenced by daily hassles, major events, and changes in coping resources, the predictive validity of the PSS is expected to fall off rapidly after four to eight weeks.

Evidence for PSS validity. In our own work (Cohen et al., 1983; Cohen, 1986), we found that the PSS provided better predictions than did life-event scales of psychological symptoms, physical symptoms, and utilization of health services. We also found that although life events did not prospectively predict smoking cessation and relapse among persons attempting to quit, persons with higher PSS scores were less likely to quit smoking and had a greater increase in posttreatment smoking rates than did those with relatively lower scores. Other investigators have reported that relatively higher PSS scores were prospectively associated with failure to quit smoking (Glasgow, Klesges, Mizes, & Pechacek, 1985), and failure among diabetics to control blood sugar levels (Frenzel, McCaul, Glasgow, &

Schafer, in press). In a cross-sectional study, higher PSS scores were associated with greater vulnerability to stressful life-event-elicited depressive symptoms (Kuiper, Olinger, & Lyons, 1986). The PSS has also been used as an outcome variable, with life events, coping processes, and personality factors prospectively predicting changes in perceived stress (e.g., Linville, 1987).

Perceived Stress or Psychological Disorder?

Because it is difficult to distinguish conceptually between perceived stress and psychological distress, the practical and conceptual viability of a perceived stress scale is controversial (e.g., Cohen, 1986; Dohrenwend & Shrout, 1985; Lazarus, DeLongis, Folkman, & Gruen, 1985). For example, feelings of stress and overload are viewed as symptomatic of psychological disorder. As a result, a correlation between a scale assessing perceived stress and one assessing psychological distress may be partly or totally attributable to the fact that some of the items in the two scales measure a similar or identical concept. In short, cross-sectional correlations between perceived stress and psychological distress may be totally artifactual, and correlations between perceived stress and physical disorders may actually reflect an association between psychological distress (as measured by questions about perceived stress) and physical disorder.

Although appraised stress may be symptomatic of psychological distress when viewed in combination with elevated scores on other symptoms, it is our contention that the perception of stress itself, as assessed by the PSS, is not merely a measure of psychological symptomatology. First, the PSS contains some items that are not typical of psychological disorder scales. These include a number of questions regarding perceived control over external demands.[2] Second, the inevitable overlap of stress and distress scales represents only one of a number of domains from which the distress scales draw. Besides items tapping perceptions of stress, common distress scales assess a broad range of symptoms including hostility, diminished self-esteem, depressed affect, anxiety, and psychosomatic complaints (e.g., PERI Demoralization Measure described in Dohrenwend, Shrout, Egri, & Mendelsohn, 1980; the General Health Questionnaire described in Goldberg, 1972).

There is no doubt that events can be appraised as stressful without resulting in these various psychological symptoms. Concretely, persons can score high on the PSS *without* elevated scores on the other dimensions of psychological distress. This contention is, in fact, supported by data from several studies in which concurrently assessed symptomatology was partialed out of the relation between the PSS and various outcomes. This conservative analysis attributes any variance common to both the PSS and psychological symptoms to the symptoms, eliminating the possibility that any remaining effect of perceived stress is attributable to the overlap between symptoms and the PSS. Studies using this procedure indicate that PSS and depressive affect scales *independently* predict physical symptomatology (Cohen et al., 1983). Moreover, the PSS prospectively predicts psychological symptomatology when concurrently assessed psychological symptomatology is partialed out of the relations between the PSS and the outcome (Cohen, 1986). Finally, other prospective analyses indicate that the PSS predicts both physical symptoms and smoking cessation even after controlling for the influence of psychological distress (Cohen, 1986). In short, there is overwhelming evidence that the PSS does not measure the same thing as standard psychological distress scales.

Other evidence for the independence of the PSS and psychological distress is provided by studies indicating that psychological distress scores of those with high levels of social support are not influenced by perceived stress levels (Cohen, Mermelstein, Kamarck, & Hoberman, 1985; Cohen, Sherrod, & Clark, 1986). To the extent that a perceived stress scale and a psychological distress symptom scale measure the same thing, relations between the two scales would not be moderated by other variables. Yet the association between the PSS and disorder is moderated by social support; persons with high levels of support show less disorder under high PSS levels than do those with low levels of support. In sum, high scores on the PSS are not the same thing as elevated scores on psychological distress, but they do place people at risk for future distress.

Reducing ambiguity in interpretation. Because of the potential overlap between perceived stress and psychological distress, cross-sectional correlations between these concepts are subject to artifact, and therefore are particularly difficult to interpret. Like any measure, perceived stress scales should be used in conceptual and methodological contexts that allow relatively clear interpretation. When intended as a predictor of psychological distress, the scale is most appropriately used in prospective studies that control for initial distress level. In short, we advise avoiding cross-sectional correlations between scales that may contain some items that assess the same or similar concepts.

The question of discriminative validity is more difficult. When a perceived stress scale is used as a predictor of a nonconfounded outcome (e.g., utilization of health services, physical health, or smoking cessation), are relations attributable to perceived stress or to psychological distress? There is no definitive answer. Because psychological disorder scales are not very good predictors of clinical disorder (see Dohrenwend, Shrout, Egri, & Mendelsohn, 1978; Lin, Dean, & Ensel, 1986), a good argument can be made that measures of psychological distress actually measure perceived stress. Consequently, what psychological distress scales and the PSS actually measure depends to a great extent on how one conceptualizes stress and disorder. At the very least, it is reasonable to argue that the PSS measures what it was designed to assess—the perceived degree to which environmental demands exceed abilities to cope.

Finally, it is important to emphasize that we are not arguing that perceived stress scales are *the* scales to use in stress research. Scales should be chosen as tools to answer specific questions and should be used in methodological contexts that help reduce ambiguities in interpretation. As discussed earlier, the PSS is especially appropriate in studies investigating factors influencing or influenced by stress appraisal.

In the remainder of this chapter, we present and discuss PSS data from a probability sample of the United States. This representative sample allows us to reexamine the psychometric characteristics of the scale, compare the usefulness of the PSS14, PSS10, and PSS4, and describe the distribution of perceived stress levels in the U.S. population. Of special interest are mean differences for subpopulation categories based on gender, age, socio-economic status, race and ethnic background, smoking, and drinking status. These data provide norms for the scale as well as evidence for differences in perceived stress across subgroups in the population. We are also able to investigate the relations between the PSS and a wide range of health outcomes, including frequency of illness, serious and nonserious symptomatology, utilization of health services, health practices, and life satisfaction.

Method

Study Population

Respondents were 960 male and 1,427 female residents of the United States, 18 years of age and older (mean age = 42.8, standard deviation = 17.2), who completed a telephone interview conducted by Louis Harris and

Associates, Inc. in 1983. The 2,387 persons meeting the criteria for inclusion in the analyses represented 69.6% of the 3,430 eligible individuals with whom telephone contact was made (926 refused to be interviewed, and 117 terminated the interview prior to completion).

Sampling Techniques

Based on Bureau of Census information, a national area-probability sample was developed from the distribution of the adult, noninstitutionalized population of the United States. Stratification was done according to geographic regions (East, South, Midwest, and West) and by size of residential community (central city, non-central city, and rural areas). With counties as primary sampling units, a random digit dialing procedure was used to select telephone numbers to be called within each sampling unit. In the event that the dialed number was busy, it was redialed as many as four times at 15-minute intervals. For a ringing but unanswered phone, up to four call-backs were made at varying times and on different days during the sampling period. A total of 7,787 numbers were called. Of these, no contact was made with 1,819, because there was no answer after five dialings (1,138), the line was busy after five calls (142), the designated respondent could not be reached during the sampling period (97), or no appropriate contact had been made at the end of the sampling period, prior to the fourth call-back (442). Of the remaining numbers, 2,538 did not meet eligibility criteria; 456 were business numbers, 1,827 were not in service, and 255 were answered by individuals with whom there was a language barrier or who had a health condition that precluded their participation.

Once contact was established, interviewers described the purpose of the study and disclosed all information required under the Privacy Act. To further ensure an unbiased sample, the interviewer asked to speak to the person in the household who was 18 years of age or over and whose birthday had been most recent. Each interview required approximately 31 minutes to complete. Professional interview techniques developed by the Harris organization were employed to minimize refusal rates. Table 3.1 presents the demographic profile of the sample population obtained through these procedures along with comparable statistics from the 1980 U.S. Census. As can be seen, in those categories for which census data were available for comparison, the distribution of the Harris sample was similar to that of the U.S. Census. The sampling error at a 95% level of confidence for the full sample of 2,387 respondents was calculated at + or −2.0%.

Measures

Respondent information fell into six major categories: (1) perceptions of stress, (2) self-reported health and utilization of health services, (3) health behaviors, (4) life satisfaction, (5) help seeking behaviors, and (6) demographic data. Some of the measures were previously validated scales, some were variations of previous scales, and others were simply individual questions. We found that some of the latter could be grouped into scales, so that related information could be analyzed together. Each category of measures is discussed in turn.

We present psychometric evidence from the Harris sample in regard to internal reliability (Cronbach's alphas) for those instruments in which items are intended to measure the same construct and hence are expected to have high interitem correlations. In contrast, most instruments based on frequencies of events—for example, life events, number of illnesses, number of nights in a hospital—assume relative independence of items and are not expected to have high interitem correlations. Consequently, internal reliability statistics are not appropriate for these instruments.

Stress measures. In addition to the 14-item PSS, there were four individual questions designed to tap the level of experienced stress, a life-events scale, and a number of questions regarding work-related stress.

The individual questions about experienced stress were:

(1) Have you ever personally experienced stress? (1 = yes, 2 = no)
(2) Are there things going on in your life now that you find very upsetting or bothersome? (1 = yes, 2 = no)
(3) How much stress do you experience during an average week? (1 = almost no stress to 4 = a lot of stress)
(4) Compared to a year ago, how much stress do you experience now? (1 = less now, 2 = about the same, 3 = more now)

The life-events scale consisted of 16 events representing potentially significant changes in the respondent's life. In all, 10 of the events are normally construed as negative (e.g., death of spouse, mate, or close family member, loss of employment, separation or divorce from spouse, serious illness or injury of respondent). Three of the events are normally considered positive (marriage, pregnancy, reconciliation with mate), and three more events could be considered either positive or negative (retirement, major change in health/behavior of family member, change in income). Respon-

Table 3.1
Comparison of Demographic Characteristics of Sample
and of 1980 U.S. Population

	Percent of Harris Sample[a]	*Percent of 1980 U.S. Census Adult Population*
Sex		
male	39.9	47.4
female	60.1	52.6
Age		
20-29	24.0	26.4
30-44	33.6	28.1
45-54	13.3	14.7
55-64	13.4	14.1
65 & over (end sign)	15.7	16.5
Total annual household income		
$15,000 or less	33.3	37.5
$15,001-$25,000	24.2	22.9
$25,001-$35,000	20.3	19.1
$35,001-$50,000	13.6	12.7
More than $50,000	8.6	7.9
Ethnic origin		
black (non Hispanic)	7.8	10.2
white (non Hispanic)	86.5	82.7
Hispanic	3.7	5.3
other minorities	2.1	1.8
Work status		
employed	63.8	58.6
unemployed	5.3	4.5

NOTE: Table 3.1 includes only those categories for which equivalent data were available from both the census and Harris Poll. For this reason, the percentages shown do not sum to 100% in every category.

a. For purposes of comparing the Harris sample with U.S. Census data, only those respondents over 20 years of age were included in these calculations, leaving N = 2268 in the Harris sample.

dents identified the events that had happened to them in the last year and rated the impact of each event on a five-point scale ranging from –2 (extremely negative) to +2 (extremely positive). Separate scores were calculated based on the total number of life events that the respondent indicated had happened, on the sum of the reported impact of the events, and on the sum of the impact of events respondents reported as having had negative impact.

The last category of measures of potential stress was concerned with tapping characteristics of respondents' employment. The people who indicated that they were employed (either full or part time or in the military) were first asked how many hours they worked during an average week. Two more questions related to work load (frequency of overtime work and how often work load caused breaks and lunch hours to be skipped) and were rated on scales of 1 (never) to 5 (very frequently). These latter two responses were combined to yield a measure of *Workload Demand.*

A final measure of job characteristics consisted of five items to tap perceptions of work responsibilities, to which subjects responded on a scale of 1 (agree strongly) to 5 (disagree strongly):

(1) I am held accountable for the development of other employees.
(2) I am responsible for counseling my subordinates or helping them solve their problems.
(3) I take actions or make decisions in my job that affect the safety or well-being of others.
(4) My responsibilities in my job are more for things than for people. (Scores were reversed on this item.)
(5) I receive appropriate recognition for performing my job well.

A principal components factor analysis with varimax rotation revealed two factors, which, when combined, accounted for 60.4% of the total variance. The first factor consisted of items 1, 2, and 5 (39.0% of the variance) and was labeled *Job Responsibilities with Feedback.* Items 3 and 4 comprised the second factor (21.4% of the variance), which was labeled *Job Responsibilities without Feedback.* Cronbach's alpha was .56 for the With Feedback measure and .42 for the Without Feedback measure.

Measures of self-reported health and utilization of health services. Respondents were asked to rate their current health status on a five-point scale ranging from 1 (excellent) to 5 (poor). They were then asked about utilization of health services within the last year:

(1) Have you been a patient in a hospital overnight during the past year? (1 = yes, 2 = no)
(2) If yes, how many nights?
(3) How many times did you personally see a doctor about your health during the past year, not counting hospitalization?

(4) Aside from these visits or when you telephoned to make an appointment, how many times in the past year did you contact a doctor or other health professional by telephone to consult about your health?

The number of nights the respondent had spent in the hospital, the number of doctor visits, and the number of times a doctor had been called were summed to provide an index of *Health Services Utilization.*

A composite score of three questions regarding effects of health status on ability to perform usual activities was obtained by asking respondents how many days during the past month illness or injury had caused them to (1) be absent from work, (2) be unable to perform routine activities, or (3) have difficulty performing routine duties. The measure of *Inability to Perform Routine Activities* for health reasons was obtained by summing the number of days given in response to all three questions.

To measure *Frequency of Serious Illness,* a 13-item scale listing a variety of health conditions (e.g., migraine headaches, hypertension, heart disease, vascular disease, respiratory illness, cancer) was employed. Respondents were asked (1) Have you ever had [this condition]? and (2) Have you had it in the past year? Scores were generated for responses to each of these questions, so that the effects of ever having had a particular illness and having had it within the past year could be examined separately.

A final measure of self-reported health status was the Psychosomatic Index, the 12-item somatization subscale of the Symptom Checklist 90 (Derogatis, Rickels, & Rock, 1976). This scale includes items such as weakness, soreness, numbness, heavy feelings, headache, nausea, and faintness. Respondents indicated the degree to which each ailment had bothered them within the last month on a scale of 1 (not at all) to 4 (quite a bit). A principal components factor analysis with varimax rotation revealed three factors, which, when combined, accounted for 48.1% of the total variance. The first factor contained five items related to nonserious health conditions (weakness, soreness, numbness, heavy feelings, and pains in lower back). A second factor was composed of symptoms that might be considered indicative of more serious illness (faintness or dizziness, pains in heart or chest, and trouble getting one's breath). The third factor contained items that might be seen as simply describing cold or flu symptoms (headaches, nausea or upset stomach, lump in throat, hot or cold spells). These factors, for descriptive simplicity, were labeled *Nonserious Symptoms, Serious Illness Symptoms,* and *Flu Symptoms;* the alpha reliability coefficients were .71, .58, and .50, respectively.

Health behaviors. Respondents answered a variety of questions that elicited information about their healthful or unhealthful behaviors. First, they were asked two questions about their sleeping habits: (1) On average, how many hours do you sleep each day in total, including naps, as well as regular nightly sleeping periods? and (2) Of the time you spend sleeping each day, how many hours of sleep do you typically get in the longest single period of sleep? Second, subjects were asked how often they ate breakfast (1 = never to 7 = daily). Third, information was solicited about frequency (1 = never to 7 = daily) and quantity (1 = 1 drink to 5 = more than 5 drinks) of alcoholic beverage consumption. Fourth, respondents rated their cigarette smoking habits on a scale of 1 = currently smoke, 2 = once smoked, but don't anymore, or 3 = never smoked. Those who indicated that they were currently smoking were asked how many packs of cigarettes they consumed daily. As a fifth measure of health behavior, subjects rated how often they exercised strenuously for at least 20 minutes on a scale of 1 (never) to 7 (daily).

Use of prescription and/or nonprescription medications was measured by responses to the question, "Do you ever take . . . ?" followed by a list of seven categories of drugs (prescription pain relievers, sleeping tablets, tranquilizers, medication for stomach distress, diet pills, over-the-counter pain relievers, and over-the-counter medication to relieve stomach distress). Two additional items asked if other prescribed or over-the-counter medications were being taken. A factor analysis (principal components with varimax rotation) yielded two factors, which together accounted for 31.6% of the total variance. The first factor consisted solely of prescription drugs (pain relievers, sleeping tablets, tranquilizers, and medications for stomach distress) and accounted for 18.2% of the variance. Nonprescription drugs and prescription diet pills made up the second factor accounting for 13.4% of the variance. Consequently, separate measures were derived by summing the number of drugs taken in two categories, one for prescription drugs and one for over-the-counter medications plus prescription diet pills.

For each type of drug taken by the respondent, a parallel question requested that frequency of usage be rated on a scale of 1 (less than one day a month) to 6 (daily). These data were subjected to the same factor analysis procedures described previously, resulting in three factors, which, in total, accounted for 40.8% of the variance. Frequency-of-use factor 1 was made up of over-the-counter pain relievers and other prescription and non-prescription drugs not specifically mentioned (15.8% of variance). The second factor included prescription pain pills, sleeping pills, and tranquilizers (12.9% of variance); the third frequency-of-use factor included both prescription and over-the-counter stomach medications and prescription diet pills (12.1% of variance). We labeled these factors *Other Drugs, Depressants,* and *Gastrointestinal/Obesity Drugs.* Separate scores for each category were derived by summing responses for the three types of drugs within that classification.

Life satisfaction measure. Using a scale of 1 (very satisfied) to 5 (very dissatisfied), respondents were asked to rate their degree of satisfaction with (1) their job, (2) themselves, and (3) life in general. Responses to these three items were summed to create a score of general life satisfaction. A principal components factor analysis produced only one factor, which accounted for 58.3% of the variance. The alpha coefficient of reliability was .63.

Measure of help-seeking behavior. Two questions were asked regarding whether, in the past year, respondents had considered seeking help for personal or emotional problems, and if so, whether they had actually sought that help. Responses to these items were then combined to generate a measure of help-seeking and were coded as 1 (considered and obtained help), 2 (considered seeking help, but did not), or 3 (did not consider seeking help).

Demographic data. Interviewers determined the respondent's sex, age, race, level of education completed, household income, and marital status. Further questions determined the number of people living in the respondent's household and how many of those were under 18 years of age. Data regarding employment included requesting the respondent's employment status and if working, his or her job title or primary job duties.

Results

The data were analyzed to provide information about the psychometric properties of the Perceived Stress Scale, the distribution of perceived stress across demographic factors, and the relation between perceived stress and a series of measures of health and health behavior. Because a large number of analyses were performed, a conservative alpha level of $p < .001$ was set for determining statistical significance. Post hoc contrasts between group means were considered *exploratory,* and Scheffé procedures were employed with alphas set at the traditional $p < .05$ level for these analyses.

Because the results reported here are based on cross-sectional data, no inferences of causality can be made. In other words, for relations reported between PSS scores and scores on other measures, we cannot say with any certainty whether stress acted as the causal agent, whether stress resulted from those related factors, or whether both factors were influenced by other variables.

Factor Analyses, Reliability Estimates, and Intercorrelations

The 14-item Perceived Stress Scale was factor analyzed, using a principal components method with varimax rotation. The principal components analysis revealed that 10 items loaded positively on the first factor at .48 or above. Items 4, 5, 12, and 13 had relatively low loadings of .17, .33, .11, and .39, respectively. The analyses further revealed that there were two factors with eigenvalues over 1.0 (Factor 1 = 3.6 and Factor 2 = 2.2), which together accounted for 41.6% of the total variance.

Examination of the highest loadings for each item indicated that the first factor (25.9% of the variance) weighted most heavily those items that were negatively worded (e.g., been upset, unable to control things, felt nervous and stressed), and the second factor (15.7% of the variance) reflected positively phrased statements (e.g., dealt successfully with hassles, effectively coping, felt confident). For purposes of measuring perceptions of stress, the distinction between the two factors was considered irrelevant. Consequently, scores for the PSS14 used in later analyses were obtained by summing responses (with the appropriate items reversed) to all 14 items. Cronbach's alpha coefficient for the internal reliability of the PSS14 was .75.

A somewhat shorter version of the Perceived Stress Scale, the PSS10, was derived by dropping the four items with relatively low factor loadings (items 4, 5, 12, and 13). The remaining 10 items were submitted to the factor analysis procedures described previously. In the principal components analysis of this shortened scale, all items loaded positively on the first factor at .42 or above. Once again, two factors emerged with eigenvalues over 1.0 (3.4 and 1.4, respectively), composed of negatively and positively worded items. Deletion of the four items resulted in a slight improvement in both the total explained variance (48.9% for both factors combined, Factor 1 = 34.4%, and Factor 2 = 14.5%) and internal reliability (alpha coefficient = .78). Thus it appears that the PSS10 may be at least as good a measure of perceived stress as the longer 14-item version of the scale.

A more abbreviated version of the PSS, a four-item scale consisting of items 2, 6, 7, and 14, was previously employed in telephone follow-up interviews in smoking cessation studies (Cohen, 1986; Cohen et al., 1983). In these prior studies, the PSS4 demonstrated adequate reliability and was shown to be a useful measure of perceived stress for situations requiring a very short scale. Responses to the four items from the present sample were factor analyzed using a principal components method. The analysis revealed only one factor with an eigenvalue over 1.0 (specifically, 1.8), which accounted for 45.6% of the variance. The alpha reliability coefficient for the PSS4 was .60.

To summarize, the three versions of the Perceived Stress Scale analyzed here all appear to demonstrate adequate internal reliability. With the large sample size provided by the Harris survey, we were able to determine that a somewhat shortened version of the original 14-item scale, the PSS10, appears to provide at least as good a measure of perceived stress as does the longer scale. The results of the preceding analyses also confirm previous indications that the PSS4 has adequate reliability for use in situations requiring a very brief measure of perceptions of stress. Normative data are reported later for all three versions of the Perceived Stress Scale (PSS14, PSS10, and PSS4).

Means and Standard Deviations

Mean scores for the entire sample (males and females combined) for the PSS14, PSS10, and PSS4 were 19.62, 13.02, and 4.49, respectively, with standard deviations of 7.49, 6.35, and 2.96. The ranges of scores for each measure were 0 to 45 (PSS14), 0 to 34 (PSS10), and 0 to 15 (PSS4). Table 3.2 presents the means and standard deviations of scores on the three Perceived Stress Scales for each category of demographic variables.

Sex. As is apparent from Table 3.2, on all three measures, females reported higher levels of perceived stress than did males. One-way ANOVAs revealed that, in all cases, these differences were statistically significant at the $p < .0001$ level or beyond.

Age. PSS scores decreased as age increased. Negative correlations between age of respondent and the three PSS measures were small but significant at $p < .001$: for PSS14, $r = -.13$; for PSS10, $r = -.13$; for PSS4, $r = -.11$. Since the age data are actually continuous, we have reported correlations with perceived stress here. However, norms (mean PSS scores and standard deviations) are reported for five age categories (18-29, 30-44, 45-54, 55-64, and 65 and over) in Table 3.2.

Income. When scores were classified by level of household income, the three PSS measures produced the same patterns of results. As Table 3.2 shows, perceptions of stress declined linearly as household income increased to the level of $35,000 per year. Beyond $35,000 per year, the trend was less consistent. Respondents with earnings between $45,000 and $50,000 per year reported less stress than did those in any of the other categories, while stress levels of those earning between $35,000 and $40,000 and those with incomes in excess of $50,000 were approximately the same as those in the $25,000-30,000 range. One-way ANOVAs indicated that the effect of household income on perceived stress was significant at $p<.0001$ for all three PSS scales.

Because response patterns were virtually identical for all PSS measures, only the results of the post hoc analyses for the PSS14 are reported here. Scheffé tests for differences between group means indicated that PSS scores for those with incomes of $5,000 or less were significantly higher than the scores of all respondents with incomes over $15,000, but did not differ from those in the $5,000-10,000 and $10,000-15,000 categories. Respondents with household incomes in the $5,000-10,000 range reported significantly higher levels of perceived stress than did those earning $25,000-30,000, $30,000-35,000, $45,000-50,000, and more than $50,000. Only those whose income was $30,000-35,000 or $45,000-50,000 reported significantly less stress than did those in the $10,000-15,000 group. None of the other comparisons between group means were significant at $p<.05$.

Education. The more education respondents had, the lower were their scores on the PSS14, PSS10, and PSS4. One-way ANOVAs showed that this effect was significant for all three measures at $p<.0001$ or better. The Scheffé procedure for testing differences between group means indicated that PSS scores were not significantly different for those with less than a high school diploma and those who were high school graduates. However, subjects with less than a high school education reported significantly more perceived stress than did all those with some education beyond a high school diploma. Of all the other possible comparisons, only the difference between high school graduates and respondents with an advanced degree was significant.

Race. In this sample, minority ethnic origin or race was associated with reports of perceived stress. Table 3.2 shows that respondents who classified themselves as "white" had lower scores on all three PSS measures than did those classified as black, Hispanic, or other minority. One-way ANOVAs

Table 3.2
Mean PSS14, PSS10, and PSS4 Scores and Standard Deviations for Demographic Categories

Category	N	PSS14 Mean	SD	N	PSS10 Mean	SD	N	PSS4 Mean	SD
Sex									
male	949	18.8	6.9	926	12.1	5.9	946	4.2	2.8
female	1406	20.2	7.8	1344	13.7	6.6	1`84	4.7	3.1
Age									
18-29	649	21.1	7.2	645	14.2	6.2	648	4.9	3.0
30-44	762	19.6	7.3	750	13.0	6.2	756	4.5	2.9
45-54	298	19.1	7.1	285	12.6	6.1	290	4.4	2.9
55-64	300	18.3	8.1	282	11.9	6.9	294	4.2	3.1
65 & over	333	18.5	7.8	296	12.0	6.3	330	4.0	3.0
Annual household income									
$5K or less	170	23.1	8.5	153	16.4	7.4	162	5.9	3.5
$5-10K	233	21.8	8.3	216	15.0	6.7	232	5.2	3.3
$10-15K	309	20.9	7.4	303	14.1	6.2	308	5.0	3.0
$15-20K	277	19.4	7.5	270	12.8	6.3	275	4.4	2.8
$20-25K	247	19.5	7.0	242	12.8	6.0	245	4.4	2.8
$25-30K	255	18.6	7.3	248	12.1	6.1	252	4.1	2.8
$30-35K	181	17.8	6.6	178	11.6	5.6	181	3.8	2.6
$35-40K	134	18.8	6.4	130	12.5	5.5	131	4.2	2.5
$40-45K	93	18.3	6.3	91	11.7	5.3	93	4.1	2.5
$45-50K	72	16.1	5.8	70	10.3	4.7	71	3.1	2.3
over $50K	189	18.4	6.3	187	11.9	5.6	187	3.9	2.5

Education completed									
less than H.S.	400	21.3	7.8	369	13.4	6.8	399	4.9	3.4
H.S. grad	820	19.9	7.8	799	13.1	6.7	812	4.6	3.1
some college	580	19.6	7.5	555	13.1	6.2	568	4.5	2.9
4 yr. college	263	18.2	6.6	262	12.0	5.6	264	4.0	2.6
some grad. school	140	18.0	6.4	137	12.2	5.4	138	4.0	2.4
advanced degree	145	17.4	6.4	142	11.4	5.2	143	3.8	2.3
Race									
white	1995	19.3	7.4	1924	12.8	6.2	1974	4.4	2.9
Hispanic	100	21.3	7.8	98	14.0	6.9	100	5.1	3.2
black	185	21.5	8.1	176	14.7	7.2	183	5.1	3.4
other minority	51	20.5	6.7	50	14.1	5.0	51	4.9	2.3
Number of people in household									
one	407	18.9	7.8	372	12.6	6.6	400	4.3	3.1
two	755	18.9	7.4	729	12.3	6.2	745	4.2	2.9
three	442	19.7	7.6	431	13.2	6.5	438	4.6	3.0
four or five	627	20.4	7.3	615	13.7	6.2	623	4.7	2.9
six or more	124	21.6	7.5	123	14.4	6.2	124	5.3	3.0
Number of children in household									
none	948	19.0	7.3	911	12.5	6.1	933	4.2	2.8
one	412	20.1	7.6	406	13.4	6.5	412	4.8	3.1
two	377	20.4	7.4	371	13.6	6.2	373	4.6	2.9
three	147	20.9	7.4	146	14.0	6.4	148	5.0	3.0
four or more	60	22.6	7.8	60	15.1	6.6	60	5.6	2.9

(continued)

Table 3.2 Continued

Category	PSS14			PSS10			PSS4		
	N	Mean	SD	N	Mean	SD	N	Mean	SD
Marital status									
widowed	215	18.9	8.0	190	12.6	6.7	214	4.3	3.1
married/living with mate	1439	19.0	7.2	1399	12.4	6.1	1427	4.2	2.8
single never wed	451	20.9	7.0	442	14.1	6.0	444	4.9	2.8
divorced	198	21.3	8.7	190	14.7	7.4	195	5.3	3.4
separated	46	23.5	7.9	43	16.6	7.1	44	6.1	3.3
Employment status									
in the military	16	17.8	5.8	16	11.4	6.4	16	2.7	3.2
retired & not working	311	18.2	7.8	280	11.7	6.4	312	3.9	3.0
employed full time	1235	18.9	6.9	1211	12.4	5.8	1223	4.2	2.7
homemaker	270	19.3	8.0	256	12.9	6.8	264	4.4	3.1
employed part time	254	21.0	7.7	250	14.3	6.6	253	5.1	3.1
student	78	22.6	7.4	77	15.3	6.6	78	5.6	3.0
unemployed	129	23.6	7.2	123	16.5	6.3	124	6.2	3.1
disabled/too ill to work	40	26.8	8.4	36	19.9	6.8	39	7.2	3.3
Profession									
proprietor	77	17.4	8.2	76	10.9	6.9	76	3.6	3.1
agriculture	22	17.6	6.1	22	10.3	5.6	22	3.9	2.3
professional	292	18.1	6.2	285	12.0	5.3	288	4.0	2.4
managerial	187	18.2	6.7	187	12.0	5.8	185	3.9	2.6
skilled	177	18.7	6.6	175	12.3	5.5	176	4.3	2.7
sales	112	19.3	7.4	110	13.0	6.3	110	4.5	2.9
clerical	244	20.0	7.8	239	13.5	6.5	243	4.7	2.9
service	200	20.5	7.4	195	13.7	6.2	199	4.8	3.0
unskilled	158	21.4	6.9	156	13.8	6.1	157	5.0	3.0

on these data revealed that the effect of race on PSS scores was statistically significant for all three measures at the p<.001 level or better. Between-group comparisons using the Scheffé procedure further revealed that means for whites were significantly lower than were means for blacks, but that the differences between mean scores for all other possible comparisons between groups were not statistically significant (due, in part, to their smaller *N*s).

Household composition. The number of people in one's household and the number of them who are children were also associated with perceptions of stress. As Table 3.2 shows, either living alone or with one other adult was least stressful. As the number of people in the household increased, so did PSS scores. Correlations between the number of people living in the respondent's household and PSS scores on the three scales were small, but significant at the p<.001 level or better: for PSS14, r = .11; for PSS10, r = .10; for PSS4, r = .11. A similar relationship was evident for number of children and PSS results. The correlations between respondents' perceived stress and number of children were all significant at p<.001 or better: for PSS14, r = .11; for PSS10, r = .10; for PSS4, r = .10. Because data collected on these two dimensions of household composition were continuous, we have reported correlations scores here. However, for the purpose of reporting mean PSS scores and standard deviations, these two variables were divided into the categories shown in Table 3.2.

Marital status. Perceptions of stress appeared to be related to marital status. One-way ANOVAs revealed that this effect was significant for each measure of stress at p<.0001. Surprisingly, respondents who were married or living with a mate did not differ in levels of perceived stress from those who reported that their spouses were deceased. These two groups had the lowest PSS scores, and Scheffé tests revealed that these scores were significantly lower than the scores of those who were single/never married, divorced, or separated. Respondents who had never been married did not differ significantly from those who were divorced or separated, nor were there significant differences between mean PSS scores of separated (but not divorced) and divorced individuals.

Employment. A final category of demographic variables concerned two aspects of respondents' employment: (1) employment status, and (2) profession. Mean PSS scores for the classifications within these two categories are shown in Table 3.2. One-way ANOVAs revealed effects for both employment variables on PSS scores that were significant at the p<.001 level or better. Those who said they were in the military, retired and not working, employed full time, or homemakers had PSS scores (on all three scales) below the overall sample means. Scores of respondents who were employed part time, students, unemployed, or disabled/too ill to work fell above the overall sample means. The Scheffé procedure for multiple comparisons between groups revealed several differences between means. Those respondents who were disabled/too ill to work reported significantly more stress than did those who were in the military, retired, employed (either full or part time), or homemakers. Additionally, individuals who were employed full time or who were retired and not working had PSS scores significantly lower than did part-time employees, students, and the unemployed. Due, in part, to varying Ns in the groups, the stress levels of part-time employees and military personnel were only significantly lower than those of the disabled/too ill to work group, and homemakers were significantly lower only than those respondents who were unemployed or disabled. Clearly, being either employed full time or retired and not working was associated with lower levels of perceived stress, and being either unemployed or disabled was related to higher reports of stress.

Data for those individuals who indicated that they were working either full or part time were further analyzed according to the job title or main duties of their jobs. For this classification, the patterns of scores were much the same on all three scales. Proprietors, agricultural workers, professionals, managers, and skilled workers scored below the overall sample means. Scores for sales workers were, on all three measures, very close to the sample means. Respondents with PSS scores above the overall sample means were clerical, service, and unskilled workers. Using the Scheffé procedure, PSS scores for unskilled workers were significantly higher than for proprietors, professionals, and managers. None of the other comparisons between groups was statistically significant.

Summary. The patterns of perceived stress scores for the demographic variables just reported indicate that a variety of personal characteristics were associated with perceptions of stress. Reported stress levels were consistently higher for females than for males. There was a small, but significant, negative correlation between PSS scores and age, suggesting that perceptions of stress tend to decline as age increases. Whites reported less stress than did those in minority groups, although only the difference between whites and blacks was statistically significant. PSS scores tended to decrease as respondents' level of formal education increased.

Factors associated with one's living and working environments were also found to be related to perceived stress. As would be expected, PSS scores generally decreased as household income increased. Reports of stress increased as the number of people living in the respondent's household increased and as the number of children in the household increased. People who were currently either married or living with a mate and those whose spouses had died reported less stress than did those who had never been married or who were divorced or separated from their mates. Finally, being unemployed and/or disabled was found to be related to high levels of reported stress, while being employed full time or retired and not working was associated with lower PSS scores. Individuals whose occupations involved relatively higher degrees of status and control (proprietors, professionals, and managers)—and one might assume, more income as well—reported significantly less perceived stress than did unskilled workers.

Evidence for Construct Validity

In this section, we examine evidence provided by the Harris Poll data relevant for establishing the construct validity of the PSS measures. Included are relations between the PSS and other stress measures, health, health service utilization, health behaviors, life satisfaction, and help-seeking. In general, we expected that increased stress as measured by the PSS would be associated with increased stress as assessed by other instruments and questions, greater help-seeking, poorer health, more health service utilization, and poorer life satisfaction.

For dichotomous and noncontinuous variables, mean scores on the PSS14, PSS10, and PSS4 were calculated. For continuous variables, scores were correlated with PSS14, PSS10, and PSS4 responses. Data are presented for the entire sample. Because many variables were not relevant to large numbers of respondents, *N*s varied widely from one measure to another. Since the patterns of results were much the same for the three PSS measures, only the results for the PSS14 are discussed in this section. However, the mean scores and correlations for all three scales are presented in the tables of results.

Comparisons between PSS scores and stress measures. Since respondents were asked how often *in the last month* they had experienced the circumstances described by the PSS, it was expected that PSS scores would be most closely related to other measures that were designed to tap perceptions of stress within the previous month. Consequently, measures with a longer time reference (such as "in the past year" or "ever") were expected to be somewhat less closely related to PSS scores. These expectations were confirmed. A t-test revealed that mean PSS scores for subjects who indicated that they had *ever* experienced stress (mean = 19.3) were significantly ($p < .0001$) lower than scores of those who said there were things in life now that were upsetting or bothersome (mean = 23.2). Similarly, as Table 3.3 shows, PSS scores were correlated with reports of the amount of stress experienced during an average week ($r = .36$, $p < .0001$) and the amount of stress experienced now as compared to a year ago ($r = .26$, $p < .0001$).

Cohen, Kamarck, and Mermelstein (1983) found that PSS scores were moderately correlated with the number of life events that respondents indicated they had experienced within the last year. They also found that the correlation increased when respondents' perceptions of the events were taken into account. As shown in Table 3.3, PSS scores were correlated with number of life events ($r = .30$, $p < .0001$). However, in the present study, consideration of respondents' reports of the impact of these events did not increase the correlation, although, as would be expected, the correlation between perceived stress and negative impact ($r = -.27$, $p < .0001$) was higher than the correlation between PSS scores and overall impact ($r = -.10$, $p < .0001$). The life-events measures used in the Cohen et al. studies consisted of 99 items related to adjusting to the demands of college life (college student sample) and 71 items related to negative life events (smoking cessation sample). On the other hand, the life-events measure used in the present study contained only 16 events, some of which were negative, some positive, and some ambiguous. It may be that this much abbreviated scale was not as sensitive a measure of perceptions of life events as those used previously.

A final category of measures of potential stress had to do with certain characteristics of employed respondents' jobs. Correlations between PSS scores and these measures are shown in Table 3.3. Number of hours per week worked was inversely related to perceived stress ($r = -.10$, $p < .0001$), indicating that the more hours per week a person spent working, the lower were perceptions of stress. This relation was consistent with the finding reported above that part-time workers reported more stress than did full-time workers.

The two factors of the Job Responsibilities Scale, responsibilities with feedback and responsibilities without feedback, both correlated positively with PSS responses, indicating that the less responsibility a worker had, the higher were perceptions of stress. Further, the correlation between PSS scores and responsibilities with feedback ($r = .14$, $p < .0001$) was higher than for responsibilities without feedback ($r = .07$, $p < .002$).

Table 3.3
Correlations Between PSS14, PSS10, and PSS4 Scores and Stress Measures

Measure	PSS14	PSS10	PSS4
How much stress do you experience during an average week? (high scores = more stress)	.36 (1697)	.39 (1655)	.29 (1683)
Compared to a year ago, how much stress do you experience now? (high scores = more stress)	.26 (1694)	.26 (1653)	.23 (1680)
Life-events scales			
Number of events	.30 (2355)	.32 (2270)	.28 (2330)
Overall impact of events	–.10 (1765)	–.09 (1701)	–.09 (1746)
Negative impact of events	–.27 (1024)	–.27 (992)	–.26 (1015)
How many hours/week do you work?	–.10 (1485)	–.11 (1457)	–.12 (1472)
Job responsibilities scales (high scores = less responsibility)			
With feedback	.14 (1375)	.14 (1351)	.14 (1362)
Without feedback	.07* (1421)	.05,ns (1398)	.06,ns (1410)
Workload demand (high scores = high demand)	.03,ns (1228)	.06,ns (1205)	.03,ns (1217)

NOTE: The number of respondents in each condition is shown in parentheses. Unless otherwise indicated, all correlations are significant at $p < .001$ or better.
*$p < .005$; ns = nonsignificant.

Surprisingly, the measure of Workload Demand was not related to PSS scores of respondents who were employed full time ($r = .03$, n.s.). Apparently, job responsibilities that cause an employee to work overtime and miss lunches and breaks were not generally associated with the employee's perceptions of stress.

In summary, PSS scores were moderately related to responses on other measures of appraised stress, as well as to measures of potential sources of stress as assessed by event frequency. It also appeared that jobs with more responsibilities, especially those in which the employee received feedback about performance, were associated with *lower* levels of stress. However, certain aspects of employment that might typically be considered stressful, such as working overtime and missing lunches and breaks, were not related to perceptions of stress.

Comparisons between PSS scores and self-reported health and utilization of health services. As Table 3.4 shows, the individual question regarding health status was correlated with reports of stress (r = .23, p<.0001); the poorer that respondents perceived their health to be, the more stress they reported. Similarly, on the individual question about hospitalization, respondents who reported being hospitalized during the previous year had higher PSS scores (mean = 20.3) than did those who had not been in the hospital (mean = 19.5), although these differences were not significant at our set criterion of p<.001 (for PSS14, p<.10; for PSS10, p<.01; for PSS4, p<.05).

As expected, scores on the Health Services Utilization Scale were positively correlated with PSS scores (r = .21, p<.0001), as were responses to the measure of inability to perform routine activities (r = .21, p<.0001). Further, the number of serious illnesses respondents had ever had (r = .15, p<.0001), as well as the number of serious illnesses experienced within the last year (r = .14, p<.0001) were both positively related to perceptions of stress.

The three factors of the Psychosomatic Index were also related to PSS scores. Symptoms of potentially serious illness were positively correlated with perceived stress (r = .27, p<.0001), and the correlation was slightly higher for both factors concerned with symptoms indicative of less serious health conditions. For the Nonserious Symptoms factor, the correlation was .31 (p<.0001), and for symptoms possibly associated with flu, the correlation was .32 (p<.0001).

In summary, these results clearly demonstrate an association between self-reported physical illness and elevated stress as measured by the PSS. Both frequency of physical illness and symptoms of physical illness were positively related to reports of stress. Moreover, perceived stress was almost as closely related to serious symptomatology as to nonserious symptoms. Because these correlations are cross-sectional, no inferences of causality can be made. Although stress may have caused health problems, it is also possible that poor health elevated stress, or that a third factor, for example socioeconomic status, influenced both stress and health.

Comparisons between PSS scores and health behaviors. In general, relations between measures of various health behaviors and perceptions of stress were not impressive, as shown in Table 3.5.

Table 3.4
Correlations Between PSS14, PSS10, and PSS4 Scores and Self-Reported Health and Health Services Utilization Measures

Measure	PSS14	PSS10	PSS4
How is your health?			
(1 = excellent to 5 = poor)	.23	.22	.20
	(2353)	(2268)	(2327)
Index of inability to perform routine activities			
(high scores = more frequent difficulty)	.21	.23	.24
	(404)	(397)	(400)
Index of ever having had serious illness			
(high scores = more illnesses)	.15	.16	.13
	(2355)	(2270)	(2330)
Index of serious illness in last year			
(high scores = more illnesses)	.14	.15	.12
	(2355)	(2270)	(2330)
Psychosomatic index factors			
(high scores = more bothered)			
Non-serious symptoms	.31	.32	.26
	(2340)	(2258)	(2316)
Serious illness symptoms	.27	.28	.22
	(2350)	(2265)	(2325)
Flu symptoms	.32	.34	.27
	(2337)	(2254)	(2314)
Health services utilization scale			
(high scores = more utilization)	.21	.22	.18
	(288)	(277)	(287)

NOTE: The number of respondents in each condition is shown in parentheses.
Unless otherwise indicated, all correlations are significant at p < .001 or better.
ns = nonsignificant.

First, for the entire sample, the total number of hours of sleep per day was not correlated with PSS scores (r = −.01, n.s.). Further, when the sample was stratified by age grouping, none of the correlations reached our criterion of p<.001, although for respondents 65 years of age and older, the negative correlation of −.13 approached significance at p<.008. The negative correlation of the PSS with number of hours in the longest period of sleep per day was small, although statistically significant (r = −.08, p<.0001), suggesting a general tendency for stress to be associated with a shorter period of sleeping. When these data were analyzed by age group, only PSS scores of respondents between 18 and 29 years of age were significantly correlated with number of hours in the longest period of sleep

Table 3.5
Correlations Between PSS Scores and Health Behavior Measures

Measure	PSS14	PSS10	PSS4
In total, how many hours/day do you sleep?	−.01,ns	−.02,ns	.01,ns
	(2347)	(2264)	(2322)
How many hours in the longest period of sleep each day?	−.08	−.07	−.05,ns
	(2308)	(2231)	(2281)
How often do you eat breakfast?			
(1 = never to 7 = daily)	−.09	−.09	−.07
	(2354)	(2269)	(2328)
How often do you drink alcohol?			
(1 = never to 7 = daily)			
Total sample	−.04,ns	−.04,ns	−.06
	(2350)	(2265)	(2324)
Drinkers only	−.07*	−.08*	−.07*
	(1568)	(1530)	(1556)
When you drink, how many drinks per day?	.10	.08	.09
	(1549)	(1513)	(1538)
If you smoke, how many packs per day?	.03,ns	.02,ns	.03,ns
	(704)	(683)	(697)
How often do you exercise strenuously for 20 min. or longer?			
(1 = never to 7 = daily)	−.06*	−.06*	−.05,ns
	(2335)	(2256)	(2313)
Licit drug use scale:			
Total number of drugs taken	.17	.19	.15
	(2355)	(2270)	(2330)
prescription drugs	.13	.16	.12
	(2347)	(2262)	(2322)
over-the-counter drugs	.12	.13	.10
	(2349)	(2266)	(2326)
Frequency of all drug usage	.16	.18	.15
	(2127)	(2059)	(2110)
depressants	.27	.26	.28
	(374)	(357)	(368)
gastrointestinal/obesity	.14	.14	.12
	(811)	(785)	(799)
other drugs	.09	.10	.08
	(2043)	(1977)	(2027)

NOTE: The number of respondents in each condition is shown in parentheses.
Unless otherwise indicated, all correlations are significant at p < .001 or better.
* p < .005; ns = nonsignificant.

(r = –.13, p<.001). For subjects between 30 and 44 years of age, the correlation was marginal (r = –.09, p<.007).

Second, the frequency with which subjects ate breakfast was also related to PSS scores (r = –.09, p<.0001). This negative correlation indicates that people under stress eat breakfast less often than do those experiencing lower levels of stress.

Third, for the total sample of both drinkers and nondrinkers, frequency of drinking alcohol was not related to PSS scores (r = –.04, n.s.). Among respondents who indicated that they drank alcohol at all, number of drinks per day was positively related to higher PSS scores (r = .10, p<.0001). However, there was a marginal inverse relation between how many days alcoholic beverages were consumed and reports of perceived stress (r = –.07, p<.002). These data suggest that increased drinking under stress occurred on specific "drinking" days of the week, perhaps on weekends.

A fourth category of health behaviors concerned cigarette smoking. A one-way ANOVA revealed that respondents who said they were currently smoking had marginally (p<.004) higher PSS scores than those who had quit smoking or had never smoked. Table 3.6 presents mean PSS scores for this measure. However, among smokers, there was no relation between perceptions of stress and how many packs of cigarettes per day were smoked (r = .03, n.s.). Fifth, there was a small and marginally significant correlation between frequency of exercise and PSS responses (r = –.06, p<.003), with increased stress associated with infrequent physical exercise.

Finally, usage of licit drugs, as measured by (1) number of different drugs taken and (2) frequency of usage, was compared to PSS scores. Perceived stress was correlated with total number of drugs taken (r = .17, p<.0001), as well as with the two subcategories: number of prescription drugs (r = .13, p<.0001) and over-the-counter drugs (r = .12, p<.0001). In all cases, taking more varieties of medication was related to higher reports of stress. Frequency of all drug usage also increased with increased PSS scores (r = .16, p<.0001), as did usage of the three subcategories of drugs: other drugs, r = .09, p<.0001; depressants, r = .27, p<.0001; gastrointestinal/ obesity drugs, r = .14, p<.0001.

In summary, perceptions of stress were only slightly related to self-reports of health behaviors. Small but statistically significant correlations were observed between elevated PSS scores and (1) shorter periods of sleep, (2) infrequent consumption of breakfast, (3) increased quantity of alcohol consumption, (4) usage of more licit drugs, and (5) frequency of licit drug usage. Marginal relations were also found between stress and smoking, lack of physical exercise, and fewer days per week of alcohol consumption (for

Table 3.6
Mean PSS Scores for Respondent Smoking Status

Status	*PSS14*	*PSS10*	*PSS4*
Currently smoke	20.4	13.7	4.8
	(708)	(686)	(700)
Once smoked, but quit	19.1	12.6	4.2
	(616)	(583)	(605)
Never smoked	19.4	12.8	4.5
	(1028)	(998)	(1022)

NOTE: The number of respondents in each condition is shown in parentheses.

those who drink). Smokers reported higher levels of perceived stress than did nonsmokers. Perceptions of stress were not associated with total hours slept per day nor, among smokers, with number of packs of cigarettes smoked per day. However, associations between stress and health practices may be underestimated because self-reports of many of these behaviors, particularly alcohol and drug consumption, may be subject to social desirability effects.

Comparison of PSS scores and Life Satisfaction Scale. Levels of perceived stress should be inversely related to reports of satisfaction with self, job, and life in general. This expectation was confirmed. High PSS scores were correlated with reports of increased dissatisfaction ($r = .47$, $p<.0001$). However, to some extent, this correlation may be artifactual, since it is possible that the two scales may be tapping the same underlying concepts.

Comparisons between PSS scores and measures of help-seeking behavior. We assumed that the need for help increases with an increasing stress level and hence predicted a positive relation between the PSS and help-seeking. Table 3.7 presents mean PSS scores for the help-seeking measure. A one-way ANOVA revealed that respondents who reported having considered seeking help in the past year for personal or emotional problems (whether they actually got help or not), had higher PSS scores than did those who had not thought about getting help ($p<.0001$). Scheffe tests for differences between group means revealed that, those who had gotten help did not differ from those who considered help but failed to receive it, but scores for both these groups were higher than scores of individuals who had not considered seeking aid. One interpretation of these results is that people think about getting help only for problems that are bothersome enough to be stressful. Perhaps those who had not considered seeking aid had no serious emotional or personal problems in the past year and so actually experienced little stress.

Discussion

The major goals of this chapter included (1) providing psychometric data on the three different versions of the PSS, (2) describing variations in stress levels for subgroups of the U.S. population, and providing PSS norms for each subgroup for use in evaluating scores from other samples, (3) comparing perceived stress scores to scores on other stress measures, and (4) examining the association between the PSS scales and a wide range of measures of health and health behavior. In this section, we discuss the evidence reported in regard to these issues, making recommendations when appropriate.

Which Scale Is Best?

The psychometric acceptability of the PSS14 was supported by evidence reported in an earlier paper (Cohen et al., 1983) and similarly supported in terms of reliability and construct validity by the data reported in this chapter. One of the unique goals of this chapter was to compare the psychometric qualities of the shorter versions of the PSS with the original 14-item scale. With the large sample size provided by the Harris survey, we were able to determine that the PSS10 provides as adequate a measure of perceived stress as the longer scale. Moreover, the PSS10 had a somewhat tighter factor structure and a slightly better internal reliability than the PSS14, and correlations between the PSS10 and various outcomes were equivalent to those found with the original scale. For this reason, we recommend use of the PSS10 in future research. The PSS4 demonstrated a moderate loss in reliability, but its factor structure and predictive validity were good. Although we recommend use of the 10-item scale when time allows, the PSS4 is appropriate for use in situations requiring a very brief measure of stress perceptions.

Table 3.7
Mean PSS14, PSS10, and PSS4 Scores for the Measure
of Help-Seeking Behavior

Behavior	PSS14	PSS10	PSS4
Considered & obtained help	22.8	16.0	5.6
	(383)	(378)	(379)
Considered, but did not obtain help	23.6	16.6	6.1
	(136)	(135)	(136)
Did not consider seeking help	18.7	12.1	4.2
	(1785)	(1709)	(1765)

NOTE: The number of respondents in each condition is shown in parentheses.

Distribution of Perceived Stress in the Population

We view the distribution of perceived stress across demographic characteristics as indicative of the likelihood that specific groups of people encounter stressful life events and/or appraise encountered events as stressful. Our data are consistent with traditional conceptions of groups who should be experiencing greater stress because of the demands of their environments and the lack of adequate resources for coping with events. These include persons with relatively low socioeconomic status (lower income, less education, more children, more persons in household), the unemployed and disabled, those in occupations with relatively low degrees of status and control, those who are divorced, separated, or never married, racial and ethnic minorities, females, and the young.

There are relatively few data on the distribution of stress in the population to compare with these. An exception is work reported by Henderson, Byrne, and Duncan-Jones (1981) on the distribution of life events in a community sample of 756 adults residing in Canberra, Australia. In their work, distributions of events were calculated from data collected from a 73-item stressful life-event interview. Data for both event frequency and event impact were similar, hence only the latter (closer to perceived stress) is discussed here. Consistent with the results presented earlier, event impact was found to decrease with age, and to be greater among the single, divorced, and separated than the married and widowed. However, no differences were found in the Australian study for either sex or income. Moreover, in contrast to our finding of a decrease in perceived stress with greater education in their study, event impact increased with increased education. The discrepancies between the two studies may be attributable to differences in the sensitivity of the stress scales, cultural differences, and differences in the range of the demographic variables under consideration (e.g., income ranged from less than $1,000 to over $15,000 in the Australian sample compared with less than $5,000 to over $50,000 in the U.S. sample).

Perceived Stress and Other Stress Measures

In order to further establish the construct validity of the PSS, we examined the relation of the PSS14, PSS10, and PSS4 with other items and scales assessing stress within the survey. As expected, PSS scores were moderately related to responses on other measures of stress, as well as to measures of potential sources of stress. However, certain aspects of employment that might typically be considered stressful, such as working overtime and missing lunches and breaks, were not related to perceptions of stress. It also appeared that jobs with more responsibilities, especially those in which the employee received feedback about performance, were associated with *lower* levels of stress. This, of course, is consistent with the idea that persons with greater control over events are less likely to perceive them as stressful.

Perceived Stress, Health, and Health Behaviors

It is generally believed that stress detrimentally influences health status and interferes with the performance of health practices. Although the cross-sectional nature of our data did not allow causal analyses, we examined the concurrent data for evidence consistent with these hypotheses. Frequency of serious illnesses, and both serious and nonserious symptoms of illness were positively related to perceived stress. Small correlations were also observed between perceived stress and health practices. Elevated PSS scores were associated with: (1) shorter periods of sleep, (2) infrequent consumption of breakfast, (3) smoking cigarettes, (4) decreased frequency but increased quantity of alcohol consumption, (5) less frequent physical exercise, and (6) increased frequency and variety of licit drug use. On the other hand, perceptions of stress were not associated with total hours of sleep per day or number of packs of cigarettes smoked per day.

Summary and Conclusion

Perceived stress is assumed to be an important mediator of the pathway linking stressful events to poorer health and health practices. The data reported in this chapter establish associations between perceived stress and illness, illness symptoms, and a wide range of health behaviors. They also indicate that persons with less power and wealth in our society are more prone to generalized perceptions of stress. These data support the traditional views regarding the distribution of stress and effects of stress on health.

The analyses in this chapter also provide evidence that the PSS does an adequate job of measuring appraised stress. With the possible exception of life satisfaction, and minor physical symptoms, there is little or no overlap between the constructs measured by the PSS and what is assessed by the outcomes scales in this study. Hence these relationship data are not subject to a "confounding" explanation. The work is, however, cross-sectional and therefore no causal inference is implied in our report.

Finally, the PSS scale has been established as an economical tool for assessing perceived stress in the population. We reiterate, however, that perceived stress scales are not always appropriate. Scales should be chosen to address specific questions being posed in a research project, and used in methodological contexts in which alternative explanations are minimized. As discussed earlier, perceived stress scales should not be used in cross-sectional studies of the relation between stress and psychological distress.

APPENDIX A
Items and Instructions for Perceived Stress Scale

The questions in this scale ask you about your feelings and thoughts during the last month. In each case, you will be asked to indicate *how often* you felt or thought a certain way. Although some of the questions are similar, there are differences between them and you should treat each one as a separate question. The best approach is to answer fairly quickly. That is, don't try to count up the number of times you felt a particular way; rather indicate the alternative that seems like a reasonable estimate.

For each question choose from the following alternatives:

0. never
1. almost never

2. sometimes
3. fairly often
4. very often

1. In the last month, how often have you been upset because of something that happened unexpectedly?
2. In the last month, how often have you felt that you were unable to control the important things in your life?
3. In the last month, how often have you felt nervous and "stressed"?
4. In the last month, how often have you dealt successfully with day to day problems and annoyances?
5. In the last month, how often have you felt that you were effectively coping with important changes that were occurring in your life?
6. In the last month, how often have you felt confident about your ability to handle your personal problems?
7. In the last month, how often have you felt that things were going your way?
8. In the last month, how often have you found that you could not cope with all the things that you had to do?
9. In the last month, how often have you been able to control irritations in your life?
10. In the last month, how often have you felt that you were on top of things?
11. In the last month, how often have you been angered because of things that happened that were outside of your control?
12. In the last month, how often have you found yourself thinking about things that you have to accomplish?
13. In the last month, how often have you been able to control the way you spend your time?
14. In the last month, how often have you felt difficulties were piling up so high that you could not overcome them?

NOTE: Items 4, 5, 6, 7, 9, 10, and 13 are scored in the reverse direction.

Notes

1. The PSS scale is reprinted with permission of the American Sociological Association, from Cohen, S., Kamarck, T., and Mermelstein, R. (1983). A global measure of perceived stress. *Journal of Health and Social Behavior, 24,* 386-396.

2. One could argue that stress itself is a symptom of distress, hence, even if a particular dimension is not tapped in both scales, it should be.

References

Averill, J. R. (1973). Personal control over aversive stimuli and its relationship to stress. *Psychological Bulletin, 80,* 286-303.

Cohen, S. (1978). Environmental load and the allocation of attention. In A. Baum, J. Singer, & S. Valins (Eds.), *Advances in environmental psychology* (Vol. 1). Hillsdale, NJ: Lawrence Erlbaum.

Cohen, S. (1986). Contrasting the hassles scale and the perceived stress scale: Who's really measuring appraised stress? *American Psychologist, 41,* 717-718.

Cohen, S., Kamarck, T., & Mermelstein, R. (1983). A global measure of perceived stress. *Journal of Health and Social Behavior, 24,* 385-396.

Cohen, S., Mermelstein, R., Kamarck, T., & Hoberman, H. (1985). Measuring the functional components of social support. In I. G. Sarason & B. R. Sarason (Eds.), *Social support: Theory, research and application.* The Hague, Netherlands: Martinus Nijhoff.

Cohen, S., Sherrod, D. R., & Clark, M. S. (1986). Social skills and the stress-protective role of social support. *Journal of Personality and Social Psychology, 50,* 963-973.

Derogatis, L., Rickels, K., & Rock, A. (1976). The SCL-90 and the MMPI: A step in the validation of a new self-report scale. *British Journal of Psychiatry, 128,* 280-289.

Dohrenwend, B. P., & Shrout, P. E. (1985). "Hassles" in the conceptualization and measurement of life stress variables. *American Psychologist, 40,* 780-785.

Dohrenwend, B. P., Shrout, P. E., Egri, G., & Mendelsohn, F. S. (1978). What psychiatric screening scales measure in the general population: Part I: Jerome Frank's concept of demoralization. In S. Sudman (Ed.), *Proceedings of the Third Biennial Conference of Health Survey Methods.* Washington, DC: National Center for Health Statistics.

Dohrenwend, B. P., Shrout, P. E., Egri, G., & Mendelsohn, F. S. (1980). What psychiatric screening scales measure in the general population: Part II: The components of demoralization by contrast with other dimensions of psychopathology. *Archives of General Psychiatry, 37,* 1229-1236.

Frenzel, M. P., McCaul, K. D., Glasgow, R. E., & Schafer, L. C. (in press). The relationship of stress and coping to regimen adherence and glycemic control of diabetes. *Journal of Social and Clinical Psychology.*

Glasgow, R. E., Klesges, R. C., Mizes, J. S., & Pechacek, T. F. (1985). Quitting smoking: Strategies used and variables associated with success in a stop-smoking contest. *Journal of Consulting and Clinical Psychology, 53,* 905-912.

Glass, D. C., & Singer, J. E. (1972). *Urban stress: Experiments on noise and social stressors.* New York: Academic Press.

Goldberg, D. P. (1972). *The detection of psychiatric illness by questionnaire.* London: Oxford University Press.

Henderson, S., Byrne, D. G., & Duncan-Jones, P. (1981). *Neurosis and the social environment.* Sydney, Australia: Academic Press.

Kahn, R. L., Wolfe, D. M., Quinn, R. P., Snoek, J. D., & Rosenthal, R. A. (1964). *Organizational stress: Studies in role conflict and ambiguity.* New York: John Wiley.

Keating, J. (1979). Environmental stressors misplaced emphasis. In I. G. Sarason & C. D. Spielberger (Eds.), *Stress and anxiety* (Vol. 6). Washington, DC: Hemisphere.

Kuiper, N. A., Olinger, J., & Lyons, L. M. (1986) Global perceived stress level as a moderator of the relationship between negative life events and depression. *Journal of Human Stress, 12,* 149-153.

Lazarus, R. S. (1966). *Psychological stress and the coping process.* New York: McGraw-Hill.

Lazarus, R. S. (1977). Psychological stress and coping in adaptation and illness. In Z. J. Lipowski, D. R. Lipsi, & P. C. Whybrow (Eds.), *Psychosomatic medicine: Current trends.* New York: Oxford University Press.

Lazarus, R. S., DeLongis, A., Folkman, S., & Gruen, R. (1985). Stress and adaptational outcomes: The problem of confounded measures. *American Psychologist, 40,* 770-779.

Lazarus, R. S., & Folkman, S. (1984). *Stress, coping, and adaptation.* New York: Springer.

Lei, H., & Skinner, H. A. (1980). A psychometric study of life events and social readjustment. *Journal of Psychosomatic Research, 24,* 57-65.

Lin, N., Dean, A., & Ensel, W. (Eds.). (1986). *Social support, life events, and depression.* Orlando, FL: Academic Press.

Linville, P. W. (1987) Self-complexity as a cognitive buffer against stress-related illness and depression. *Journal of Personality and Social Psychology. 52,* 663-676.

Sarason, I. G., Johnson, J. H., & Siegel, J. M. (1978). Assessing the impact of life changes: Development of the life experiences survey. *Journal of Consulting and Clinical Psychology, 46,* 932-946.

Seligman, M.E.P. (1975). *Helplessness: On depression, development and death.* San Francisco: W. H. Freeman.

Vinokur, A., & Selzer, M. L. (1975). Desirable versus undesirable life events: Their relationship to stress and mental distress. *Journal of Personality and Social Psychology, 32,* 329-377.

Worchel, S. (1978). Reducing crowding without increasing space: Some applications of an attributional theory of crowding. *Journal of Population, 1,* 216-230.

Worchel, S., & Teddlie, C. (1976). The experience of crowding: A two factor theory. *Journal of Personality and Social Psychology, 34,* 30-40.

4

The Other Side of Perceived Control: Disadvantages and Negative Effects

SUZANNE C. THOMPSON
PAUL R. CHEEK
MELODY A. GRAHAM

T he hypothesis that perceptions of control ameliorate the effects of stressful situations has generated several decades of research. Despite the intuitive appeal of this idea, the findings on the effects of control indicate a more complicated relationship. Reviews of the control and stress literature have concluded that under some conditions perceptions of control do reduce stress and arousal, but the availability of a control response does not necessarily reduce stress; its effects depend upon the meaning of control in that situation (Averill, 1973; Thompson, 1981). Perceptions of control also appear to be less effective in reducing stress during administration of a stressor than during the anticipatory or postevent periods (Thompson, 1981). In general, the negative side of having control has been ignored, although there has been some interest in the idea that perceptions of control are not always adaptive and, at times, may actually increase stress or pain (Burger, McWard, & LaTorre, 1986; Rodin, Rennert, & Solomon, 1980; also see Folkman, 1984, for an interesting analysis of control in terms of Lazarus' theory of coping), in general, the negative side of having control has been ignored. The purposes of the present chapter are to examine the hypothesis that situations that engender feelings of control are sometimes maladaptive, and to explore the conditions that lead to positive or negative effects of control.

First, it is necessary to consider what is meant by "perceptions of control." If control is defined as the ability to get desired outcomes, or as a contingency between actions and outcomes with feedback showing that progress is in the desired direction (Fisher, 1984), then it is difficult to see how control might be undesirable or maladaptive. By definition, people would prefer a condition that allowed them to achieve their desires. Such a state would also appear to be more adaptive and less stressful than a condition without that feature.

However, this definition does not adequately capture many of the manipulations or naturally occurring variations in control that research has examined. These include the opportunity to avoid an aversive outcome by performing well on a task; being involved in one's own health care; practicing health-promoting behaviors; self-administration of a noxious stimulus, such as drawing a blood sample; being the one to make a choice or a decision; instruction in cognitive techniques that could be used to reduce pain or stress; and receiving information about what to expect in a situation, which presumably allows one to prepare for a stressful event and therefore reduce its impact.

There are four characteristics of these control options that are important to consider. First, they are often *perceptions* of control that may or may not be veridical. The perception could be inaccurate and, if so, control efforts would fail. Second, in most situations, the control available is *probabilistic*; that is, one's efforts may make it more likely to get a desired outcome, but success is not certain. Thus even if one's perceptions of control were accurate, one's efforts toward control could lead to failure. Third, the desired outcome in a potential control situation is frequently *multidimensional*; that is, more than one type of goal is desired. A decision about a health issue, for example, could also have implications for other goals, such as self-esteem, interpersonal relationships, and finances. Exercising control might make the desired health outcome more likely, but could adversely affect some other goals. Fourth, perceived control is often the *potential* to affect an outcome. It may be rather costly to actualize that potential and attempt to have control in a situation. The costs may involve considerable effort, financial loss, hassle, worry, and/or increased stress.

To illustrate these points, consider the example of stroke patients who want to avoid having a second stroke. Many stroke patients believe that they can avoid a recurrence of stroke if they watch their diets and avoid stress in their lives (Thompson, Sobolew, Graham, & Janigian, 1987). This control is a perception; for any one patient, dietary and stress-related changes may or may not make a difference. The control is probabilistic because even if life changes may *reduce* the risk of a second stroke, a second stroke incident could still occur. These characteristics of control mean that control efforts can result in failure. In addition, the situation has multidimensional outcomes because stroke patients may not be concerned just with recurrence of a stroke, but also with the quality of their relationships with others, with their financial situations, or with maintaining positive affect. The control available is also a potential that must be exercised to be effective. Exercising it may involve a restrictive and difficult diet or avoiding certain social situations or reducing work activities. Thus attempting to avoid a second stroke may adversely affect other outcomes.

These four characteristics of control options make it reasonable to assume that perceived control is not always desired and actually can be maladaptive.

Factors That Influence the Effects of Control

Although there has been very little research on the negative aspects of control, a number of researchers have found that manipulations designed to increase control, and therefore to reduce stress, anxiety, or pain, have had the opposite effect or were not effective. We next consider research findings concerning a number of factors that might be expected to influence the adaptiveness of perceived control.

Effort and Attention

There is some evidence that control options that require effort and attention to execute are no more effective than not having control, or can actually increase arousal in comparison to situations in which no control is available to influence a stressful event. Solomon, Holmes, and McCaul (1980) found that self-reported anxiety about receipt of a painful shock was reduced if subjects believed they could avoid the shock by successful performance on a task, but only if the task required low effort. A high-effort-task control option produced as much anxiety as the condition without control. A second measure of stress, physiological arousal, was reduced during the pretask anticipatory period if subjects believed they would later have the control option, but not during the performance period when the control had to be exercised. Difficult-to-exercise control was more arousing than was low-effort control and just as arousing as a situation in which no control was available. In Manuck, Harvey, Lechleiter, and Neal's (1978) study, subjects who could control the receipt of unpleasant noise by their performance on a difficult cognitive task showed greater physiological arousal than did subjects with no control option available. Other studies have also found that having to perform well on a task to avoid electric shock is more arousing than is administration of the shock without an opportunity to avoid it (Elliott, 1969; Houston, 1972). It appears that control options that require attention and effort may at times increase, rather than reduce, stress.

Amount of Control

Mills and Krantz (1979) raise the possibility that high levels of control may be more stressful than moderate levels of control. Their study investigated the effects of two different control manipulations: information about the procedures, and a choice to be made by the participant. Donors at a blood bank were given no control, one control option, or two options (information and a choice of arm to be used in the procedure). Stress experienced by the patient was assessed through observation of nursing staff interventions to aid the patient, and through nurse and patient reports of patient distress. Both information and choice, administered alone, reduced stress during the donation, but donors who received both information and choice were more stressed during donation than were the single-option groups and reported the most pain in the postsession period. Corah and Boffa (1970) also found that the availability of one type of control (either an "escape" condition or a choice condition) was more effective in reducing sound-discomfort ratings than was the combination of both types of control.

In contrast to these studies, Sherrod, Hage, Halpern, and Moore (1977) found that both control over the initiation of aversive noise and control over its termination resulted in better concurrent and posttask performance. The combination of both types of control led to the least performance degradation in comparison to a group who did not receive aversive noise.

Perceptions of control, however, did not affect the perceived stressfulness of the noise.

Thus there is some evidence to suggest that higher levels of control or combinations of control options may increase stress, but not in all circumstances. Perhaps an increase in control is maladaptive only when it increases the effort and attention necessary to exercise the control. In the Sherrod et al. (1977) study, the control option was a one-time decision to turn on or turn off the noise tape, whereas in Mills and Krantz's (1979) study, the choice and information conditions may have signaled to the blood donors that their task was to control their reactions throughout the procedure. The potential increase in control under these circumstances may have made the task more difficult.

Lack of Information

Information can function as a control option by allowing individuals to prepare for a noxious event, as in the Mills and Krantz (1979) study. Information may also be a precondition that determines whether or not individuals will desire or choose to use other types of control. Rodin, Rennert, and Solomon (1980) suggest that individuals will not be motivated to have or exercise control if sufficient information to evaluate the alternatives effectively is not available. They found that subjects expended less effort on a task that would assure them of an opportunity to select their own portion of food if they had not previously sampled the food portions that were available. Presumably, without sampling, subjects did not have enough information about the choices to be motivated to exert control. Condry (cited in Rodin, Rennert, & Solomon, 1980) independently varied the amount of choice available to subjects and the amount of information subjects had about those choices. His results showed that subjects in the high-choice/low-information groups expended the least effort on the task and had the most negative attitude toward it.

Thus it appears that the availability of control without sufficient information to use it effectively is not seen as desirable.

Preferred Coping Styles

The possibility that the effects of control depend on individuals' preferred styles of dealing with stress has also been investigated. The idea is that those who do not expect control (i.e., people with an external locus of control) or those who deal with stress by repression or denial would be more stressed by situations in which control is available. Several studies have found that sensitizers benefited from information about self-control options following stressful medical procedures but that the same information was counterproductive for repressors or deniers (Andrew, 1970; Shipley, Butt, & Horowitz, 1979; Shipley, Butt, Horowitz, & Farbry, 1978). However, Houston (1972) found no support for the idea that locus of control interacted with the effects of a control option on measures of anxiety and arousal while anticipating the delivery of shock, although short-term memory performance was better when subjects were in situations that matched their dispositional expectations for control. In addition, weight-loss programs appear to be more effective when the design of the program matches preferences for control, that is, people who were internal in health locus of control lost more weight in individual programs and externals lost more weight in group programs (Wallston, Wallston, Kaplan, & Maides, 1976).

Individuals also seem to prefer and seek out situations that match their desired level of control. For example, compared to externals on health locus of control, internals prefer control in health-related areas (Wallston, Smith, King, Forsberg, Wallston, & Nagy, 1983), are more involved in their postoperative care (Johnson, Leventhal, & Dabbs, 1971), and are more likely to practice preventive dental care (Williams, 1972). These findings indicate that control options that are incongruent with an individual's desired or expected level of control will not be preferred and, in some cases, may actually be maladaptive.

Unsuccessful Control Attempts

Perceptions of control may also be maladaptive when the attempt to exercise control is ineffective and leads to failure. There are several reasons to suspect that it is more stressful to experience a failure when one has tried to achieve success or avoid the negative outcome than if one expected or accepted the failure.

Research done with animals is suggestive here. Weiss (1971a) proposed that ulceration in rats in stressful situations increases when the number of coping attempts is high and feedback that the attempts are successful is low. He found that animals that had an effective way to delay shock but did not receive feedback about the success of their attempts had more severe ulceration than did animals without a way to control the shock (Weiss, 1971b). Thus, in rats, it is not adaptive to increase coping attempts without providing feedback that those efforts are effective.

Although this intriguing hypothesis does not appear to have been tested with human subjects, there is research showing that humans will refrain from exercising control in situations in which the probability of success is not high. Rothbaum, Weisz, and Snyder (1982) reviewed the evidence that those who see a fairly high chance of failure, either because of the structure of the situation or because of low self-esteem, will attempt to avoid the disappointment of failing to obtain a sought-after goal by not exercising the available control. Disappointment when one's expectations are not fulfilled is one way in which exercising control can be stressful.

Lack of preparation for failure. Besides disappointment, there are a number of other reasons why an unsuccessful effort to control one's environment can increase stress. One possibility is that those who expect control and attempt to exercise it may be cognitively unprepared for failure. This assumes (a) that certain cognitive states or perspectives reduce the aversiveness of stressful events, like failure, and (b) that exercising control is not conducive to those perspectives.

The evidence regarding the first assumption, that certain cognitive perspectives can reduce stress, is fairly clear. The distinction between actively trying to control one's environment and managing one's emotional reactions by adapting to the environment is a well-known one, especially in many Eastern philosophies, and has been applied to describing different ways that people cope with stressful experiences. Rothbaum, Weisz, and Snyder (1982), for example, make a distinction between primary control (changing the environment to achieve desired outcomes) and secondary control (changing oneself to fit better with the environment). Primary control is the type of perceived control being discussed in this chapter. Secondary control involves making attributions about one's limited ability, about chance, or about powerful others, all of which help one to understand and give meaning to uncontrollable events so they are more easily accepted and, therefore, less stressful. Finding meaning may also be achieved by reevaluating a negative, stressful experience in a more positive light: for example, comparing oneself to others who are worse off, finding benefits in the experience, considering worse alternatives, or changing to goals that are more easily achieved in the new circumstances. A number of studies have found that these ways of giving meaning to an undesirable situation are associated with less stress and better psychological adaptation

(Chodoff, Friedman, & Hamburg, 1964; Taylor, Wood, & Lichtman, 1983; Thompson, 1985). Thus individuals who adopt these cognitive orientations in situations in which control is not possible or not exercised are likely to be better prepared for the stressful consequences.

The second assumption, that attempting to exercise control to get a desired change in the environment is not compatible with adapting to the situation, is more problematic. Intuitively, it would seem that emphasizing one's limited ability or the role of external factors or highlighting the positive aspects of an undesired state would reduce the motivation to attempt control. Thus those who were cognitively best prepared for a negative experience would be least likely to try to avoid it. Conversely, those who expect to be able to exert control and avoid a negative outcome would not be well prepared for failure and, therefore, might be more devastated by it. In support of this point, Rothbaum, Weisz, and Snyder (1982) suggest that those relying mainly on primary control are likely to experience helplessness when the efforts to exert control are unsuccessful and the undesired event occurs. However, they also maintain that individuals are able to use both primary and secondary control in many situations. Indeed, the most adaptive posture is seen as a balance of both processes. Some of the examples they use to illustrate this point, however, indicate that they mean that it is adaptive to try to control some outcomes but to accept other outcomes, whereas the present analysis is concerned with the possibility of adapting to a particular undesired situation while at the same time trying to control or avoid it.

A study done by Folkman and Lazarus (1980) may be more relevant. Respondents were asked to indicate how they coped with real life events over the course of seven months and were found to use *both* problem-focused techniques (attempting to change the event) and emotion-focused strategies (attempting to control their emotions) for over 98% of the reported events. So this study does indicate that problem- and emotion-regulating strategies are not incompatible.

Another possibility is that some individuals are particularly adept at both trying to achieve desired outcomes and preparing themselves for failure at the same time, whereas others are less likely to use this approach. Norem and Cantor (1986) have studied those who use a strategy of defensive pessimism to manage their anxiety about achievement situations. Defensive pessimists, despite a high level of past achievement, expect failure on an upcoming task and use their anxiety about this to motivate themselves to try hard on the task. So, for these individuals, trying to exercise control and being prepared for failure (at least, to the extent that they are prepared because failure is expected) are not incompatible.

Thus the second assumption, that those who try to change a situation are less likely also to adapt to it cognitively, has intuitive appeal but apparently no research support. Until further research can clarify the relationship between primary and secondary control, the hypothesis that expecting and exercising control leaves one less prepared for failure remains an open question.

Being held responsible by others. Control efforts that fail may also be maladaptive if others hold the person responsible for the negative outcome. For example, a person may not want control over deciding where a group of friends should go on vacation because, if the vacation turns out badly, he or she may be held responsible for the outcome.

Although no research has been conducted directly on the hypothesis that control may be maladaptive if others hold one responsible for the negative outcome, there is evidence that having control over a negative situation leads to blame for the situation by others. For example, Weiner, Amirkhan, Folkes, and Verette (in press) manipulated the amount of control that subjects thought a confederate had over a negative outcome (being late for a joint experiment). Tardy confederates who offered an excuse involving events that were beyond their control provoked less anger, resentment, irritation, and dislike than did confederates who offered an excuse involving controllable events or no excuse at all. This suggests that having control over a negative situation is likely to lead to being held responsible for the situation by other people. Not only are others more likely to blame an individual for an event or hold the person responsible who had control over the outcome, but they are more likely to evaluate the person negatively (Snyder & Higgins, in press). Thus, in situations in which people find it stressful or harmful to be evaluated negatively by others, control may not be desired and may increase stress.

Holding oneself responsible. Another reason unsuccessful efforts to exert control may lead to more stress than relinquishing control is that attempts to control a situation may lead to blaming oneself for the negative consequences when the control effort fails. An important question here is whether or not it is maladaptive to hold oneself responsible for a negative event. The evidence concerning the effects of self-responsibility on psychological adaptation to stressful events is quite mixed. Some studies find worse outcomes among those who hold themselves responsible (Abrams & Finesinger, 1953; Graham, Thompson, Estrada, & Yonekura, in press; Meyer & Taylor, 1986), some studies find no relationship between self-responsibility and coping (Taylor, Lichtman, & Wood, 1984), and in a number of studies, self-responsibility is associated with better coping (Bulman & Wortman, 1977; Baum, Fleming, & Singer, 1983; Tennen, Affleck, & Gershman, 1986).

Janoff-Bulman (1979) proposed that two types of self-blame can be distinguished: characterological self-blame that involves attributions to stable aspects of oneself (e.g., ability, character), and behavioral self-blame, in which blame is assigned to one's own modifiable behavior. She predicted that characterological self-blame should be maladaptive, but behavioral self-blame should be associated with successful adjustment. This is an important distinction; however, it does not always successfully predict when self-blame will or will not be adaptive. One limitation is that behavioral and characterological measures of self-blame often are highly correlated (Thompson & Janigian, 1987) and can have similar effects on coping (Meyer & Taylor, 1986; Thompson & Janigian, 1987).

Taylor (1983) suggested that it is difficult to find consistent effects of causal attributions for real world events because the attributions are unlikely to have the same meanings in all situations. In some cases, self-blame may be associated with mastery, whereas in other situations it may produce guilt and self-recrimination. Thompson and Janigian (1987) have attempted to identify the types of situations in which self-responsibility will be adaptive or maladaptive. They propose that in situations that arouse concern about one's enduring abilities or dispositions (achievement situations), self-responsibility will be associated with poor psychological adjustment. However, in situations in which the central concern is understanding why the event occurs, what it means, and how to avoid it in the future (accident situations), self-responsibility is more likely to be adaptive.

In one study, Janigian and Thompson (1985) asked respondents to recall an important achievement failure and an important accident failure that had occurred in the past year, make attributions for them, rate how much they could avoid a similar event in the future, and judge their present emotional reactions to the events (e.g., helpless, depressed, incompetent). Blaming oneself (both characterologically and behaviorally) was significantly related to feeling worse about oneself and more incompetent in achievement situations but not in accident situations. Self-blame was correlated with greater perceptions of future avoidability and less helplessness for accidents, but not for achievement situations.

In a second study, respondents kept daily records of the most negative event that had happened to them each day, and made similar ratings of attributions, future avoidance, emotional reactions, and unfairness (Thompson & Janigian, 1987). Blaming oneself for an accident situation did not appear to be maladaptive: Those who did so felt the situation to be fairer, judged that they could avoid a future occurrence, and did not feel worse emotionally. However, for achievement failures, self-blame was related to worse emotional outcomes. A difference between the effects of behavioral and characterological self-blame was found on the unfairness and future-avoidability ratings: Those who blamed their behavior for the achievement failure found the event to be fairer and more avoidable; characterological self-blame was not related to fairness and avoidability. Thus holding oneself responsible for a negative event may not be adaptive if the situation arouses concern about one's enduring abilities or dispositions.

It is interesting to note that people will often refrain from exercising control in a situation that has likelihood of failure, presumably to avoid internal attributions for the failure. The research on self-handicapping shows that in achievement situations in which failure is anticipated, subjects will often choose a condition that increases their chances of failure, but that has the advantage of avoiding the costs of self-responsibility (Jones & Berglas, 1978). It appears that self-responsibility for achievement failures is not seen as desirable. It is under these circumstances, then, that one would expect failure to be more stressful in a situation in which one had attempted control than had one not attempted control (and hence would not hold oneself responsible).

Disconfirmations of Control

A more extreme situation than a single control failure occurs when individuals discover that they never had, or no longer have, control over an important area of life. Some theorists have suggested that belief in control may be maladaptive if the situation turns out, in fact, not to be controllable; in those circumstances it may be more distressing if one originally believed that one had control than if one did not (Folkman, 1984; Wortman & Brehm, 1975). Two studies provide some support for this hypothesis. Scheppele and Bart (1983) found that rape survivors who had been attacked in what they considered safe situations (by men they trusted, or at home with the doors locked, or when they were following the "rules of rape avoidance") were more likely to have a severe fear reaction in the aftermath of the rape than were those who were attacked in unsafe situations. The researchers suggested that the loss of controllability contributed to the extreme distress experienced by those who believed themselves to be safe; those attacked in less safe situations did not feel that they had been actively attempting to avoid rape and so were less likely to experience a loss of controllability.

Schulz and Hanusa (1978) assessed the long-term psychological and physical effects of participation in a research study that manipulated control among retirement home residents. There were four groups in the original study: those who could control the frequency and duration of visits from college undergraduates, those who could predict but not control the visits, those visited on a random schedule, and those who did not receive visits (Schulz, 1976). At the end of the visitation period, it was found that those in the control and predict groups were significantly superior to the other two groups on health and psychological-state measures. However, in the follow-up studies, conducted 24, 30, and 42 months later, the control and predict groups had declined dramatically after the intervention ended and were actually lower in psychological functioning than the other two groups, although this difference was not statistically significant. The random-visits and no-visits groups remained fairly stable over time. Furthermore, the control and predict groups had a marginally significant higher mortality rate than had the two comparison groups. The authors speculated that the violation of control expectancy that occurred when the original study ended may have been responsible for the precipitous decline in residents who had experienced control or predictability of visitations.

These studies indicate that the violation of an expectation that one has control may be more stressful than an initial (and continued) perception of no control. However, Taylor (1983) argues that initial perceptions of control are adaptive even if they are disconfirmed. In a study of breast cancer patients, she found anecdotal evidence that disconfirmations of control over recurrences of the disease were not emotionally devastating. Women were able to find other ways to enhance control when they were ineffectual in controlling one area.

There have been too few studies of disconfirmations of control to reach any definite conclusions about their effects. At the least, it appears that, under some circumstances, they can lead to increased stress. It may be the case, however, as Taylor (1983) suggests, that control can often be found in other areas when one type has been disconfirmed.

Availability of a More Effective Agent

Control may also not be preferred in situations in which another agent is seen as possessing greater skills or knowledge than oneself. Transferring control to that person is likely to be seen as a more effective way of getting desired outcomes than is exercising the control oneself. Burger, McWard, and LaTorre (1986) tested this idea by giving subjects the choice of drawing their own blood sample or having another person do it. When the other agent was the experimenter, who was presumed to be experienced and knowledgeable, 70% preferred not to draw their own blood; but only 38% made this choice when the other agent was an inexperienced assistant. Thus most subjects did not choose to have control if a more effective agent was available.

Unresolved Questions

The foregoing results are relevant to a more basic question addressed by Rodin, Rennert, and Solomon (1980), and Burger, McWard, and LaTorre (1986): Is control intrinsically motivating, or is it desired only because it increases the chances of good outcomes? That is, is control valued for its own sake, as has been proposed by a number of theorists (deCharms, 1968; White, 1959), whether or not its use is likely to be effective? Rodin, Rennert, and Solomon (1980) showed that subjects will not work to gain an opportunity to make a choice in situations in which they are already assured of obtaining a good outcome; the attainment of control was motivating only when it increased the chances of getting a good outcome. In addition, contrary to the assumption of control theorists such as White (1959) that perceived control enhances self-esteem, they found that the opportunity to make a choice (in this case, to invent one's own questions as an interviewer) led to lower self-esteem.

The conclusion that control may not be intrinsically motivating (at least, not as a universal or absolute value) fits with the other research we have reviewed indicating that control is not desired or adaptive under some circumstances. In summary, when using control is difficult, requiring effort, time, and attention; when there is not sufficient information to use it effectively; when control is contrary to one's preferred style; when control options do not have a high probability of success, or actually result in failure or in the disconfirmation of control; and when a more effective agent is available, then the opportunity to control one's environment is less likely to be preferred and may increase distress.

A second question about control that our review raises is whether perceptions of control are ever maladaptive or undesirable if no attempt is made to exercise the control. Many of the negative effects of perceived control that have been covered here occur when individuals attempt to *act upon* their perception of control and are unsuccessful, or incur other costs by their actions. It might be argued that it is not the perception of control that is problematic, but the attempt to exercise the control. However, there are three reasons to conclude that perceptions of control are also important. First, an obvious point is that perception of control and the exercise of control are intimately linked: Perceiving that one has control is a necessary condition for attempting to exercise the control. Thus manipulations that are designed to increase perceptions of control also increase the probability that the control will be exercised (and that the negative consequences of attempting to exert control will occur). Second, several of the studies covered earlier in this chapter indicate that perceptions of control can be undesirable even when no attempt is made to use the control. For example, repressors are more stressed when given information about self-control options (Andrew, 1970), and subjects who thought they were going to control the course of an interview had lower self-esteem (Rodin, Rennert, & Solomon, 1980). Third, those who are believed to have control may be held responsible by themselves or others for *not* exercising it. The Weiner et al. (in press) study is an example of a situation in which individuals are evaluated negatively for outcomes that they had the power to avoid. Although we did not cover any research addressing this point, it also seems likely that individuals could experience regret or guilt if they believed that they had the potential to control a situation and did not do so. Thus perceptions of control can be undesirable and lead to poor outcomes even if no attempt is made to exercise the control.

Preferences for No Control

We have reviewed the evidence that people may prefer not to have control under certain circumstances. However, it is not known how often people encounter situations in which no control is preferred, or how common are the various factors that affect desire for control. These are important issues because if no control is only rarely preferred over having control, then preferences for no control may have little importance for practical issues, such as interventions to increase perceived control in health care settings.

The best way to study these issues would be with a diverse sample of individuals from the general population and with a wide array of situations.

However, as a first approximation, we have used a more restricted sample. College students (28 females and 16 males) were asked to relate an incident in which they preferred or chose not to have control in each of three areas: academic, interpersonal, and health. They described each incident, rated its frequency and importance, stated whether or not they had actually exercised the control, and discussed why they did not want control in that situation. From an inspection of their answers, post hoc coding categories were developed and are listed in Table 4.1. Five categories referred to the amount of effort involved in exercising the control, four categories to the effect that using control would have on other desired outcomes, two categories to the benefits of not having control, and the other three categories referred to a concern with the effects of failure, the availability of a more effective agent, and an attitude of fatalism.

All subjects, except two, were able to recall an incident in which they did not want control for each of the three areas. The incidents that subjects described were quite diverse; they included actions that could affect grades or classes, being the one to make a group decision, approaching a potential romantic partner, breaking up a relationship, intervening to avert a potentially bad situation, expressing one's opinions, weight loss, exercise, choosing a type of contraception, playing sports and risking further injury, and responding to symptoms that might indicate a health problem.

Respondents gave one reason for not preferring or choosing control for 65% of the incidents, two reasons for 27% of the incidents, and more than two reasons for 8%. It is interesting to note that two of the categories support the point made in the previous section that perceived control can be undesirable because failing to exercise it would lead to guilt or to being blamed by others. Several respondents mentioned that an advantage of not having control is that one can avoid performing an unpleasant behavior and have an acceptable excuse that others will find acceptance or not experience guilt.

The most common types of reason for avoiding control in the academic area were not caring enough about the outcome to make an effort (e.g., "When my lab group was dividing up the work, it wasn't important enough to me to argue for what I wanted to do."), and the side effects of the exercise of control on other outcomes (e.g., "I didn't try to get a grade changed because it would be embarassing to talk to the professor."). Frequently cited reasons for not preferring control in the interpersonal realm were uncertainty about failure (e.g., "I didn't approach someone I wanted to get to know because I was afraid she would reject me.") and side effects (e.g., "I didn't want to control the plans for our trip because I might be seen as pushy."). For health issues, the most common reasons given were

Table 4.1
Percentages of Subjects Citing Reasons for Not Wanting Control

Reason given	Academic	Interpersonal (all in percentages)	Health
Amount of effort			
hassle	2	7	14
stress	9	0	7
didn't care enough	23	7	16
easier not to	0	2	9
too lazy	9	2	9
Effects on other outcomes			
side effects	18	18	2
hold self responsible	0	2	0
others would hold self responsible	11	14	9
interfere with desired outcome	5	5	7
Benefits of no control			
lessen guilt	0	5	6
make a good excuse	7	0	5
Uncertain — might fail	11	25	9
More effective agent	14	9	27
Fatalism	11	5	5

NOTE: The percentages in each column do not sum to 100% because multiple reasons were sometimes given.

identifying a more effective agent (e.g., "My trainer knows better than I when I'm healthy and can play, so I let him decide.") and not caring enough to make the effort (e.g., "I didn't try to control my weight because it just wasn't that important to me.").

Importance ratings of these incidents were made on a 7-point scale (1 = unimportant, 7 = important). The mean rating was 5.1. Frequency ratings were made on a 4-point scale (1 = had never happened before, 2 = had happened once before, 3 = occasionally happened, 4 = frequently happened), and here the mean rating was 2.5.

These data suggest two points. First, the types of events in which control is not sought or desired are not rare. The mean rating of frequency indicates that the particular type of event cited by respondents had happened, on average, between two times and occasionally. It seems reasonable to think that there are also other types of situations in which control is not desired, but which were not mentioned by respondents in the present study. Second, the factors that respondents cited as influencing their preferences for no control were the ones that past research has suggested are important. In the area of health, these students were particularly cognizant of how the effort involved in exercising control and the availability of a more effective agent affected their preferences.

Thus at least for a college student population, incidents in which individuals are aware of not desiring control are not rare.

Practical Implications for Health Settings

Many studies have found that individuals can benefit from perceptions of control over aversive events. (See Averill, 1973; Miller, 1979; or Thompson, 1981, for reviews.) The perception that one has a response available to influence the timing or the effect of a stressful situation appears to be particularly useful in the anticipatory period as one awaits the event (Thompson, 1981). The benefits that can be derived from the availability of a control response make interventions to enhance control a promising strategy in health settings in which individuals frequently have to undergo stressful or painful diagnostic or treatment procedures, or are faced with unpredictable, life-threatening outcomes such as the recurrence of cancer or a second stroke. However, as our review of factors affecting control has suggested, perceptions of control are not always desired or beneficial. The solution is not to forego efforts to enhance perceived control, but rather to offer control in circumstances in which the results are most likely to be beneficial. In this section, we discuss some issues that should be considered in the design of interventions to enhance perceptions of control.

Control Response and Outcome

Some ways of exerting control are more costly, requiring attention, effort, time, and other resources, while other types of control are more easily achieved. As discussed earlier, there is evidence that control attempts that are more difficult to execute may increase the stress of a situation. Also, the stress, effort, and hassle involved in using control were frequently mentioned by respondents in our study as reasons to prefer not having or using control.

The outcomes that control manipulations are intended to affect also vary in their importance to the individual. Some outcomes that one could affect might be very trivial and of little concern, such as which bed one is assigned to in a room or when one is scheduled for x-rays, while other outcomes are of major importance.

Although there is no direct evidence on this point, it seems likely that preferences for control and the adaptiveness of having control depend on a cost-benefit comparison of the resources required to exercise the control relative to the importance of the potential outcome. Control options that exact high costs may still be beneficial if they increase the chances of getting a very important outcome, whereas even minimally costly control may not be desired or adaptive if the outcome is not important.

The obvious implication is that interventions to enhance patients' perceptions of control should be used in areas in which the outcome is a meaningful one, especially if exercising the control requires attention and involvement. Making even a minor decision may involve more effort than a person would want to invest for a trivial difference in outcomes. For example, one could conceivably increase hospital patients' perceptions of control by giving them a number of trivial choices to make—for example, color of hospital gown, which dessert for dinner, a bath at 3:00 or 4:00—but the enhanced control would most likely not be beneficial because the effort involved in making these decisions is not worth the difference in outcomes they produce.

Another factor to consider is whether or not individuals feel that they have enough information in the case of a decision or the necessary skills in the case of a behavioral response to use the control option successfully. Increased participation in treatment decisions, such as a choice between a radical or conservative treatment for cancer, should be accompanied by understandable information about the risks, benefits, and likely outcomes of each procedure. It is also important that this information comes from an impartial source, someone with no investment in the results of the decision. If patients are to be offered control, then the choice should not be an illusory one that is based on a biased presentation of information that appears to lead to only one conclusion. Thus control options should be worth the effort and resources they require and they should be accompanied by sufficient information to make the choice an informed and meaningful one.

The Effects of Failure

The consequences of a control effort that is unsuccessful, perhaps making the situation worse rather than improving it, should also be considered. The research on this issue is too sparse to reach any firm conclusions, but it is at least a possibility that believing in and attempting to exercise control leaves one cognitively unprepared for failure, and that an unambiguous disconfirmation of expected control is more maladaptive than an initial perception of no control. Until further studies can clarify these issues, it would be wise for researchers to pilot test interventions intended to enhance control to see if unsuccessful use of the control or a loss of control at the end of the study is detrimental.

Some control failures may also lead to individuals blaming themselves for the outcome and/or being held responsible by others. For example, promoting the view among cancer patients and their families that patients' positive attitudes can help prevent a recurrence is likely to increase patients' perceptions of control. However, if there is a recurrence, patients may be seen as failures by themselves or their families for their inability to maintain the proper attitude. It seems reasonable to imagine that being seen by others as causing a negative event would increase stress, so interventions with the potential to increase blame from others should be used only if there is evidence that this outcome is outweighed by other benefits. As discussed earlier, self-blame may be maladaptive primarily if it raises concerns about important abilities or dispositions. Thus in many situations there will be no harm in feeling responsible for the outcome; in fact, positive effects may accrue from feelings of the fairness of events or the future avoidability of similar events. But, again, the likelihood of such effects should be checked in the particular situation pertaining to the intervention.

Circumstances in Which Control Is Offered

Patients enter a health care setting to receive treatment from medical experts who are concerned about the patients' health. Although many interventions to increase patients' own control may be welcomed and highly beneficial to patients, there is a danger that the offer of control itself may undermine patients' expectations about providers' expertise and concern. Janis (1984) points out that an emphasis on patient control and responsibility could be interpreted as a lack of concern or an unwillingness on the part of the health care provider to take charge of the situation. Offers of, or demands for, patient involvement and control in a medical setting could also raise questions about the expertise of the health professional or the effectiveness of the treatment strategy (Johnson, 1984). For example, a patient who is told that there are several courses of treatment, each with certain risks and benefits, and that it is up to him or her to decide among them may conclude that physicians do not know what to do and have relegated the decision to the patient to avoid responsibility. The resulting lower levels of trust in the expertise and caring of medical providers could increase patient anxiety and/or lead to noncompliance with the treatment regimen.

Despite these potential problems, we are not suggesting that patients not be offered control in medical settings. Rather, the implication is that some thought should be given to the meaning that the offer of control will have to patients. Is the message inadvertently being given that the providers cannot figure out what to do, so the decision is being left up to the patient?

There are several ways of thinking about this issue. One is that if the health professionals are, in fact, unsure about the diagnosis or course of treatment, then the patient should be aware of this, regardless of whether or not it undermines faith in the expertise of the providers. However, this approach needs an accompanying warning: In cases in which medical knowledge is sound, care should be taken to ensure that the offer of participation or control does not lead to the unwarranted conclusion that the providers are lacking in expertise or concern.

Another way of approaching this issue is to see offers of control as involving a trade-off between short-term and long-term effects. Some control options may increase anxiety and concern about the treatment in the short run, but may be more adaptive when a longer time period is considered. For example, it may be initially stressful to be offered a choice of treatment options, but several months later those who made the choice may be better off, even if the outcome is not positive. As discussed earlier, self-responsibility is associated with feelings of fairness and, if the proffered choices or decisons do not relate to one's abilities and dispositions, it also does not lead to worse emotional outcomes. Research is needed to test these ideas in medical settings, but it is at least a working hypothesis that in the long run participation in decisions may be beneficial.

Individual Preferences for Control

A final factor that affects when control will be desired and adaptive is the individual's preferences for control over health-related outcomes. As reviewed earlier in the chapter, people who have an external locus of control and those who handle stress through repression are less likely to prefer control or to find it beneficial. Clymer, Baum, and Krantz (1984) point out that not everyone wants to be an active, informed participant in his or her own health care, and that the failure to consider these individual differences may result in interventions that increase stress and poor outcomes for some participants.

One solution would be to take measures of preferences for control over health outcomes in the medical setting and then tailor interventions to individual needs. Krantz, Baum, and Wideman (1980) report that the Krantz Health Opinion Survey (Krantz, 1978) reliably distinguishes between those who want and those who do not want an active role in self-care. Auerbach, Martelli, and Mercuri (1983) used this scale success-fully to predict the effects of different types of information given to dental patients. However, this approach has practical limitations. If interventions to enhance control are to be adopted and widely used in routine medical care, then the suggested interventions should be ones that are easy to implement. It seems unlikely that most physicians would administer a questionnaire to each patient, score it and then refer to it before consulting with patients. It may be possible to devise a simple measure of preferences, consisting of two or three questions that a care provider could ask patients directly; but until a measure of preferences for control is devised that can easily and routinely be administered, it is not practical to suggest that this become a regular part of health care.

Conclusion

We have reviewed the evidence suggesting that control is not always desirable and discussed some implications of these findings for interventions in health care settings. There are two points that deserve final emphasis. The first is that research on the effects of control interventions should anticipate and include measures to assess negative effects and limitations on the effectiveness of the options. When feasible, manipulations of variables that might affect the outcome of the control manipulation, such as information and effort, should be included in the design. Studies that go beyond a focus on the main effect of control and examine factors that improve or detract from its effectiveness would be particularly useful.

The second point is that considerable research is needed before firm conclusions can be reached about the effects of control in health settings. Answers to some of the basic questions raised in this chapter are still largely speculative. For example, what are the effects of disconfirmations of control? Can people exercise control and still adequately prepare themselves for failure? Is it adaptive to be offered control even if it undermines one's faith in the health professional? These are important issues to be resolved before firm recommendations about patient treatment are made.

Health psychologists are now at a point where they can move beyond the simple perspective that control is always good and the more control the better. Further research can probe more deeply into the considerable complexity of these issues.

References

Abrams, R. D., & Finesinger, J. E. (1953). Guilt reactions in patients with cancer. *Cancer, 6,* 474-482.

Andrew, J. M. (1970). Recovery from surgery, with and without preparatory instruction, for three coping styles. *Journal of Personality and Social Psychology, 15,* 223-226.

Auerbach, S. M., Martelli, M. F., & Mercuri, L. G. (1983). Anxiety, information, interpersonal impacts, and adjustment to a stressful health care situation. *Journal of Personality and Social Psychology, 44,* 1284-1296.

Averill, J. R. (1973). Personal control over aversive stimuli and its relationship to stress. *Psychological Bulletin, 80,* 286-303.

Baum, A., Fleming, R., & Singer, J. E. (1983). Coping with victimization by technological disaster. *Journal of Social Issues, 39*(2), 117-138.

Bulman, R. J., & Wortman, C. (1977). Attributions of blame and coping in the "real world": Severe accident victims react to their lot. *Journal of Personality and Social Psychology, 35,* 351-363.

Burger, J. M., McWard, J., & LaTorre, D. (1986, May). *Relinquishing control over aversive stimuli.* Paper presented at the meeting of the Western Psychological Association, Seattle.

Chodoff, P., Friedman, S. B., & Hamburg, D. A. (1964). Stress, defenses and coping behavior: Observations in parents of children with malignant disease. *American Journal of Psychiatry, 120,* 743-749.

Clymer, R., Baum, A., & Krantz, D. S. (1984). Preferences for self-care and involvement in health care. In A. Baum, S. E. Taylor, & J. E. Singer (Eds.), *Handbook of psychology and health: Vol. II. Social psychological aspects of health.* Hillsdale, NJ: Lawrence Erlbaum.

Corah, N. L., & Boffa, J. (1970). Perceived control, self-observation, and response to aversive stimulation. *Journal of Personality and Social Psychology, 16,* 1-4.

deCharms, R. (1968). *Personal causation: The internal affective determinants of behavior.* New York: Academic Press.

Elliott, R. (1969). Tonic heart rate: Experiments on the effects of collative variables lead to a hypothesis about its motivational significance. *Journal of Personality and Social Psychology, 12,* 211-228.

Fisher, S. (1984). *Stress and the perception of control.* Hillsdale, NJ: Lawrence Erlbaum.

Folkman, S. (1984). Personal control and stress and coping processes: A theoretical analysis. *Journal of Personality and Social Psychology, 46,* 839-852.

Folkman, S., & Lazarus, R. S. (1980). An analysis of coping in a middle-age community sample. *Journal of Health and Social Behavior, 21,* 219-239.

Graham, M. A., Thompson, S. C., Estrada, M., & Yonekura, M. L. (in press). Factors affecting psychological adjustment to a fetal demise. *Journal of Obstetrics and Gynecology.*

Houston, K. B. (1972). Control over stress, locus of control, and response to stress. *Journal of Personality and Social Psychology, 21,* 249-255.

Janigian, A. S., & Thompson, S. C. (1985, April). *Attributions of responsibility for negative events and failures.* Paper presented at the annual meeting of the Western Psychological Association, San Jose, CA.

Janis, I. L. (1984). Improving adherence to medical recommendations: Prescriptive hypotheses derived from recent research in social psychology. In A. Baum, S. E. Taylor, & J. E. Singer (Eds.), *Handbook of psychology and health: Vol. II. Social psychological aspects of health.* Hillsdale, NJ: Lawrence Erlbaum.

Janoff-Bulman, R. (1979). Characterological versus behavioral self-blame: Inquiries into depression and rape. *Journal of Personality and Social Psychology, 37,* 1798-1809.

Johnson, J. E. (1984). Psychological interventions and coping with surgery. In A. Baum, S. E. Taylor, & J. E. Singer (Eds.), *Handbook of psychology and health: Vol. II. Social psychological aspects of health.* Hillsdale, NJ: Lawrence Erlbaum.

Johnson, J. E., Leventhal, H., & Dabbs, J. M. (1971). Contribution of emotional and instrumental response processes in adaption to surgery. *Journal of Personality and Social Psychology, 20,* 55-64.

Jones, E. E., & Berglas, S. (1978). Control of attributions about the self through self-handicapping strategies: The appeal of alcohol and the role of underachievement. *Personality and Social Psychology Bulletin, 4,* 200-206.

Krantz, D. S. (1978). *The Krantz health opinion survey: A scale for the prediction of health care preferences.* Unpublished manuscript, University of Southern California.

Krantz, D. S., Baum, A., & Wideman, M. V. (1980). Assessment of preferences for self-treatment and information in health care. *Journal of Personality and Social Psychology, 39,* 977-990.

Manuck, S. B., Harvey, A. H., Lechleiter, S. L., & Neal, K. S. (1978). Effect of coping on blood pressure responses to threat of aversive stimulation. *Psychophysiology, 15,* 544-549.

Meyer, C. B., & Taylor, S. E. (1986). Adjustment to rape. *Journal of Personality and Social Psychology, 50,* 1226-1234.

Miller, S. M. (1979). Controllability and human stress: Method, evidence, and theory. *Behavior Research and Therapy, 17,* 287-304.

Mills, R. T., & Krantz, D. S. (1979). Information, choice, and reactions to stress: A field experiment in a blood bank with laboratory analogue. *Journal of Personality and Social Psychology, 37,* 608-620.

Norem, J. K., & Cantor, N. (1986). Defensive pessimism: Harnessing anxiety as motivation. *Journal of Personality and Social Psychology, 51,* 1208-1217.

Rodin, J., Rennert, K., & Solomon, S. K. (1980). Intrinsic motivation for control: Fact or fiction. In A. Baum & J. E. Singer (Eds.), *Advances in environmental psychology: Applications of personal control.* Hillsdale, NJ: Lawrence Erlbaum.

Rothbaum, F., Weisz, J. R., & Snyder, S. S. (1982). Changing the world and changing the self: A two-process model of perceived control. *Journal of Personality and Social Psychology, 42,* 5-37.

Scheppele, K. L., & Bart, P. B. (1983). Through women's eyes: Defining danger in the wake of sexual assault. *Journal of Social Issues, 39*(2), 63-80.

Schulz, R. (1976). Effects of control and predictability on the physical and psychological well-being of the institutionalized aged. *Journal of Personality and Social Psychology, 33,* 563-573.

Schulz, R., & Hanusa, B. H. (1978). Long-term effects of control and predictability-enhancing interventions: Findings and ethical issues. *Journal of Personality and Social Psychology, 36,* 1194-1201.

Sherrod, D. R., Hage, J. N., Halpern, P. L., & Moore, B. S. (1977). Effects of personal causation and perceived control on responses to an aversive environment: The more control, the better. *Journal of Experimental Social Psychology, 13,* 14-27.

Shipley, R. H., Butt, J. H., & Horowitz, B. (1979). Preparation to reexperience a stressful medical examination: Effect of repetitious videotape exposure and coping style. *Journal of Consulting and Clinical Psychology, 47,* 485-492.

Shipley, R. H., Butt, J. H., Horowitz, B., & Farbry, J. E. (1978). Preparation for a stressful medical procedure: Effect of amount of stimulus preexposure and coping style. *Journal of Consulting and Clinical Psychology, 46,* 499-507.

Snyder, C. R., & Higgins, R. L. (in press). Excuses: Their effects and their role in the negotiation of reality. In C. R. Snyder & C. Ford (Eds.), *Coping with negative life events: Clinical and social psychological perspectives.* New York: Plenum.

Solomon, S., Holmes, D. S., & McCaul, K. D. (1980). Behavioral control over aversive events: Does control that requires effort reduce anxiety and physiological arousal? *Journal of Personality and Social Psychology, 39,* 729-736.

Taylor, S. E. (1983). Adjustment to threatening events: A theory of cognitive adaption. *American Psychologist, 38,* 1161-1173.

Taylor, S. E., Lichtman, R. R., & Wood, J. V. (1984). Attributions, beliefs about control, and adjustment to breast cancer. *Journal of Personality and Social Psychology, 46,* 489-502.

Taylor, S. E., Wood, J. V., & Lichtman, R. R. (1983). It could be worse: Selective evaluation as a response to victimization. *Journal of Social Issues, 39*(2), 19-40.

Tennen, H., Affleck, G., & Gershman, K. (1986). Self-blame among parents of infants with perinatal complications: The role of self-protective motives. *Journal of Personality and Social Psychology, 50,* 690-696.

Thompson, S. C. (1981). Will it hurt less if I can control it? A complex answer to a complex question. *Psychological Bulletin, 90,* 89-101.

Thompson, S. C. (1985). Finding positive meaning in a stressful event. *Basic and Applied Social Psychology, 6,* 279-295.

Thompson, S. C., & Janigian, A. S. (1987). *Attributing responsibility to the self for negative events.* Unpublished manuscript, Pomona College, Claremont, CA.

Thompson, S. C., Sobolew, A., Graham, M., & Janigian, A. (1987). *Psychosocial adjustment following a stroke.* Unpublished manuscript, Pomona College, Claremont, CA.

Wallston, B. S., Wallston, K. A., Kaplan, C. D., & Maides, S. A. (1976). Development and validation of the health-related locus of control (HLC) scale. *Journal of Consulting and Clinical Psychology, 44,* 580-585.

Wallston, K. A., Smith, R. A., King, J. E., Forsberg, P. R., Wallston, B. S., & Nagy, V. T. (1983). Expectancies about control over health: Relationships to desire for control of health care. *Personality and Social Psychology Bulletin, 9,* 377-385.

Weiner, B., Amirkhan, J., Folkes, V. S., & Verette, J. (in press). An attributional analysis of excuse giving: Studies of a naive theory of emotion. *Journal of Personality and Social Psychology.*

Weiss, J. M. (1971a). Effects of coping behavior in different warning signal conditions on stress pathology in rats. *Journal of Comparative and Physiological Psychology, 77,* 1-13.

Weiss, J. M. (1971b). Effects of punishing the coping response (conflict) on stress pathology in rats. *Journal of Comparative and Physiological Psychology, 77,* 14-21.

White, R. W. (1959). Motivation reconsidered: The concept of competence. *Psychological Review, 66,* 297-323.

Williams, A. F. (1972). Personality characteristics associated with preventive dental practices. *Journal of American College of Dentists, 39,* 225-234.

Wortman, C. B., & Brehm, J. W. (1975). Responses to uncontrollable outcomes: An integration of reactance theory and the learned helplessness model. In L. Berkowitz (Ed.), *Advances in experimental social psychology* (Vol. 8, pp. 277-336). New York: Academic Press.

5

Social Support and the Cancer Patient

SHELLEY E. TAYLOR
GAYLE A. DAKOF

Over the last two decades, research has examined the possibility that social and emotional ties, otherwise known as social support, can foster good psychological and physical health. *Social support* has been defined as "an interpersonal transaction involving one of the following: (1) emotional concern (liking, loving, empathy), (2) instrumental aid (goods or services), (3) information (about the environment), or (4) appraisal (information relevant to self-evaluation)" (House, 1981, p. 39). Social support can come from family members, such as a spouse, partner, or child; from friends or professional caregivers; from social and community ties, such as clubs or religious organizations; or from groups especially organized to provide social support (i.e., social support groups, such as Alcoholics Anonymous).

The research to date clearly indicates that social support can reduce the psychological impact of stressful events (e.g., Billings & Moos, 1982; Kaplan, Robbins, & Martin, 1983; Lin, Simeone, Ensel, & Kuo, 1979; Williams, Ware, & Donald, 1981). The influence of social support on physical health is somewhat less clear. Some studies have indicated that individuals with high levels of social support are less likely to develop serious illnesses (e.g., Berkman & Syme, 1979; Jackson, 1956; Nuckolls,

Cassel, & Kaplan, 1972; for a review, see Wallston, Alagna, DeVellis, & DeVellis, 1983). Other studies have failed to find lower levels of illness among individuals with high levels of social support (Wallston et al., 1983). However, the evidence consistently suggests a relationship between social support and prospects for recovery. People who are already ill seem to recover more quickly if they have high levels of social support (Chambers & Reiser, 1953; Cobb, 1976; Dimond, 1979; Robertson & Suinn, 1968; for reviews, see DiMatteo & Hays, 1981, and Wallston et al., 1983).

How social support may enable people to cope with stressful events has been a particular research focus. Two hypotheses have been explored. One, termed the *direct effects hypothesis,* maintains that social support is beneficial during nonstressful times as well as stressful times. The other, termed the *buffering hypothesis,* maintains that the health and mental health benefits of social support are chiefly evident during periods of high stress. According to the buffering hypothesis, social support acts as a resource and reserve that blunts the effects of stress or enables an individual to cope with high levels of stress more effectively. There is research evidence to support both hypotheses, and they are not mutually exclusive (for a review, see Cohen & Wills, 1985).

Social Support and Cancer

The occurrence of cancer is a highly stressful event that is receiving increasing research attention as its incidence rises. At the present time, nearly one out of every three individuals will develop at least one malignancy in his or her lifetime (American Cancer Society, 1986). Because cancer is an ongoing stressor that continually requires physical and psychological adjustments even in the best of cases, it is a chronically stressful event. Patients with active cancers face potential physical deterioration and the debilitating effects of certain treatments such as chemotherapy or radiation therapy. Even patients whose cancers are in remission may have physical disabilities to manage as well as ongoing concerns about whether or not the cancer will recur (Dunkel-Schetter, 1984). Social support is a potential resource to help cancer patients deal with these fears and ambiguities (Bloom, 1982; Carey, 1974).

As is true for other stressful events, research suggests that social support is psychologically beneficial for cancer patients. Numerous studies have suggested a positive relationship between emotional support from family members and degree of physical and psychological adjustment to cancer (Bloom, 1982; Carey, 1974; Cobliner, 1977; Currier, 1966; Dunkel-Schetter, 1984; Funch & Mettlin, 1982; Giacquinta, 1977; Grandstaff, 1976; Kaplan, Smith, Grobstein, & Fischman, 1973; Klein, Dean, & Bogdonoff, 1976; Lichtman & Taylor, 1986; Lichtman, Taylor, & Wood, in press; Morris, 1979; Sutherland, Orbach, Dyk, & Bard, 1953; Weidman-Gibbs & Achterberg-Lawlis, 1978; Weisman, 1979). Moreover, the causal connections between social support and adjustment have been demonstrated in longitudinal studies indicating that social support at the time of diagnosis is associated with less emotional distress and longer life (e.g., Funch & Marshall, 1983).

Although the research literature consistently suggests a relationship between social support and positive adjustment among cancer patients, it should be noted that there are many problems with this literature. Methodological standards have not been uniformly high. Outcome measures of psychosocial functioning and, to some degree, physical functioning have been variable and often fail to capture the multifaceted nature of these variables (Dunkel-Schetter, 1984; Wortman, 1984). There is controversy over how social support should be defined and measured. Many of the samples on which the research evidence is based are small and unrepresentative. Nonetheless, the consistency of the research evidence suggesting a link between social support and adjustment among cancer patients is impressive.

Thus there is clear evidence that social support can be helpful to cancer patients. However, there is also some suggestion that cancer may threaten the availability of social support. Work by Wortman and Dunkel-Schetter (1979), Dunkel-Schetter and Wortman (1982), and Silver and Wortman (1980) has suggested that sometimes victims, such as cancer patients, do not receive either enough social support or enough appropriate social support. These authors suggested that cancer patients can be inadvertently victimized by their families and friends. Cancer creates two conflicting reactions in significant others: first, feelings of fear and aversion to cancer, and second, beliefs that appropriate behavior toward cancer patients requires maintaining a cheerful, optimistic facade. The conflict between these reactions may produce ambivalence toward the patient and anxiety about interacting with him or her. Consequently, significant others may physically avoid the patient or may avoid open communication about the disease.

These discrepancies in behavior (i.e., positive verbal but negative nonverbal behavior) can lead a cancer patient to feel rejected or abandoned by loved ones.

Research evidence concerning this so-called victimization hypothesis is mixed. On the one hand, the available research suggests that the majority of cancer patients perceive the degree of social support that they receive as adequate or outstanding (Dunkel-Schetter, 1984; see Lichtman & Taylor, 1986, for a review). On the other hand, cancer patients sometimes report guarded communications from family members (Cobb, 1976; Gordon et al., 1980; Klagsbrun, 1971; Lichtman & Taylor, 1986; Wellisch, Jamison, & Pasnau, 1978). Peters-Golden (1982) found that breast cancer patients reported that social support was often not available to them, and when it was, it was sometimes inappropriate (see also Wortman, 1984). In extreme cases, a patient may even be blamed for his or her cancer (Abrams & Finesinger, 1953; Giacquinta, 1977; Vettese, 1976).

In this chapter, we will review a program of research that we have undertaken with our associates over the past eight years. The interest of the senior author in this problem was initially sparked by a cancer conference, which posed the question: What does your discipline tell us about how to define and meet the needs of the cancer patient? In putting together a talk on the contributions of social psychology to an understanding of cancer, she was struck, first, by the wealth of social psychological findings that were potentially applicable to defining and meeting the cancer patient's needs, and second, by the total absence of direct research on this problem area in social psychology. Consequently, the potential to make a contribution was one impetus for conducting this research. A second impetus for both authors was a growing feeling that basic social psychological processes such as interpersonal interaction, causal attributions, or beliefs in personal control cannot be fruitfully studied in the laboratory alone. Without input from real-world situations, the theories concerning these variables fail to incorporate real-world contingencies that may greatly modify the meaning and consequent effects of these very important variables.

In presenting our program of research, we will concentrate on two major issues: Do cancer patients experience social support or lack of support from their significant others following the cancer experience? When problems with social support from significant others emerge, what is the nature of those problems? In addressing these issues, we will examine both global measures of social support and more recent evidence on specific social support transactions.

Social Support Following Cancer: Empirical Evidence

In our first study of social support (Lichtman & Taylor, 1986; Lichtman, Taylor, & Wood, in press), we conducted interviews with 78 breast cancer patients. Patients were recruited through a three-physician private oncology practice in Los Angeles. The sample ranged in age from 29 to 78 with a median age of 53. Overall, 71% were married, 19% were divorced, separated, or never married, and 10% were widowed. A total of 49% of the sample was employed either full-time or part-time. The sample was largely middle and upper-middle class, with the median level of education being one year of college. All but two of the women in the sample had had their breast cancer treated surgically either by lumpectomy (31%) or by mastectomy (67%). Some 31% had good prognoses, and 69% had fair to poor prognoses.

Each patient was interviewed by a trained psychological interviewer who followed a structured set of questions. The interviews typically lasted approximately an hour and a half and covered: basic demographic data; details about the woman's cancer experience; questions regarding attributions for cancer and beliefs about the ability to control the cancer; life changes experienced since cancer; perceptions of marital, family, and social relationships following cancer; perceptions of own adjustment; the amount of information the respondent had about cancer and how she had acquired it; and social comparisons made with respect to cancer.

In the section concerning social support, the patient was asked first to rate separately the degree of support she had received from her spouse or partner, if relevant, from other family members, and from her friends (4-point scales). Then she was asked to identify and describe any particular relationships in which she had experienced a lack of support when she was expecting it (open-ended questions). She was also asked whether or not people treated her any differently after the cancer (4-point scale), and if so, who and in what way (open-ended question). She next rated the openness and honesty of communication between herself and other people (5-point scale). The patient was asked if her social life had changed in any respect, and if so, how. Her answer was coded by the interviewer as increased, stayed the same, or decreased. Next she was asked if she was spending more, the same, or less time with her friends, with her immediate family, and with her extended family (3-point scales). In the section dealing with the relations between the patient and her spouse or partner, the patient was asked to rate her degree of satisfaction with the relationship prior to the cancer and her current satisfaction (5-point scales). Next she was asked how open and honest communication was between them (5-point scale). Patients were also asked how much they had been able to share their concerns with the significant other (5-point scale).

Overall, the amount of social support reported by these women was high; 75% rated the amount of support received from their spouse as "a great deal," which was the highest level; 77% reported a great deal of support from other family members; and 81% reported a great deal of support from friends. When asked how open and honest communications with other people were after the cancer, 80% of the sample rated them in the two highest categories, with only 7% in the two lowest categories. Generally, then, respondents reported a high level of social support and ability to communicate with their significant others following cancer. However, we caution against generalizing too far from this sample since it was female, heavily middle to upper-middle class, and had a cancer site typified by a generally favorable prognosis.

To address further the social support experiences associated with cancer, we conducted a questionnaire survey of Southern California cancer patients (Taylor, Falke, Shoptaw, & Lichtman, 1986; Taylor, Falke, Mazel, & Hilsberg, in press). Because a portion of the research addressed the cancer support-group experience, we attempted to recruit approximately half of our respondents from cancer support groups and half from general cancer practices. To recruit those who had attended cancer support groups, we obtained lists of Southern California area support groups, contacted the group leaders, and obtained mailing lists of the group members. To recruit cancer patients who had not attended support groups, we selected Southern California oncologists randomly from the University of California Cancer Center lists. Physicians were sent a contact letter that was followed by phone calls to obtain mailing lists of patients.

In all, we contacted 1,068 potentially eligible individuals. The final sample of 668 individuals represents a response rate of 62.5%. However, we subsequently completed a survey of nonrespondents and discovered that a substantial percentage either had died prior to our initial contact with them or were ineligible to participate (e.g., children or hematology patients inadvertently included on oncologists' patient lists). When we applied the estimated rates of deceased individuals and ineligible individuals to our sample, the response rate increased to approximately 80%.

Respondents ranged in age from 21 to 89 with a median age of 58. The sample was disproportionately female (521 or 78% of the sample), and Caucasian (93%). Subjects with all types of cancers participated in the study, and as would be expected, there were high percentages of patients with breast, gastrointestinal, and lymphatic cancers.

On the whole, the results from the study were consistent with the previous study, suggesting that cancer patients report positive, socially supportive experiences following cancer. A full 86% indicated that their spouses had been very helpful or helpful in addressing the needs that cancer brought on; 80% indicated that other family members had been very helpful or helpful; and 81% indicated that friends had been very helpful or helpful. Moreover, these reports did not vary systematically by sex, socioeconomic status, site of cancer, or prognosis.

However, in response to the question, "Do you wish you could talk more freely or openly about your cancer with family or friends?", 55% indicated they wished very much or somewhat that they could do so. A substantial minority (36%) also endorsed the statement, "Sometimes I feel that my family members don't really understand what I am going through."

To summarize, then, if we look at these data in the context of the Wortman and Dunkel-Schetter (1979) hypothesis that cancer patients are inadvertently victimized by their families and friends, we might conclude that the weak version but not the strong version of their hypothesis is supported. That is, generally, cancer patients do not report a high level of difficulties with social support following cancer. However, a minority (approximately 20%) are at least somewhat dissatisfied with their social support, and a substantial number report some concerns over whether or not their families truly understand their experiences. But, since neither our studies nor the work summarized by Wortman and Dunkel-Schetter included comparison groups (e.g., matched healthy controls or groups with other chronic illnesses), we do not know if this desire for more open communication and understanding is unique to cancer patients. For instance, it would not be implausible to think that approximately one-half to one-third of the general population, if asked, would indicate that their families "do not really understand" them, and that they wish they could talk more freely and openly to significant others. Thus answers to questions about the prevalence and type (if any) of communicative and interpersonal problems resulting from cancer must await further empirical investigation.

Social Support and Adjustment

In our research, we also examined whether social support was associated with positive adjustment, as previous work has found (e.g., Billings &

Moos, 1982; Kaplan et al., 1983; Lin et al., 1979; Williams, Ware, & Donald, 1981). In the interview study of breast cancer patients, we employed multiple measures of psychological adjustment: the patient's self-rating of psychological adjustment on a 5-point scale; the oncologist's rating of the patient's adjustment using the Global Adjustment to Illness Scale (GAIS—a standardized 100-point measure that has been used previously with cancer patients); the interviewer's rating of the patient on the GAIS; the spouse or partner's rating of the patient's adjustment on a 5-point scale; the patient's self-ratings of anxiety (4-point scale); and depression (4-point scale); and two objective measures of psychological adjustment, the Index of Well-Being developed by Campbell, Converse, and Rogers (1976), and the Profile of Mood States (POMS—McNair, Lorr, & Droppleman, 1971). These measures were subjected to a principal components factor analysis with a quartimax rotation to produce a single factor. The resulting scores for each subject were combined, weighted by their factor loadings, and standardized. This constituted our composite measure of adjustment. In the survey study, adjustment was assessed by the POMS, and interviewer and physician GAIS ratings.

When we correlated perceived social support from family and friends with psychological adjustment, the results were significant in both studies (Falke, 1987; Lichtman, Taylor, & Wood, in press). Depending upon the particular measure of support used, the correlations in both studies typically centered around .30. For example, in the breast cancer study, women were better adjusted who perceived supportiveness from their families ($r = .26, p < .01$) and friends ($r = .35, p < .001$), as were women who reported that they could share concerns with their husbands ($r = .32, p < .01$), who reported open and honest communications with their husbands ($r = .34, p < .002$), or who reported open and honest communications with others around them ($r = .21, p < .03$). Patients who said that their social life had increased since the cancer showed better adjustment than those who had reported a decrease ($r = .29, p < .004$). This is approximately the level of association that might be expected, since there are other factors such as type of surgery, prognosis, and beliefs in personal control that are known to be significant predictors of adjustment to cancer, and these were unmeasured constructs in the foregoing analyses.

It is important to note that in examining these correlational relationships, it is not possible to make a definitive statement regarding the causal direction. It is possible that people who are well-adjusted to their cancer either make more effective use of the social support that is available to them, or profit from social support by not driving it away. Maladjusted cancer patients may drive off people who could otherwise provide them with social support. On the other hand, it is also possible that more social support helps to produce better patient adjustment.

Problems in Social Support

When cancer patients do experience problems of social support, what is the nature of these problems? Our initial study of 78 breast cancer patients addressed this issue. Although relatively few individuals in that sample reported rejection by family and friends, 42% of the sample indicated that they had been surprised by at least one occurrence of rejection or isolation by a particular person. This lack of support came from the patient's mother in 26% of the cases, a close friend in 23% of the cases, a casual friend in 21% of the cases, and the spouse in 32% of the cases (Lichtman & Taylor, 1986; Lichtman, Taylor, & Wood, in press).

The problems that cancer patients typically experienced with their mothers were either withdrawal or oversolicitousness. For example, one woman, representative of several, stated about her mother:

She won't even discuss the cancer with me; she pretends it never happened.

In contrast, other women reported incidents like the following:

My mother drove me nuts. She would wake me up from a sleep to make sure I was O.K. She scared the hell out of me.

With respect to friends, typically our patient sample did not experience rejection from them, and in fact patients often grew closer to their female friends following breast cancer. However, it was not uncommon for a patient to report that one particular friend cut off all contact and communication following the cancer episode. For example,

I had one friend who wouldn't talk to me. Couldn't even face me. That had an effect on how I now look at people.

A similar incident:

> I had one girlfriend who had just had a baby. After I finished radiation therapy, we had gotten together. We went over to her house and she kept the baby away from me. It was real strange. When we left, I said to my husband, "You know Sue thinks I am contagious," and that was the last we ever heard from them.

A full third of the women we interviewed in the breast cancer study indicated that, despite general satisfaction with the support they received from their spouses following the cancer episode, a particular persistent communication difficulty occurred between themselves and their spouses (Lichtman & Taylor, 1986; Lichtman, Taylor, & Wood, in press). Typically, the form of this communication difficulty was that patients indicated a need for more opportunities to express freely their fears and anxieties about cancer recurrence and death, whereas their spouses expressed the belief that talking about it would be maladaptive to the patient's adjustment and might even lead to a recurrence.

Contributing to this difficulty was an apparent difference in temporal perspective about the cancer. The patients felt that the cancer was still an ongoing threat, and they needed to express their fears several months or even years later. Family members, on the other hand, sometimes expressed the thought that the cancer was a crisis that had been successfully resolved, and so did not require further discussion after the crisis period had ended.

One woman still close to the breast cancer episode spoke about her husband's attitude.

> It's five years before they consider you are cured. Well, for his peace of mind as far as he is concerned, it's over and done with. The issue is closed. He doesn't want to talk about it.

As the husband put it:

> We never talked about death. That was my private concern and I didn't want to let on about that either. You must say "O.K. you had the operation. It's over and done with, let's get back on the track." So I never talked about it.

This particular communication difficulty, namely that victims wanted to talk about the incident and significant others avoided communication about it, appears to be a typical problem for victims other than cancer patients as well. In Silver and Wortman's (1980) analysis of undesirable life events, they observed that victims dealing with a variety of losses, including the death of a spouse or child, often needed to air their feelings about the event months or even years later. However, family and friends often discouraged these efforts on the grounds that it was time for the patient to put the incident to rest. Silver and Wortman suggested that nonvictims may have incorrect ideas about how quickly people can overcome victimizing events. Nonvictims may believe that victims can voluntarily control their negative thoughts and emotions when this may not be the case.

Overall, one can ask the question, Who is right? Should patients put the incident behind them or should significant others be more open to communication about the issue? That question cannot be answered definitively. However, in our breast cancer data set (Lichtman, Taylor, & Wood, in press), we found that couples who shared their realistic thoughts, such as worries about recurrence or death, and those who appeared to be more sensitive to each other's emotions and thoughts had higher marital adjustment. Moreover, patients' self-reports that communications with a spouse were open and honest were positively correlated with patients' emotional adjustment ($r = .34$). These results tentatively suggest that it may be better for patients to air their grievances and concerns than for them to follow what appear to be frequent wishes of spouses and family members that the concerns be put out of mind and kept covered up.

Socially Supportive and Unsupportive Transactions

To this point, we have focused primarily on relatively global reports of social support and lack of it. However, there are several lines of work in the social support literature suggesting that a more fine-grained approach to social support is appropriate. The first is a general caution raised by social support researchers (Barrera, 1981; Dunkel-Schetter, Folkman, & Lazarus, in press; Wortman, 1984) that the field must focus on specific social support transactions and not merely on measures of the perceived availability of social support. That is, to appreciate fully what kinds of actions, information, and comments are helpful from others, researchers need to look at specific instances of social support efforts.

In addition, as noted earlier, social support researchers have created taxonomies of social support such as emotional concern (liking, loving, and empathy), instrumental aid (providing goods or services), information about the environment, or appraisal information relevant to the victim's self-evaluation (House, 1981; Schaefer, Coyne, & Lazarus, 1981). These distinctions imply that different types of support may serve different functions.

Another reason for focusing on specific social support transactions stems from the fact that not all kinds of social support may be equally beneficial from the same individuals (Brown & Harris, 1978; Gottlieb, 1981; Hirsch, 1980; Shinn, Lehmann, & Wong, 1984). Researchers have suggested that if social support efforts come from the wrong person, or if the wrong kind of support is offered, it may actually exacerbate stress (Cohen & McKay, 1983; Suls, 1982; Wortman, 1984). In her study of cancer patients, Dunkel-Schetter (1984) found evidence for this position. She asked cancer patients to describe the most helpful and most unhelpful things anyone had done since their cancer diagnoses. When possible, responses were coded into four categories: emotional support, instrumental support, informational support, and appraisal support. Her respondents indicated that family, medical caregivers, and, to a lesser extent, friends were all extremely helpful in providing social support during the cancer episode. However, different types of support were reported to be helpful from different individuals. Overall, instances of emotional support were perceived as most helpful by 81% of respondents. Informational support, that is the provision of specific information to the cancer patient by another person, was perceived as extremely helpful by 41% of respondents. Providing direct aid and giving patients appraisal support were much less frequently perceived as extremely helpful, each by 6% of respondents.

More interesting were the patterns of which kinds of support were desirable from whom. Somewhat surprisingly, emotional support was perceived as helpful regardless of whether it came from family, friends, or medical personnel. In fact, the lack of emotional support from physicians and other medical caregivers was commonly perceived as unhelpful. In contrast, information and advice were perceived as helpful when they came from medical caregivers, but were often perceived as unhelpful if they came from family and friends. Clearly, then, when one considers adequacy of social support for cancer patients, one must examine not only the overall amount of support an individual receives, but who is providing what kind of support.

A Recent Study

To address this issue, we selected a subset of individuals from the larger interview study we had conducted on social support (Taylor et al., 1986). Respondents were selected from the larger sample on the basis of gender (equal representation of men and women), age (between 30 and 70), prognosis (split on good and fair/poor prognosis), and whether or not the individual had participated in a cancer support group. All sites of cancer were included. Of those contacted, four declined participation yielding a response rate of 93%.

A total of 55 people, 30 women and 25 men, with a median age of 54 participated in the interview study. In all, 83% (N = 47) were married, and 84% had children; 31 (56%) were employed, mostly in white collar or professional jobs, and the median yearly family income was between $40,000 and $49,000. Some 93% had completed high school, and 29% were college graduates. Overall, 44% were Protestant, 25% were Jewish, 13% were Catholic, and 18% indicated either another or no religious affiliation.

All participants had first had their cancer diagnosed or had sustained a recurrence (whichever was most recent) within the previous six years (M = 3.2 years, SD = 1.7); 11 study participants (20%) were receiving treatment for their cancer at the time of the interview. Using medical chart materials, an independent oncologist rated prognosis on a five-point scale ranging from 1 (very guarded or grave prognosis) to 5 (probable cure). Overall, 36 patients had cancers that were rated 4 or 5 (in remission), and the remainder (N = 19) had prognostic ratings of 1, 2, or 3 (active cancers).

A total of 27% had never attended a support group, 22% had attended only briefly, and 50% had at one time been regular attenders. Only 10 patients (18%), however, were regularly attending support group meetings at the time of the interview.

Each study participant was asked about the social support or nonsupport received from each of seven sources: spouse, other family members, friends, casual acquaintances, other cancer patients, physicians, and nurses. The specific questions were: (1) In the time since your diagnosis, what is the most helpful thing that (support target) has said or done to help you with your cancer? and (2) In the time since your diagnosis, what has your (support target) said or done that you experienced as most annoying, or that upset you, made you angry, or just somehow rubbed you the wrong way? Subjects' responses were coded into categories for data analytic purposes. Codes to the open-ended questions were developed after a careful examination of a random sample of responses. The interrater reliability over all codes was excellent (Cohen's Kappa = .79 [Cohen, 1960], and percentage agreement over occurrences = 92%). A third judge coded all questions on which the two original judges disagreed.

Some Results

The most commonly reported helpful and annoying or upsetting actions provided by each of the seven potential social support providers were as follows. From the *spouse,* three behaviors were mentioned as most helpful. They included physical presence (just being there) (35%), expressions of concern and love (33%), and a calm acceptance of the participant's illness and its consequences (30%). The following quote about a patient's husband illustrates two codes, physical presence and expression of concern and love:

> He was always there beside me, even when I was throwing up from the chemotherapy. He still loved me even when I lost my hair.

Other helpful actions from spouses were the provision of practical assistance (20%) and expression of optimism about the patient's prognosis or ability to live successfully with the cancer (20%). (The total exceeds 100% because several respondents indicated more than one helpful action.)

The most annoying behaviors that patients reported from their spouses included being critical of how the patient was handling the cancer (20%), minimizing the impact of the cancer (13%), and expressing too much worry and pessimism about the illness (13%). One woman described how her husband was critical of her:

> I might be okay for months, and then all of a sudden, and I still don't know why, I'll feel insecure and depressed. He gets angry at my inability to mentally tolerate these things. So, of course, I get angry at him cause I say to myself, "You don't know what it's like."

Overall, 39% of the married respondents could not think of an unsupportive spousal act.

In response to the question inquiring about the helpful social support provided by *other family members,* 68% of respondents with children reported about a helpful example of support provided by their children. Most commonly, helpful experiences centered on three behaviors: expressions of concern and affection (40%), mere presence (29%), and practical assistance such as providing transportation, preparing meals, and providing postsurgical care (24%).

In response to the question asking about family behaviors that were most upsetting, the two most frequently mentioned acts were family members minimizing the seriousness of the cancer (18%), or criticizing the patient's response to the cancer (13%).

From *friends,* the most helpful efforts at support were showing love and concern (30%), providing practical assistance (24%), and calmly accepting the illness (23%). In the following quote, a patient describes how his friends' calm acceptance of his cancer was helpful:

> I faced it and my friends faced it. They just accepted it. So I had cancer, and you know it was no big deal. Because that's the way I wanted it. I didn't want no big deal, crying the blues and all that kind of stuff.

With respect to unhelpful or upsetting behaviors, 17% (33% of respondents who had any complaints about their friends) reported that the most annoying or upsetting thing a friend did was to avoid social contact with them. This pattern reflects the same problem reported by the breast cancer patients. As in that study, the finding presented here does not denote social rejection from friends generally, but that respondents were often bothered by a particular friend who withdrew from them. In addition to concern over being avoided, 13% of respondents were upset by friends who were overly pessimistic about their cancer or cancer in general.

Respondents' views of what was helpful and unhelpful from *acquaintances* were, on certain dimensions, similar to what they said about friends. For example, being concerned (16%) and calm (14%) were helpful and being pessimistic (20%) was experienced as unhelpful. But they also had very different experiences with these two groups of people. Practical assistance was more frequently helpful from friends, but infrequently mentioned with respect to acquaintances (only 7%). Social avoidance was the single most frequently mentioned complaint about friends, but only rarely mentioned for acquaintances (4%). The two most frequently mentioned examples of nonsupport from acquaintances were their pessimism about cancer (20%), and rude or inappropriate remarks about the illness (13%). Examples of responses that were coded as rude and inappropriate include comments about the patient's hair (e.g., "Your hair has grown in all grey"), physical damage resulting from surgery (e.g., "How can you still feel like a woman?"), and other miscellaneous rude remarks (e.g., "I thought you had died!"). In some cases, the acquaintances' inappropriate or pessimistic comments stemmed from the fact that they did not know that the person with whom they were speaking was a cancer patient. In other cases, acquaintances seemed simply not to know how to act or what to say, and as a result said or did the wrong thing.

With respect to *other people who had or have had cancer,* the most frequently reported helpful behavior was their ability to offer the special kind of understanding that one gets from sharing a similar experience (27%), as the following quote illustrates:

> I don't have to say much to another breast cancer patient for her to understand. The most common one is what happens a week to a few days prior to getting a check-up. All you got to do is say, "My check-up is in three days," and they know what that experience is like. Its almost like a club. When you get hypersensitive to an unusual symptom or feeling, you only have to say a few words and they understand.

The provision of useful information about cancer and its treatment (25%), and acting as a good role model (21%) were also common helpful behaviors offered by others with cancer. The single most unsupportive thing that others with cancer did was to deal with their own cancer in a way that the respondent thought was self-destructive or foolish (23%) such as being pessimistic or continuing to smoke.

Concerning health care professionals, respondents indicated that the most helpful things provided by *physicians* were medical information (38%), effective medical care (27%), and expressions of optimism about the prognosis or the patient's ability to live with the cancer (27%). As examples of nonsupportive physician behaviors, respondents reported that not giving sufficient medical information (25%), and failure to express concern and empathy (16%) were the most unhelpful things their physicians did. From *nurses,* the most helpful behaviors were being concerned and empathetic (24%), being generally pleasant and kind (18%), providing practical assistance (i.e., nursing care—18%), and providing information (16%). As for unsupportive actions, 20% mentioned technical incompetence, 14%

mentioned minimizing the impact of the illness, and 11% reported that being unconcerned with the patient as a person were the most annoying or upsetting acts.

In outlining general trends regarding helpful actions, it is evident that to a greater or lesser extent, concern and empathy—the warm aspects of interpersonal relationships—were perceived as helpful from all sources. These results are consistent with Dunkel-Schetter's (1984) findings. Emotional support was most important from close others (spouse, family, and friends), but it was clearly important from medical personnel as well. With the exception of this dimension, however, there seemed to be considerable specificity in the socially supportive actions that were experienced as helpful by different providers. Intimates' most helpful actions included love and concern, physical presence, calm acceptance of the disease, and to a lesser extent, practical assistance. Other people with cancer provided information about the disease, the special understanding that comes from being a similar other, and a good role model. Medical personnel provided capable medical care, medical information, and optimism.

It is notable that very few respondents reported that being permitted to express the full range of their emotions (ventilation) was a helpful function with regard to the cancer. This missing finding was unexpected. It is commonly assumed, both by professionals and layman, that "getting concerns off your chest" is beneficial, yet very few respondents mentioned this as a socially supportive function.

Patients generally reported different unhelpful efforts from different categories of people. From the spouse, being critical of how the patient was handling the illness was the most frequently cited unhelpful experience. These incidents often appeared to be misfired efforts at social support in that, based on the examples reported, spouses were apparently attempting to provide useful feedback, which was experienced by the patients as critical.

Regarding friends, the most common complaint was that at least one friend avoided social contact with them, and this appears to be a fairly robust finding. As for acquaintances, pessimism and rude remarks about cancer were experienced as most upsetting. Finally, respondents reported that the most unhelpful acts experienced from health care professionals involved their failure to provide information, human concern, or technically competent medical care.

As noted earlier, social support researchers have been alert to the possibility that different types of social support may be valuable from different individuals in a social network, and our data largely support that caution. However, a parallel point suggested by these data should also be noted, namely that different kinds of social support may be valuable for different individuals undergoing the same stressful event. Our data suggest relatively little consensus about what types of behaviors are seen as supportive and unsupportive from particular targets in the social support network. For example, one individual may consider the spouse just being there to be a sign of support, whereas another individual may experience the spouse's presence as supportive only if it is accompanied by expressions of concern and love. Similarly, one individual may find the physician's medical attention to the cancer to be sufficiently helpful, whereas another individual may feel a need for emotional support as well.

It should be noted that there were relatively few instances in which a behavior seen as helpful by one individual was seen as unhelpful by another. For example, no respondent suggested that expressions of emotional concern from a medical caregiver were unhelpful. On the other hand, consensus regarding supportive and unsupportive behaviors was never greater than 35%, indicating that there is clear variability in what is seen as helpful or unhelpful from the same target. These findings suggest that, while medical caregivers, family and friends, and others in a cancer patient's network can be appraised of the kinds of actions that are typically perceived as supportive and unsupportive by cancer patients, they must also be alert to the fact that there are considerable individual differences in these preferences. Thus recommendations regarding supportive or unsupportive behaviors should be tempered with knowledge about particular patients and their preferences for certain kinds of actions. These results emphasize the importance of social support transactions in a general context of open communication, in which feedback is solicited and provided regarding what is helpful and unhelpful.

Summary and Conclusions

Overall, it appears that cancer patients report relatively few serious problems in their social support network (see also Jamison, Wellisch, & Pasnau, 1978; Revenson, Wollman, & Felton, 1983; Smith, Redman, Burns, & Sagert, 1985). Spouses, children, and close friends appear to provide much appreciated and adequate support. These findings should be qualified by the fact that our samples and those of other researchers who have studied social support and cancer have disproportionately included middle- and upper-middle-class patients, and it is possible that poverty-level and working-class patients may experience more significant gaps and problems in their social support network.

Despite general reports of satisfaction with social support from others, patients do appear to want different things from different people in their networks. Thus a continued research focus on specific acts of helping does appear to be a useful one. Our studies, of course, do not strictly provide a transactional analysis of social support because only patients and not the support providers were interviewed. However, given the dearth of literature in the area regarding what acts are perceived as supportive and unsupportive from different people, a focus on patient reports seemed to be appropriate in highlighting distinctive socially supportive and unsupportive actions. Such an analysis can provide a basis for a more informed theoretical analysis of the functions of social support, and it can also suggest specific interventions that may augment the support received by victims such as cancer patients.

References

Abrams, R. D., & Finesinger, J. E. (1953). Guilt reactions in patients with cancer. *Cancer, 6,* 474-482.

American Cancer Society. (1986). *Cancer facts and figures 1986.* New York: Author.

Barrera, M. (1981). Social support in the adjustment of pregnant adolescents: Assessment issues. In B. Gottlieb (Ed.), *Social networks of social support* (pp. 69-96). Beverly Hills, CA: Sage.

Berkman, L. F., & Syme, S. L. (1979). Social networks, host resistance, and mortality: A nine-year follow-up study of Alameda County residents. *American Journal of Epidemiology, 109,* 186-204.

Billings, A. G., & Moos, R. H. (1982). Social support and functioning among community and clinical groups: A panel model. *Journal of Behavioral Medicine, 5,* 295-312.

Bloom, J. R. (1982). Social support, accommodation to stress, and adjustment to breast cancer. *Social Science and Medicine, 16,* 1329-1338.

Brown, G. W., & Harris, T. (1978). *Social origins of depression.* London: Tavistock.

Campbell, A., Converse, P. E., & Rogers, W. L. (1976). *The quality of American life: Perceptions, evaluations, and satisfactions.* New York: Russell Sage.

Carey, R. C. (1974). Emotional adjustment in terminal patients: A quantitative approach. *Journal of Counseling Psychology, 21,* 433-439.

Chambers, W. N., & Reiser, M. F. (1953). Emotional stress in the precipitation of congestive heart failure. *Medicine, 15,* 38-60.

114   THE SOCIAL PSYCHOLOGY OF HEALTH

Cobb, S. (1976). Social support as a moderator of life stress. *Psychosomatic Medicine, 38,* 300-314.

Cobliner, W. G. (1977). Psychosocial factors in gynecological or breast malignancies. *Hospital Physician, 10,* 38-43.

Cohen, J. (1960). A coefficient of agreement for nominal scales. *Educational Psychology Measures, 20,* 37-46.

Cohen, S., & McKay, G. (1983). Interpersonal relationships as buffers of the impact of psychosocial stress on health. In A. Baum, S. E. Taylor, & J. E. Singer (Eds.), *Handbook of psychology and health* (Vol. 4, pp. 253-267). Hillsdale, NJ: Lawrence Erlbaum.

Cohen, S., & Wills, T. A. (1985). Stress, social support, and the buffering hypothesis. *Psychological Bulletin, 98,* 310-357.

Currier, L. M. (1966). The psychological impact of cancer on the cancer patient and his family. *Rocky Mountain Medical Journal, 68,* 43-68.

DiMatteo, M. R., & Hays, R. (1981). Social support and serious illness. In B. H. Gottlieb (Ed.), *Social networks and social support in community mental health* (pp. 117-147). Beverly Hills, CA: Sage.

Dimond, M. (1979). Social support and adaptation to chronic illness: The case of maintenance hemodialysis. *Research in Nursing and Health, 2,* 101-108.

Dunkel-Schetter, C. (1984). Social support and cancer: Findings based on patient interviews and their implications. *Journal of Social Issues, 40*(4), 77-98.

Dunkel-Schetter, C., & Wortman, C. B. (1982). The interactional dynamics of cancer: Problems in social relationships and their impact on the patient. In H. S. Friedman & M. R. DiMatteo (Eds.), *Interpersonal issues in health care* (pp. 69-100). New York: Academic Press.

Dunkel-Schetter, C., Folkman, S., & Lazarus, R. S. (in press). Correlates of social support receipt. *Journal of Personality and Social Psychology.*

Falke, R. L. (1987). *The use of support groups by cancer patients.* Unpublished doctoral dissertation, University of California, Los Angeles.

Funch, D. P., & Marshall, J. (1983). The role of stress, social support and age in survival from breast cancer. *Journal of Psychosomatic Research, 27,* 77-83.

Funch, D. P., & Mettlin, C. (1982). The role of support in relation to recovery from breast surgery. *Social Science and Medicine, 16,* 91-98.

Giacquinta, B. (1977). Helping families face the crisis of cancer. *American Journal of Nursing, 77,* 1585-1588.

Gordon, W. A., Freidenbergs, I., Diller, L., Hibbard, M., Wolf, C., Levine, L., Lipkins, R., Ezrachi, O., & Lucido, D. (1980). Efficacy of psychosocial intervention with cancer patients. *Journal of Consulting and Clinical Psychology, 48,* 743-759.

Gottlieb, B. H. (1981). Preventive interventions involving social networks and social support. In B. H. Gottlieb (Ed.), *Social networks and social support* (pp. 201-232). Beverly Hills, CA: Sage.

Grandstaff, N. W. (1976). The impact of breast cancer on the family. *Frontiers of Radiation Therapy Oncology, 11,* 743-759.

Hirsch, B. J. (1980). Natural support systems and coping with major life changes. *American Journal of Community Psychology, 8,* 159-179.

House, T. A. (1981). *Work stress and social support.* Reading, MA: Addison-Wesley.

Jackson, J. K. (1956). The problem of alcoholic tuberculous patients. In P. F. Sparer (Ed.), *Personality stress and tuberculosis* (pp. 504-538). New York: International Universities Press.

Jamison, K. R., Wellisch, D. K., & Pasnau, R. O. (1978). Psychosocial aspects of mastectomy: I. The woman's perspective. *American Journal of Psychiatry, 134,* 432-436.

Kaplan, B. H., Robbins, C., & Martin, S. S. (1983). Antecedents of psychological stress in young adults: Self-rejection, deprivation of social support, and life events. *Journal of Health and Social Behavior, 24,* 230-244.

Kaplan, D. M., Smith, A., Grobstein, R., & Fischman, S. E. (1973). Family mediation of stress. *Social Work, 17,* 60-69.

Klagsbrun, S. C. (1971). Communications in the treatment of cancer. *American Journal of Nursing, 71,* 944-948.

Klein, R. F., Dean, A., & Bogdonoff, M. D. (1976). The impact of illness upon the spouse. *Journal of Chronic Disease, 20,* 241-248.

Lichtman, R. R., & Taylor, S. E. (1986). Close relationships and the female cancer patient. In B. L. Andersen (Ed.), *Women with cancer: Psychological perspectives.* New York: Springer-Verlag.

Lichtman, R. R., Taylor, S. E., & Wood, J. V. (in press). Social support and marital adjustment after breast cancer. *Journal of Psychosocial Oncology.*

Lin, N., Simeone, R. S., Ensel, W. T., & Kuo, W. (1979). Social support, stressful life events, and illness: A model and an empirical test. *Journal of Health and Social Behavior, 20,* 108-119.

McNair, D.M., Lorr, M., & Droppleman, L. F. (1971). *EITS manual for the profile of mood states.* San Diego, CA: Educational and Industrial Testing Service.

Morris, T. (1979). Psychological adjustment to mastectomy. *Cancer Treatment Review, 6,* 41-61.

Nuckolls, K. B., Cassel, J. C., & Kaplan, B. H. (1972). Psychosocial assets, life crisis, and the progress of pregnancy. *American Journal of Epidemiology, 95,* 431.

Peters-Golden, H. (1982). Breast cancer: Varied perceptions of social support in the illness experience. *Social Science and Medicine, 16,* 483-491.

Revenson, T. A., Wollman, C. A., & Felton, B. J. (1983). Social support as stress buffers for adult cancer patients. *Psychosomatic Medicine, 45,* 321-331.

Robertson, E. K., & Suinn, R. M. (1968). The determination of rate of progress of stroke patients through empathy measures of patient and family. *Journal of Psychosomatic Research, 12,* 189-191.

Schaefer, C., Coyne, J. C., & Lazarus, R. S. (1981). The health-related functions of social support. *Journal of Behavioral Medicine, 4,* 381-406.

Shinn, M., Lehmann, S., & Wong, N. W. (1984). Social interaction and social support. *Journal of Social Issues, 40*(4), 55-76.

Silver, R. L., & Wortman, C. B. (1980). Coping with undesirable life events. In J. Garber & M.E.P. Seligman (Eds.), *Human helplessness: Theory and application* (pp. 279-340). New York: Academic Press.

Smith, E. M., Redman, P., Burns, T. L., & Sagert, K. M. (1985). Perceptions of social support among patients with recently diagnosed breast, endometrial, and ovarian cancer. *Journal of Psychosocial Oncology, 3,* 65-81.

Suls, J. (1982). Social support, interpersonal relations, and health: Benefits and liabilities. In G. S. Saunders & J. Suls (Eds.), *Social psychology of health and illness* (pp. 255-277). Hillsdale, NJ: Lawrence Erlbaum.

Sutherland, A. M., Orbach, C. E., Dyk, R. B., & Bard, M. (1953). The psychological impact of cancer and cancer surgery: I. Adaptation to the dry colostomy; preliminary report and summary of findings. *Cancer, 5,* 857-872.

Taylor, S. E., Falke, R. L., Mazel, R. M., & Hilsberg, B. L. (in press). Sources of satisfaction and dissatisfaction among members of cancer support groups. In B. Gottlieb (Ed.), *Creating support groups: Formats, processes, and effects.* Beverly Hills, CA: Sage .

Taylor, S. E., Falke, R. L., Shoptaw, S. J., & Lichtman, R. R. (1986). Social support, support groups, and the cancer patient. *Journal of Consulting and Clinical Psychology, 54,* 608-615.

Vettese, J. M. (1976). Problems of the patient confronting the diagnosis of cancer. In J. W. Cullen, B. H. Fox, & R. N. Isom (Eds.), *Cancer: The behavioral dimensions* (pp. 275-282). New York: Raven.

Wallston, B. S., Alagna, S. W., DeVellis, B. M., & DeVellis, R. F. (1983). Social support and physical health. *Health Psychology, 2,* 367-391.

Weidman-Gibbs, H., & Achterberg-Lawlis, J. (1978). Spiritual values and death anxiety: Implications for counseling with terminal cancer patients. *Journal of Counseling Psychology, 25,* 563-569.

Weisman, A. D. (1979). A model for psychosocial phasing in cancer. *General Hospital Psychiatry, 1,* 187-195.

Wellisch, D. K., Jamison, K. R., & Pasnau, R. O. (1978). Psychosocial aspects of mastectomy: II. The man's perspective. *American Journal of Psychiatry, 135,* 543-546.

Williams, A. W., Ware, J. E., Jr., & Donald, C. A. (1981). A model of mental health, life events, and social supports applicable to general populations. *Journal of Health and Social Behavior, 22,* 324-336.

Wortman, C. B. (1984). Social support and the cancer patient. *Cancer, 53* (Suppl. 10), 2339-2360.

Wortman, C. B., & Dunkel-Schetter, C. (1979). Interpersonal relationships and cancer: A theoretical analysis. *Journal of Social Issues, 35*(1), 120-155.

PART II
HEALTH PROMOTION

6

Health Promotion Programs:
An Introduction

SHIRLYNN SPACAPAN
STUART OSKAMP

T hree parallel trends in the area of health care have been prominent in the last decade. First, U.S. health care costs have been skyrocketing; they now consume over 10% of the gross national product and are still climbing. Second, health professionals have been putting greatly increased emphasis on behavioral life-style character-istics as important contributing factors to many serious diseases. For instance, the Surgeon General's report, *Healthy People*, cited individual behaviors like smoking and diet as major contributors to the leading chronic diseases (Califano, 1979). Third, the U.S. public has become involved in many types of programs to promote wellness, such as exercise, aerobics, jogging, and weight control. Whether these trends are causally related is impossible to say but it is clear that they have mutually supportive—perhaps even synergistic—effects.

This section of our volume discusses health promotion programs from three different perspectives. The authors of the following chapters are among the best-known psychologists who have been working in the field of health promotion. Their chapters examine two of the major settings for health promotion—the worksite and the community—and discuss the relative costs and benefits of health promotion programs. In this chapter we will briefly sketch the major types of health promotion programs, ranging from individual approaches to community campaigns, and mention psychological research that seems to be relevant to them. However, one major fact is clear: The field of health promotion is still very new, and research in the field is in its infancy.

Types of Health Promotion Programs

Individual health promotion approaches are at the least organized end of the continuum but probably involve more people than all other types put together. Millions of people have adopted each of the health fads that have swept across America. The most prominent recent examples include jogging, home weight training, home aerobics, and now, walking. In fact, in just a few years there has been an increase of over 50% in the number of Americans who exercise regularly (American Fitness and Running Association, 1981). For many decades, various diets have had their periods of popularity, typically introduced with extravagant claims of scientific support. Often these diet and exercise fads have been accomplished by a plethora of self-help books (see, for example, Cooper, 1982). Though some of these health crazes have had questionable benefits, or even negative effects, others appear to have well-supported health benefits. For example, smoking is one of the most important risk factors for several of the leading causes of death in America, and individual attempts to stop smoking, though often unsuccessful, have enabled about 30 million Americans to kick the cigarette habit (Schachter, 1982). Similarly, there is evidence that attempts at self-cure of obesity are more successful than attempts that involve participating in therapy or other organized weight-loss programs (Schachter, 1982).

Commercial health promotion programs are typically organized because they have to show a profit. They often follow and build on the fads of individual exercise, diet, or treatment. At the individualistic end of this group are vitamin and health food stores that push particular food supplements or diets with claims for their health benefits. Among the more group-oriented current examples are gyms featuring aerobics classes, health clubs with tennis, racquetball, or body-building equipment, commercial weight-loss programs (e.g., Nutri-Systems), and highly advertised smoking-cessation programs (e.g, Schick). While many of these programs have their own claims for miraculous health benefits—some private alcohol-abuse treatment centers claim more than a 90% success rate (Hunter, 1982)—psychological literature evaluating these programs is virtually nonexistent.

Many *group or organizational* health promotion programs are similar to commercial ones, except that they are nonprofit. Examples include YMCAs and YWCAs with exercise classes, swim programs, and other sports. Other programs in this category are self-help groups, many of them widespread and long-standing in the United States—for example, Alcoholics Anonymous, Synanon, and TOPS (Take Off Pounds Sensibly). Typically these approaches stress group meetings for social support, transmission of knowledge, and modeling of changed behavior, and many also rely on one-to-one support and assistance, as in a "buddy system." A final kind of organizational health promotion effort is programs conducted by employers at the worksite, and this is the topic of Chapter 7.

In the psychological literature, there is very little published work that evaluates these nonprofit health promotion programs. Brandsma, Maultsby, and Welch (1980), for example, compared one Alcoholics Anonymous group against three other alcohol abuse programs (e.g., behavior and insight therapy groups). Although there were some methodological problems with this experiment, results indicated that the different groups were approximately equal in treatment effectiveness. Other research on the Alcoholics Anonymous program by Miller and Hester (1980) revealed that this program may be more effective for some personality types than for others. Some of the research on group health promotion programs has examined specific components of one program, rather than pitting one program against another. Levitz and Stunkard (1974), for example, studied four different treatment conditions among 16 matched TOPS groups over a 12-week period. Four groups received the standard TOPS program, four groups received additional nutrition training, and eight received additional behavior modification training (four of them from TOPS personnel and four from a psychiatrist). The superiority of the behavior modification component was evidenced by lower attrition rates, greater weight loss at the end of the study, and greater weight loss one year later.

Finally, *community* programs are at the broad, inclusive end of the continuum. Though such all-encompassing programs within a town or city are much rarer than the previously mentioned types, two excellent samples are described in Chapter 8. Many cities have community centers that offer various kinds of health outreach activities, and a few have tried to extend these efforts to all or most community citizens. Sometimes this is a brief effort, often combined with extensive media publicity, as in the annual day designated for the nationwide "Great American Smokeout." Sometimes it may continue for weeks, as in the antismoking "cold turkey" project in Greenfield, Iowa (Ryan, 1973), the national antismoking campaign in Finland (McAlister, Puska, Konkela, Pallonen, & Maccoby, 1980), and the diet and exercise program run by the Swedish National Board of Health and Welfare (Stunkard, 1975).

There are differing views on the benefits of each of these types of health promotion, ranging from strongly supportive through skeptical to down-right negative. Chapter 9 examines a number of the arguments pro and con and suggests ways in which careful research can establish the relative balance of risks and benefits for major health promotion programs. Such research is badly needed to help direct efforts and funds in the most productive directions, in order to advance public health and reduce the very great societal costs of ill health.

Chapter by James Terborg

In the following chapter, James Terborg presents a comprehensive overview of worksite health promotion programs. Noting that there has been a marked upsurge in the number of companies sponsoring activities to promote employee health, Terborg details the current status of worksite health promotion, illustrating his review with examples of programs at one large corporation and one small, family-owned business. In a previous chapter he documented the research on specific components (e.g., exercise, smoking cessation, weight loss, stress management) of such worksite programs (Terborg, 1986). Here, he takes a more general view and discusses the worksite as an advantageous context for health promotion, as contrasted with medical and community settings.

Organizations have potential advantages over clinical settings in dealing with the classic problems of participation in and adherence to programs of long-term behavior change. Terborg notes that social forces operating at the worksite can be manipulated to encourage both participation in and adherence to a health promotion program. These forces include social support and other mediators discussed earlier in this volume, as well as competition and the effects of public commitment to a course of action, and also the customary employer-employee contract involving rewards and responsibilities for performance.

One of the unique contributions of this chapter is in Terborg's discussion of how to assess program effectiveness. In this connection, he suggests that the very "threats to validity" (Cook & Campbell, 1979) that researchers usually strive to avoid may be used as "leverage points" to enhance the success of a worksite health program. To use one of his examples, a traditional researcher would not want to measure the effects of an organization's smoking cessation program soon after the death of the company president from a smoking-related disorder, because any effects of the program would be confounded with the historical event of the president's death. But a practitioner would be wise to instigate just such a program quickly, capitalizing on the event and enhancing the probability of a successful program. To this end, Terborg calls for implementation effectiveness studies to point the way to successful health promotion intervention in organizations, as well as the customary treatment effectiveness, or feasibility, studies.

Throughout this chapter, Terborg provides many concrete examples, as well as noting opportunities for future research. For instance, he illustrates how the physical environment at work can be manipulated to support health promotion efforts through such simple changes as removing cigarette machines, providing free fruit instead of candy, restricting smoking in offices, and displaying signs that prompt healthy behavior. At the same time, however, he notes that little systematic research has been done on smoking restrictions, leaving us with a lack of information as to whether such restrictions increase the likelihood of smoking cessation or result in psychological reactance in the form of increased smoking elsewhere. His concrete examples offer practitioners helpful translations from the conceptual level to the "real world" of workplaces. Similarly, his suggestions of opportunities for research should challenge investigators in the field and help to set the future research agenda for health promotion activities at the worksite.

Chapter by Nathan Maccoby

In Chapter 8, Nathan Maccoby notes that the advantages of organizations as a context for health promotion are not limited to the traditional corporate workplace. He stresses that other organizations such as families, clubs, churches, schools—even supermarkets—can be linked together as agents in a communitywide effort to promote health.

Like the other authors in this volume, Maccoby emphasizes that behavior plays a critical role in many of the risk factors contributing to the major causes of death in Western society. He recommends community education as a way to help individuals reduce their health-risk behaviors, or to prevent such behaviors from being learned in the first place. Maccoby illustrates such community education programs through a description of the design, procedure, and results of the now-famous Three-Community Study (TCS) conducted by the Stanford Heart Disease Prevention Program. This was a landmark interdisciplinary study, noteworthy for turning away from a medical model directed at high-risk individuals to a community model using combinations of carefully designed mass media messages and face-to-face instruction to facilitate cardiovascular risk reduction.

The positive results of the TCS, indicating that mass media *can* increase people's awareness of risk factors and lead to a change toward healthier behaviors, prompted the Stanford group to undertake an even more ambitious study, the current Five-City Project (FCP). In addition to replicating and extending the results of the TCS, a major goal of the FCP is to create self-sustaining health promotion structures and a model for cost-effective community health promotion.

One of the unique contributions of this chapter is in Maccoby's discussion of the theoretical perspectives that were integrated in the design and implementation of the FCP's educational program. He shows how academic research can provide a useful foundation for practical interventions. For instance, the communication-behavior-change framework (see McGuire, 1969) influenced the content chosen for the educational materials, the social marketing framework of Kotler and Levy (1983) directed the design and distribution of health education products, and a community organization framework guided efforts toward the diffusion and institutionalization of change. The lively presentation of this chapter provides a clear and succinct overview and update of the pioneering Stanford health promotion projects.

Chapter by Robert M. Kaplan

As Robert M. Kaplan notes in our closing chapter, it is difficult to estimate the costs and benefits of many health promotion efforts. However, he stresses that public policy on health promotion and medical care should be guided by a consideration of the relative costs of competing alternatives for producing enhanced health.

As he has emphasized before (e.g., Kaplan, 1985), health status is the logical focus for health promotion interventions and research, yet many providers do not set their goals in terms of health outcomes per se. For instance, some programs have attempted to modify blood triglyceride levels through diet, yet the relationship between triglyceride levels and health outcomes is not strong. In defining health status, Kaplan distinguishes between risk factors and health outcomes and warns that health status cannot be perfectly predicted even if one knows the relevant risk factors. He also distinguishes mediators of health status (like those discussed in the first half of our volume) from risk factors, and suggests that examining mediators is appropriate once health status is defined. He holds that good measures of health outcomes should combine mortality and morbidity, since the two most important objectives of health care systems are prolonging life and improving the quality of life.

The General Health Policy Model developed by Kaplan and his colleagues has three measurement components. The first component involves classifying individuals according to their objective physical states (e.g., degree of mobility, physical activity, and social activity). The second component involves weighting each of the objective states by their desirability or value, and the third component involves multiplication of the value term by the months or years spent by an individual in each of the states. As the chapter title indicates, the value component of the model is the major focus in attempts to define the quality of life as related to health outcomes. To illustrate the crucial nature of value weightings, and the trade-off between treatment costs and benefits, Kaplan points out the unpleasant side-effects of treatments for diabetes and high blood pressure— side-effects that may be more aversive to individuals than present or future suffering with the presenting medical symptoms. In considering health promotion programs, it is important to note that interventions vary widely in their potential to ensure good health—for instance, smoking cessation produces substantial benefits; heart disease prevention measures have possible benefits; and exercise programs have an unknown balance of risks and benefits.

A unique contribution of Kaplan's chapter is the exploration of the possibility that some health promotion efforts are damaging or dangerous in and of themselves. A recent example is accounts in the popular press indicating that intensive exercise may have more negative health effects than benefits (see McGuire, 1987). As an extreme example of this point, Kaplan notes that reducing a child's dietary fat intake may possibly reduce his or her risk of eventual heart disease, but can have the more immediate negative consequence of reducing, as well, physical height and weight.

Appropriately for the final chapter in this volume, Kaplan emphasizes two points that deserve spotlighting: First, there are numerous opportunities for the application of social psychology in the developing field of health promotion. Second, substantial and careful research is necessary to help guide public policy toward an efficient and effective use of our scarce health-care resources.

References

American Fitness and Running Association. (1981). *Statistical report*. Washington, DC: Author.

Brandsma, J. M., Maultsby, M. C., & Welch, R. J. (1980). *The outpatient treatment of alcoholism: A review and comparative study*. Baltimore: University Park Press.

Califano, J. A. (1979). *Healthy people: The Surgeon General's report on health promotion and disease prevention*. Washington, DC: U.S. Government Printing Office.

Cook, T. D., & Campbell, D. T. (1979). *Quasi-experimentation: Design and analysis issues for field settings*. Chicago: Rand McNally.

Cooper, K. H. (1982). *The aerobics program for total well-being*. New York: Evans.

Hunter, C., Jr. (1982). Freestanding alcohol treatment centers—A new approach to an old problem. *Psychiatric Annals, 12*, 396-408.

Kaplan, R. M. (1985). The connection between clinical health promotion and health status. *American Psychologist, 39*, 755-765.

Kotler, P., & Levy, S. J. (1983). Broadening the concept of marketing. In P. Kotler, O. C. Ferrel, & C. Lamb (Eds.),*Cases and readings for marketing for nonprofit organizations* (pp. 3-40). Englewood Cliffs, NJ: Prentice-Hall.

Levitz, L., & Stunkard, A. J. (1974). A therapeutic coalition for obesity: Behavior modification and patient self-help. *American Journal of Psychiatry, 131*, 423-427.

McAlister, A., Puska, P., Konkela, K., Pallonen, V., & Maccoby, N. (1980). Mass communication and community organization for public health education. *American Psychologist, 35*, 375-379.

McGuire, R. (1987, August 25). Lite exercise. *Los Angeles Times*, Part 5, pp. 1, 6.

McGuire, W. J. (1969). The nature of attitudes and attitude change. In G. Lindsey & E. Aronson (Eds.), *The handbook of social psychology* (2nd ed., Vol. 3, pp. 136-314). Reading, MA: Addison-Wesley.

Miller, W. R., & Hester, R. K. (1980). Treating the problem drinker: Modern approaches. In W. R. Miller (Ed.),*The addictive behaviors*. Oxford: Pergamon.

Ryan, F. J. (1973). Cold turkey in Greenfield, Iowa: A follow-up study. In W. L. Dunn, Jr. (Ed.), *Smoking behavior: Motives and incentives*. Washington, DC: Winston.

Schachter, S. (1982). Recidivism and self-cure of smoking and obesity. *American Psychologist, 37,* 436-444.

Stunkard, A. J. (1975). From explanation to action in psychosomatic medicine: The case of obesity. *Psychosomatic Medicine, 37,* 195-236.

Terborg, J. R. (1986). Health promotion at the worksite: A research challenge for personnel and human resources management. In K. H. Rowland & G. R. Ferris (Eds.), *Research in personnel and human resources management* (Vol. 4, pp. 225-267). Greenwich, CT: JAI.

7

The Organization
as a Context
for Health Promotion

JAMES R. TERBORG

Americans are becoming more concerned about their health. More and more people are making positive lifestyle changes to reduce their risk of disease and to increase their physical, emotional, and mental well being. People are eating more foods low in dietary cholesterol and saturated fats, the prevalence of smoking among adults is decreasing, and more people are exercising and controlling their weight (U.S. Department of Health and Human Services, 1985).

The trend toward healthier life-styles appears to be a major shift in social values and not merely a passing fad. Several writers have examined this shift and concluded that Americans are becoming more concerned about disease prevention and, more importantly, health promotion (Green, Wilson, & Lovato, 1986; Matarazzo, 1984; Terborg, 1986a). The proliferation of marketing campaigns built on health and fitness themes reflects the extent to which positive life-style changes have become a part of our

AUTHOR'S NOTE: Support for writing this chapter was provided by Oregon Research Institute. I thank Lynda Van Dusen for typing the manuscript. I also thank Dennis Ary, Russ Glasgow, and Ed Lichtenstein for many helpful suggestions. Finally, I thank the editors for their patience, encouragement, and advice.

society, at least among the middle and upper class. Health and fitness is a growth industry.

The concern for health also is becoming more evident in the workplace. Historically, most large companies and many small companies provided medical and disability insurance as a fringe benefit. Also, all organizations are legally required to comply with OSHA standards regarding occupational safety and to make contributions to worker's compensation insurance to cover costs associated with job-related illnesses and injuries. However, the vast majority of companies have been far more interested in the broader issues of competitiveness and profitability than in employee illness and injury. Not surprisingly, the related topics of employee fitness and wellness, as contrasted with employee illness and injury, have received even less attention.

In the past decade, however, there has been a dramatic increase in corporate concern about employee health, fitness, and wellness. Perhaps as many as 50,000 companies have sponsored activities designed to promote employee health, and more than 1,500 companies offer comprehensive health promotion programs at the worksite (Fielding, 1984; Terborg, 1986a). The Association for Fitness in Business, which is the primary professional association for directors of corporate health promotion programs, was founded in 1975 with 25 members and today has over 3,000 members. Although large companies with substantial numbers of managerial and professional employees are most likely to sponsor health promotion at the worksite, there is growing interest in occupational health promotion programs among all types of organizations in both the public and private sectors (Davis, Rosenberg, Iverson, Vernon, & Bauer, 1984; LaRosa & Haines, 1986; Terborg, 1986a).

This chapter examines the worksite as a context for health promotion. The chapter begins with a brief review of the current status of health promotion programs at the worksite. This includes descriptions of the health promotion programs developed at one very large company, Control Data, and one small company, Scherer Brothers Lumber Company. The chapter then discusses characteristics of worksite-based health promotion programs that may differentiate them from programs offered in community, hospital, or clinic settings. Emphasis is placed in three areas: (a) contextual features of the worksite that make it a particularly good place for offering health promotion programs, (b) methods and techniques to facilitate employee participation in health promotion programs and to enhance adherence and long-term maintenance of behavior change, and (c) methodological issues in program evaluation, including cost effectiveness analysis and cost benefit analysis. The chapter concludes with a discussion of organization-level factors associated with the adoption and institutionalization of health promotion programs in the worksite. Throughout the chapter research questions and needs are identified.

Overview of Worksite Health Promotion Programs

Description and Content

Worksite health promotion consists of an ongoing series of activities funded or endorsed by the organization that are designed to promote the adoption of personal behavior and corporate practices conducive to employee fitness, health, and wellness (Terborg, 1986a).

Worksite health promotion activities can take many forms, ranging from distributing free materials from voluntary organizations (e.g., pamphlets on how to stop smoking) to the construction of a million-dollar multipurpose fitness facility with professionally trained staff, the latest in exercise equipment, and a broad range of screening, education, and behavior-change programs. Health promotion programs at the worksite vary tremendously in structure, content, and scope, and this makes it difficult to compare programs and results.

Although there is no such thing as the "typical" worksite health promotion program, there are some features shared by most *comprehensive* programs. Comprehensive programs usually begin with a companywide needs assessment designed to gauge employee interest and to determine organizational needs. This is followed by administration of a health-risk-appraisal instrument or some other type of health screening device. Health-risk appraisals are used to determine the degree to which employees are at risk for premature morbidity and mortality because of such characteristics as high blood pressure, smoking, obesity, poor dietary and nutrition habits, and sedentary life-styles. Employees receive feedback and counseling based on their health-risk profiles and are encouraged to participate in appropriate health-risk-reducing activities (e.g., attend a stop-smoking class during lunch breaks). Follow-up administration of the health-risk-appraisal instrument and some type of evaluation of participant satisfaction with the program are conducted periodically to assess program effects. Formal documentation of program evaluation, however, is seldom undertaken. Reviews of the literature show that very few experimental or quasi-experimental studies have been done (Falkenberg, 1987; Fielding, 1984; Terborg, 1986a; Wolfe, Ulrich, & Parker, in press).

The most commonly offered health promotion activities deal with exercise, stress management, smoking cessation, weight loss, nutrition, and hypertension detection and control (Fielding, 1984; Terborg, 1986a). Employees usually participate on their own time, and a fee may be required for some activities, although one survey suggested that approximately one-third of programs allowed participation on company time, and a small number of companies paid for all costs (Kondrasuk, 1984). The annual cost to the company for each participant in a comprehensive health promotion program ranges from $100 to over $1,000, with typical costs in the $400-$500 range (Fielding, 1984).

As companies gain experience with health promotion activities there is a tendency to expand the program to other areas and to offer participation to employees' spouses and families, as well as to retirees. Table 7.1 presents a partial listing of different activities that could be offered to various age groups of employees, employee dependents, and retirees. As the table shows, health promotion at the worksite can be much more than a smoking-cessation class and a room with some free weights and an exercise bicycle. For example, the wellness program developed by the Adolph Coors Company—in addition to offering traditional classes in such areas as exercise, weight loss, smoking cessation, stress management, and diet and nutrition—offers family-oriented fitness programs, specially designed aerobics classes for older employees, pre- and postnatal pregnancy exercise programs, pre- and postnatal dietary and nutritional programs, classes in anger management, classes in parenting skills, screening for breast cancer and skin cancer for employees and spouses, dental education, alcohol use education, and rehabilitation for employees with cardiac and orthopedic needs.

Examples of Health Promotion at Two Companies

To give a more concrete picture of worksite health promotion, here are descriptions of two very different companies: Control Data, a Fortune 500 company, and Scherer Brothers Lumber Company, a family-owned business. These companies were chosen primarily because they have

Table 7.1
**Examples of Health Promotion Activities at the Worksite
for Different Age Groups**

Age Group	Activities
Infants	employer-sponsored day care programs parent education and support groups maternity and paternity leave flexible work schedules for parents breast feeding information and education prenatal health information prenatal exercise classes protection from work hazards associated with reproductive risk
Children	family hours for use of the fitness facility exercise classes to develop balance and coordination social games to develop cooperation swimming and water safety classes health classes employer-sponsored day care programs
Adolescents and Young Adults	family hours for use of the fitness facility youth sports and activities family sports and activities health and safety classes
Adults	high blood pressure detection and treatment diabetes detection and treatment biannual medical checkups for employees over 50 years of age health risk appraisal and health counseling health and safety classes behavior-change classes smoking restrictions or bans healthy food in vending machines and in cafeteria policies and programs to ensure a safe and healthy work environment reduction and management of work stress
Older Adults	health counseling about age-related health risks exercise classes for older adults social activities for older adults programs to ease transition to retirement expansion of worksite health promotion programs to retirees

SOURCE: Adapted from Green (1984). Copyright 1984 by Annual Reviews Inc. Adapted by
permission.

received considerable attention within the corporate wellness literature. The following descriptions are more like studies than rigorous program evaluation. The evaluation of worksite health promotion programs is discussed more extensively later in the chapter.

Control Data. Control Data's "StayWell" program was conceived in 1977 and initiated in 1979 in response to rising health-care costs (see Fielding, 1984; Glasgow & Terborg, in press; Jose, Anderson, & Haight, 1987; Naditch, 1986, for a complete description of Control Data's program; and Terborg, 1986a, for reviews). A preliminary cross-sectional study demonstrated that employees at elevated health risk because of smoking, sedentary life-styles, obesity, and high blood pressure were likely to have higher health-care costs, spend more time in the hospital, have more absences from work because of illness, and report more health-related limitations at work than were employees not at risk in these areas. Partially based on these data, the decision was made to continue development of the program.

The StayWell program has since undergone extensive pilot testing and revision. By the end of 1985, the program was available to over 70% of Control Data's full-time employees at most major company locations throughout the United States; it is also marketed to other organizations. The program is offered free to all employees and spouses. Employees participate on their own time, except for the orientation and health-risk-appraisal sessions, which are offered on company time.

The program begins with an employee and organizational health needs assessment. This is followed by preimplementation site planning. Orientation sessions are next, at which time employees are invited to participate in a health-risk appraisal and health screen. Those who complete the health-risk appraisal are given interpretation and counseling and are encouraged to participate in education and behavior-change classes in the areas of fitness, smoking cessation, stress management, nutrition, weight reduction, or back care. Classes can be self-study, computer-based, or led by a trained instructor. Instructor-led classes meet in 30-minute and 60-minute time blocks to make participation convenient to employees on restricted work schedules (e.g., production employees who may only have 30-minute lunch breaks). In addition to ongoing classes, StayWell action teams are formed at each worksite. Action teams are employee-led groups that focus on site-specific wellness activities or worksite issues, such as changing the food in the cafeteria and vending machines or making safety glasses available for home use. In addition, Control Data publishes a quarterly wellness news magazine and sponsors special campaigns and events to promote various wellness concerns.

Evaluation data on the program, as reported by Jose, Anderson, and Haight (1987), are encouraging. At the end of 1985, 62% of eligible employees had participated in at least one health promotion activity. Perhaps more important, however, are estimates of participation rates in education and behavior-change classes among employees with the highest health-risks. These participation levels reportedly reached 54% for over-weight employees, 46% for hypertensives, 45% for those with elevated blood cholesterol, 33% for those with sedentary life-styles, and 23% for smokers. Self-reported smoking prevalence dropped from 34% to 24% in sites that used StayWell, while it declined from 35% to 30% in non-StayWell sites. Of particular interest was the finding that nearly 1,200 more employees quit smoking at StayWell sites than actually completed the stop-smoking class. This "spill-over effect" was attributed to positive health changes in the worksite culture as a result of the StayWell program. From a public health perspective, changes in worksite culture and values that result from the successful implementation of a health promotion program may be one of the most important outcomes of the program. Corporatewide changes in culture and values may result in positive health effects among nonparticipants as well as among participants in the health promotion program.

In addition, compared to employees in other companies that are just starting health promotion programs, Control Data employees appear to be getting more exercise and are more likely to use seat belts. Subsequent data also suggest that employees with elevated health-risks have higher health-care costs and take more sick leave than do employees with no health-risks. Finally, by estimating the excess cost in health-care claims associated with elevated health-risk and multiplying it by the reduction since 1980 in the number of Control Data employees who are at risk, the annual savings in health-care claims is estimated to be approximately $1.8 million.

Control Data is a very large company with many resources at its disposal to ensure the proper design, implementation, and evaluation of a comprehensive health promotion program. Economies of scale also give large companies like Control Data a favorable position from which to estimate possible health cost savings. Small- and medium-sized companies, however, face a different set of questions when attempting to adopt a worksite health promotion program.

Scherer Brothers Lumber Company. Scherer Brothers, a lumber and building supply company located in Minnesota, is expected to have sales of approximately $67 million for 1987, or about the same sales volume as a large Sears store. The company is family owned and managed by the sons of Clarence and Munn Scherer who founded the business in the 1930s. It is frequently mentioned in articles on health promotion that appear in the popular press, as in a feature article in *Inc.* magazine (Hyatt, 1986), which provided the basis for the following description.

Scherer Brothers Lumber Company had a history of living up to the macho image of the northwoods lumberjack, and beer kegs often sat in the lumberyard. This image had its costs, however. Clarence Scherer died from alcohol abuse, and his brother is a recovering alcoholic. A few years after Clarence Scherer's death, one overweight employee died at work from a heart attack, another was killed in an accident related to smoking, and a third committed suicide soon after he was forced to quit working because of arteriosclerosis. Four deaths in a short period of time had a significant impact on the culture of this small company.

One of the sons, who was a dedicated marathoner, decided it was time to make some changes. The first thing he did was organize a wellness committee. After getting some suggestions from employees, the company unplugged the cigarette machine and hired a smoking-cessation expert to assist employees who wanted to quit smoking. Next they bought a blood pressure kit, held a weight-loss seminar, and replaced the candy machines with free fruit. The company started to pay for drug and alcohol treatment, and they initiated a well-pay plan whereby employees with no unauthorized absences could earn up to three days' extra pay a year. They introduced an incentive program to reduce on-the-job injuries, offered free annual physical checkups to employees over the age of 55, reduced the noise level in the lumberyard, installed orthopedically designed seats in all of their trucks, and began providing all office and supervisory staff members a free, healthy lunch. They also began distribution of a newsletter, sponsored sports teams, and offered educational programs. Roger Scherer, the current president, lost 20 pounds in a weight-control program he took with 12 other workers. Greg Scherer quit chewing tobacco and started running to work in the mornings.

The health promotion program at Scherer Brothers Lumber Company has all the signs of being successful. The company estimates an annual cost of $107,300 for their health and safety program, but annual savings in health insurance, worker's compensation insurance, absenteeism, and unemployment tax are estimated at $204,000. This does not include the intangibles of better employee morale and improved job performance.

Scherer Brothers has created a culture that promotes employee health and safe work practices. They spend money on the programs their employees need, and the Scherer family members set positive examples for their employees. They were able to accomplish this without health-risk appraisals, computer-assisted instruction, or construction of a costly exercise facility. Rather, people at the top were convinced of the value of what they were doing, they led by example, and they truly cared about the health and safety of their employees.

Promoting Health in Work Organizations

This section describes why the worksite is an excellent context for conducting health promotion activities and for doing applied social psychological research. A general discussion of advantages and facilitating conditions associated with health promotion at the worksite is followed by a more extensive treatment of two major issues in the occupational health promotion field, which are (a) how to enhance employee participation, adherence, and long-term behavior change; and (b) how to evaluate the effects of occupational health promotion programs.

Facilitating Conditions of Worksite Health Promotion Programs

There are three major reasons why the worksite is an advantageous place for conducting health promotion activities and for doing research on health promotion: (a) very large numbers of people are employed on a regular basis, (b) there is a potential for manipulation of the social and physical environments, and (c) the possibility of reduced health-care costs and increased productivity make health promotion programs at the worksite attractive to organizations.

Labor force participation rates. First, in contrast to community- and clinic-based programs, the worksite presents an excellent opportunity to affect directly the daily activities of a significant number of people. Nearly 105 million people go to work on a regular basis, and over 70% of adults between the ages of 18 and 65 are employed (U.S. Bureau of the Census, 1986). The specific labor force participation rates for males and females of various age groups are shown in Table 7.2.

Table 7.2
Labor Force Participation Rates by Age and Gender for 1986

Age	*Participation (%)* Males	Females
20-24	85.0	71.8
25-34	94.7	70.9
35-44	95.0	71.8
45-54	91.0	64.4
55-64	67.9	42.0
65+	15.8	7.3

It is important to note that labor force participation is substantial among people over the age of 40 because this is the time when morbidity and mortality statistics start to reflect the health consequences of elevated health-risk factors (Belloc, 1973). For example, the prevalence rate of high blood pressure (140/90 mm Hg or above) among employed males between the ages of 45 and 54 is more than 100% higher than the prevalence rate for employed males between the ages of 25 and 34. Furthermore, the incidence of cardiovascular disease among employed males between the ages of 45 and 54 with high blood pressure is approximately 2.8 times the rate of cardiovascular disease for those of the same age but without high blood pressure (U.S. Department of Health and Human Services, 1985). Jose, Anderson, and Haight (1987) found similar patterns using health-care costs in their analysis at Control Data. These data show that not only does health risk increase with age, but the health consequences of such risk factors become exacerbated for people over the age of 40.

It is also useful to recognize that for many people with limited incomes and minimal exposure to traditional forms of health care, the worksite may be the primary channel of health promotion. The Zeitgeist of the health and fitness movement with its memberships at health clubs, cook books promoting gourmet foods low in cholesterol and high in fiber, and registration in aerobic exercise classes, has not reached the poor, the uneducated, and single parents working in low-income jobs (Becker, 1986). A public health perspective suggests that companies should target employees most likely to benefit from worksite health promotion programs. Health promotion programs at the worksite, however, appeal most to middle- and upper-income employees, who may benefit less than lower-income workers from participation in the programs. A research challenge is to learn how to increase participation rates among employees who work at lower levels of the organizational hierarchy.

Another advantage of high labor force participation is that companies keep records on employees. This makes it much easier to conduct longitudinal studies that require follow-up data collection, especially in view of the fact that the health effects of life-style changes can take several years to occur. Clinic- and community-based health promotion programs historically have difficulty keeping track of people over long periods of time. But even when employees quit, the organization often has a forwarding address.

Opportunities for intervention. The second reason that worksites provide advantageous contexts for health promotion activities is that they provide many opportunities for intervening in the work environment and in the social system.

The work environment can be changed to promote healthy behaviors. Syme (1986) reviewed the literature on health promotion and concluded that individual-treatment programs of behavior change, as often found in clinical settings, are seriously limited because people have difficulty modifying well-established habits. One promising alternative is to modify the environment. Syme (1986) believes that such interventions are likely to be more practical and more effective in the long run. At the worksite, environmental changes may include restrictions on smoking, availability of nutritious foods and snacks in the cafeteria and in vending machines, and cues for healthy behavior (e.g., signs at elevators suggesting use of the stairs).

Social support has been shown to be important for participation, adherence, and long-term behavior change, although the results are somewhat equivocal (Brownell et al., 1986; Lichtenstein, Glasgow, & Abrams, 1986). Also, most general models of behavior explicitly include social and normative variables as important constructs (Bandura, 1977; Fishbein, & Ajzen, 1975; Triandis, 1980). Because people go to work on a regular basis, identify themselves as employees of the company, and are usually able to recognize many of their co-workers, the workplace provides a social context that can be a powerful reinforcer and punisher of behavior. Standing in front of a group of co-workers whom you see nearly every day and pledging to quit smoking is more likely to create behavioral commitment than doing the same thing in front of a group of strangers whom you will see once a week for 12 weeks in a smoking-cessation class at the local hospital.

At a minimum, it is more convenient to attend and participate in health promotion activities at the worksite than to go to a clinic or to an exercise facility. Convenience is a major factor encouraging participation and adherence (Dishman, Sallis, & Orenstein, 1985; Fielding, 1984).

Economic incentives. The third reason that organizations provide advantageous contexts for implementation of and research on health promotion is the possibility of economic benefits to organizations that sponsor health promotion programs. Simply stated, organizations are looking at health and fitness programs as a means to improve employee morale *and* to reduce medical costs.

More and more employees are requesting health promotion programs as a fringe benefit. Evidence, though mostly anecdotal, suggests that the availability of a health promotion program helps with recruiting, improves employee morale, increases employee performance, and reduces absenteeism and turnover (Terborg, 1986a). In addition, data are beginning to accumulate that show an association between employee health and fitness and total health-care costs, although the causal link is not well understood (Bellingham, Johnson, McCauley, & Mendes, 1987; Terborg, 1986a).

The fact that organizations are adopting health promotion programs because of self-interest means that companies are more receptive to social and environmental interventions, and this in turn increases opportunities for research and evaluation. If companies did not see any value to worksite health promotion, it would be almost impossible to conduct research or to bring about change, with the possible exception of change resulting from city, state or federal legislation. Of interest, the prevalence of local legislation restricting smoking is on the increase (Rigotti, 1986). However, if Kelman's (1961) work on compliance and internalization generalizes to organizations, organizational compliance with government regulations is not likely to produce the same impact as organizational change resulting from the internalization of new values and beliefs.

In summary, organizations are good contexts for conducting health promotion activities and for doing research on health promotion because (a) significant numbers of people go to work on a regular basis, (b) the worksite offers a potential for environmental and social interventions, and (c) companies are pursuing health promotion out of self-interest, which means there may be many opportunities for doing research on the adoption, institutionalization, and evaluation of worksite health promotion programs.

Participation, Adherence, and Long-Term Behavior Change

A major and continuing problem in health promotion involves the issues of (a) recruitment to and participation in a behavior-change program, (b) adherence to a prescribed regimen, and (c) maintenance of long-term behavior change. The following discussion of these issues will mention advantages as well as possible disadvantages associated with the application of motivational and behavior-change techniques.

Participation, adherence, and long-term behavior change are important variables for health promotion because many of the risk factors associated with health-care utilization have behavioral antecedents. Table 7.3 lists the 10 health conditions that account for the largest health-care expenditures for U.S. adults under the age of 65. Smoking, alcohol and drug abuse, poor diet, obesity, high blood pressure, stress, diabetes, and lack of exercise are risk factors associated with most of these conditions. Altogether, over $128 billion are spent annually on health care for these conditions in this segment of the population (Herzlinger & Calkins, 1986). It has been estimated that this figure could be reduced by as much as 50% if people would adopt healthy life-styles (Harris, 1980). Table 7.4 shows the estimated prevalence of several of these risk factors in the adult working population. The information presented in Tables 7.3 and 7.4 suggests that the worksite can provide a potentially important leverage point for improving health.

All of these risk factors can be modified through sustained behavior change. However, people most at risk are often those least likely to begin behavior-change programs (Fielding, 1984). Also, of those who do start a behavior-change program, at best between 60% and 80% will adhere to recommendations in the short-term, and at best up to 50% will successfully modify their behavior in the long-term (Heiby & Carlson, 1986). Typical rates for short-term and long-term adherence are much lower. These findings hold true for individuals of all ages, males and females, all social classes and ethnic groups, and for all degrees of symptomatology (DiMatteo & DiNicola, 1982). Furthermore, the pattern holds for pharmacological regimens, such as taking a pill once a day to control hypertension, and for nonpharmacological regimens, such as reducing the amount of salt in one's diet; it holds for modifying addictive behaviors such as smoking or alcohol abuse, and for nonaddictive behaviors such as eating more fiber and fresh vegetables; and it holds for initiating new behaviors such as starting a regular exercise program, and for stopping a harmful

Table 7.3
Conditions Having the Largest Health Care Expenditures
for U.S. Adults Under the Age of 65

Condition	Annual expenditures in billions of dollars	Risk Factors
Digestive diseases	26.1	smoking, alcohol, diet, obesity, stress
Injury and poisoning	15.0	stress, alcohol, drugs
Mental disorders	14.6	stress, alcohol, drugs
Respiratory diseases	13.2	smoking
Cardiovascular diseases	13.1	smoking, hypertension, hypercholesterolemia, lack of exercise, obesity, diabetes, stress
Nervous system diseases	13.0	hypertension, smoking hypercholesterolemia, stress, diabetes
Genitourinary	10.7	hypertension, diabetes
Musculoskeletal diseases	9.8	obesity, stress
Neoplasms	8.3	smoking, alcohol, diet, obesity
Skin diseases	5.0	obesity

SOURCE: Herzlinger & Calkins (1986). Copyright 1986 by *Harvard Business Review*. Adapted by permission.

behavior such as smoking cigarettes (DiMatteo & DiNicola, 1982).

Health promotion programs offered at the worksite would seem to have several potential advantages over programs offered through clinical or community settings in dealing with participation, adherence, and long-term behavior change. Research has only begun to explore some of these advantages. Table 7.5 contains a partial listing of topics, ideas, and techniques that can be effectively implemented at the worksite. The topics are organized under three headings: (a) social forces, (b) rewards and response costs, and (c) environmental facilitators.

Social Forces

As noted earlier, the worksite provides for more continuous social contact among participants than do clinic- or community-based health promotion interventions. This implies that social forces operating at the worksite are powerful points for intervention. Outside of the family, co-workers might be the most influential social force affecting behavior

Table 7.4
Estimated Prevalance of Risk Factors Among
the U.S. Adult Working Population

Risk factor	Percentage of estimated prevalance
High blood pressure (> 140/90 mmHg)	13-26
Smoking	13-54
Elevated cholesterol (> 240 mg/dl)	20-45
Obesity (> 120% of ideal)	14-61
Chronic alcohol consumption (> 14 servings/week)	4-23
Sedentary lifestyle	40-80

maintenance and behavior change. Although there are many questions about how to operationalize social forces (Levy, 1986), and empirical findings are inconsistent, data do suggest that social forces have an effect on participation, adherence, and long-term behavior change (Brownell et al., 1986).

Social support can take many forms. From Bandura's (1977) social learning theory we can look at modeling, encouragement, and social reinforcement as three potentially potent social forces. These forms of support can come from peers, supervisors, colleagues, and/or subordinates. Other forms of social support that have been found to increase participation, adherence, and long-term behavior change include buddy systems (Janis, 1983) and group cohesion (Lando, 1981). Research has only begun to explore this area, however, and a considerable amount of work needs to be done.

Anecdotal evidence suggests that the public display of support and actual behavior change on the part of top management and other powerful people within the organization can be an important symbolic act that helps change company norms and values. Company and work-group norms shape behavior by indicating to organization members which behaviors are acceptable and overtly encouraged and which behaviors are unacceptable and overtly discouraged. Although meaningful changes in corporate culture, work-group norms, and other similar concepts are recognized by organizational change agents as being essential for sustained behavior

Table 7.5
Topics and Techniques for Increasing Participation, Adherence, and Long-term Behavior Change in Health Promotion Programs at the Worksite

Social forces

family support	symbolic acts
role models	group norms
peer support	corporate culture
supervisor support	social competition
subordinate support	co-worker harassment
buddy system	critical mass
group cohesion	behavior contracting

Rewards and response costs

financial incentives	gifts and prizes
size of incentive	payroll deductions
schedule of payoff	group incentives

Environmental facilitators

smoking restrictions or bans	bicycle storage
improved ventilation	signs and cues that promote
no cigarette machines	health and safety
healthy food in vending machines and in the cafeteria	fitness facilities
	convenience of facilities
nutritional labels on foods and beverages	trained staff
portable blood pressure and heart rate monitors	quality equipment
	action teams to promote health and safety
scales for body weight	availability of safety equipment

change (Allen & Allen, 1986), there has been little systematic research on this form of social influence with regard to employee health and safety (Terborg, 1986a). Preliminary research, however, indicates that differences exist across worksites in norms regarding smoking, and that these differences are related to individual employee attitudes and beliefs (Sorenson, Pechacek, & Pallonen, 1986). Research also suggests that health-promotion interventions can change subjective norms and perceptions regarding healthy life-style habits at the worksite (Bellingham, Johnson, McCauley, & Mendes, 1987; Jose, Anderson, & Haight, 1987). Corporate culture and work-group norms are very important social forces that shape employee behavior. Unless these social forces are changed to support employee health and safety behaviors, other behavior-change techniques are likely to be ineffective in the long-term. Research is needed to understand better how to change corporate culture and work-group norms.

Social competition at the worksite is an intervention that has yielded very promising results, especially in the areas of smoking cessation and weight loss. Competition can be between different groups in the same organization (e.g., the production department versus the marketing department) or between different organizations. Klesges and Glasgow (1986) reported the results of a smoking-cessation competition between two rival banks. It was striking that 88% of smokers in the competition condition participated in the smoking-cessation program, whereas only 53% of smokers in control group organizations participated in an identical smoking-cessation program. This study demonstrated that competition can increase participation rates. Brownell, Cohen, Stunkard, Felix, and Cooley (1984) examined the effects of worksite competition on weight loss. They found that competition had a substantial effect on adherence. Of the 213 employees who signed up for the program, only one employee dropped out before the program was completed. In addition, survey data suggested that employees and managers thought the weight-loss competition improved morale.

Competition may work for several reasons. First, it may increase employee awareness and initial motivation to change. Because much of our behavior is habitual, one of the most important steps in behavior change is to get people to stop and observe their own behavior so that they can break their habits. Second, competition often involves goal setting and feedback. A considerable amount of research on employee motivation and on operant conditioning documents the effectiveness of these manipulations for motivation and change (Pinder, 1984). Third, in some competitions, financial rewards and other incentives may be contingent on winning. Again, a substantial amount of research supports the use of rewards and incentives (Pinder, 1984).

In spite of the early successes associated with worksite competitions, more research is needed to understand better the processes involved. So far, competition seems to be a powerful intervention that affects participation rates and adherence. However, competition may not work equally well in all organizations and would be ill-advised in a company that was actively trying to promote unity and cooperation among its departments or staff. Also, competition may produce excessive social pressure such that people feel coerced by their peers to participate or to meet their outcome criteria. Finally, the aftereffects of competition have not been systematically explored. A specific question is: Once the competition is over, do we find sustained behavior change or does the lack of competition function as a cue for relapse?

The effects of social forces as reinforcers have been examined in health promotion research. For example, studies have looked at the recruitment of employees as "buddies" to assist in behavior change (Lando, 1981). But social forces can also punish behavior change. There is some evidence that harassment may have more impact than support (Lichtenstein, Glasgow, & Abrams, 1986). Imagine being the only employee in a work group that is trying to quit smoking, while your co-workers continue to smoke, offer you cigarettes, and taunt you about quitting! Other studies suggest that the anticipation or experience of negative social consequences may be a more salient predictor of behavior than the anticipation or experience of positive social consequences (Kanouse & Hanson, 1972; Katz, Gutek, Kahn, & Barton, 1975).

A related point is based on the the concept of critical mass. Glasgow and Terborg (in press), in their review of cardiovascular programs at the worksite, could find no studies that explicitly looked at the number or proportion of people who must engage in a novel health activity before that activity becomes accepted. When a small group of employees change their habits in atypical ways (e.g., stretching before beginning work in the morning), they may be viewed as eccentric and subject to ridicule. But, when a critical mass of influential employees engage in such behaviors, the nature of social forces may shift from punishing the behavior to reinforcing the behavior. This area is wide open for systematic research.

Finally, because people go to work on a regular basis, they have continuous contact with peers and co-workers. In this context, use of behavioral contracting and other manipulations that explicitly tie a person's subsequent behaviors to earlier statements and acts might be particularly effective in obtaining adherence and long-term behavior change. Salancik (1977) proposed that people can become highly committed to future behavior patterns if they perceive that their initial action was volitional rather than constrained, if the initial action involved some cost or investment on the part of the individual, if the initial action was taken in a public context, and if the initial action was irrevocable. Dawley uses several of these techniques in his smoking-cessation program (Dawley, Fleischer, & Dawley, 1984). People enter the program voluntarily, they are asked to make an investment of time or money, they make a pledge in front of the group that they will quit smoking, and they have their picture taken with the group. Once such a public commitment to quit smoking is made, the person will have a more difficult time justifying nonadherence and relapse, especially to members of the group. These procedures might be even more powerful if performed at the worksite with co-workers that one sees nearly every day. Imagine making a pledge in front of your co-workers that you will quit smoking on July 1st, and having a picture of you making the pledge distributed throughout the worksite. The social pressure to keep your pledge would undoubtedly be very strong.

In summary, social forces have been shown to be good predictors of participation, adherence, and long-term behavior change. Because people go to work on a regular basis and become linked in continuing social networks, the worksite offers a context in which social forces should be especially powerful in changing and maintaining behavior. This discussion has only briefly touched on some of the techniques and research needs in this area.

Rewards and Response Costs

A second potential advantage of worksites over clinic- and community-based health promotion programs is the opportunity and justification for manipulating financial rewards and nonmonetary incentives. Because companies will benefit from any reductions in health-care costs, sick leave, and turnover, and from any increases in work performance that result from a health promotion program, there is an economic incentive for companies to reinforce health promotion at the worksite. Terborg (1986a), for example, estimated that companywide savings could be as high as $1,500 per employee. Also, employees are used to being paid for what they do at work, and they may already have part of their wages based on performance incentives. Thus it would not seem strange for companies to offer rewards and incentives to people who adopt healthy behaviors and life-styles, just as they offer rewards and incentives to high performers.

In spite of the demonstrated effectiveness of rewards and incentives, there is almost no systematic and controlled research on their use for health promotion at the worksite. A review of the literature estimates that a very small percentage of companies with health promotion activities use rewards and incentives (Shepard & Pearlman, 1985). Where such incentives are used, a glance through the scientific literature and the popular press reveals that considerable variability exists in the dollar amount of the award, the schedule of payoff, and the criteria for receipt of the reward. For example, rewards for successfully completing a smoking-cessation program and remaining abstinent from smoking for from six months to a year range from $150 to $1,000. Smoking status may be based on self-report or on biochemical verification. The dollar amounts can be paid in one lump sum at the end of the period, or in installments over time, or paid contingent on satisfying certain requirements, such as $100 for attending all of the smoking-cessation classes and another $100 for being abstinent at six months. Reports of rewards and incentives in weight-loss competitions range from $1 per pound to $30 per pound and also show evidence of considerable variability in schedule of payoff.

Learning theory suggests that immediate and continuous reinforcement should work best in changing behavior, and that stretching the schedule to a variable ratio or variable interval should work best in maintaining the new behavior (Kazdin, 1980). Learning theory also suggests that the strength of the behavior change is positively related to the size of the reward (Kazdin, 1980). However, there are no studies that have systematically examined these predictions in the context of worksite health promotion programs. In addition, the functional relationship between reward size and behavior change may be more complicated than previously thought. Research demonstrates that the rate of change in a behavior varies with the change in the size of the reward such that increasing reward values above a certain amount have gradually diminishing effects (McDowell, 1982). Thus we really know very little about how to design effective reward and incentive systems for worksite health promotion programs.

It also is possible to design systems that punish the undesired behavior rather than reinforce the desired behavior. Reinforcement, however, is usually recommended over punishment as a behavior-change technique (Kazdin, 1980). Punishment also becomes a sensitive issue in organizations, especially when unions are involved (Pinder, 1984). However, in spite of this negative view of punishment, several studies exist in the literature that have investigated a response-cost approach to behavior change. Response cost is a form of punishment that involves the removal or loss of something valuable if the desired response is not made. In studies that have used the response-cost approach, employees deposit a specified amount of their own money into a fund through prearranged payroll deductions. Employees get their money back only if they successfully change their behaviors, and reimbursement can be periodic or in lump-sum payments. Studies on weight loss and smoking cessation indicate that greater short-term success is associated with larger deposits and more frequent payback periods, although the results are mixed (Follick, Fowler, & Browne, 1984; Forster, Jeffery, Sullivan, & Snell, 1985; Jeffery, Gerber, Rosenthal, & Lindquist, 1983; Paxton, 1981).

Some companies also use combinations of the reinforcement and response-cost approaches (Shepard & Pearlman, 1985). This may take the form of the employee paying a deposit for a smoking-cessation class and getting back the deposit plus a bonus, either money or a prize, such as a vacation, if the employee is abstinent at the end of a specified period. Nonabstinence means that the deposit is forfeited to a charity or it may be put into a pool for distribution to employees who successfully change their behaviors.

There may be considerable merit to behavior-change programs that combine reinforcement with response costs. Reinforcement may increase the overall participation rate in the program. But the simple promise of a reward may not be enough to build strong commitment to adhering to a difficult behavior-change program. Conversely, while response costs might depress initial participation rates, this manipulation might be especially effective in sustaining motivation. Research on decision making by Kahneman and Tversky (1984) has shown that people have a strong aversion to loss. Specifically, given equal probabilities of both outcomes, the loss of $100 is more averse than the gain of $100 is attractive. Extending this finding to the use of response costs in health promotion, we might expect that the possible loss of a $100 deposit if the employee fails to lose 20 pounds would be more motivating than would the possible gain of a $100 bonus if the employee succeeds. An effective motivational program might be one that uses a large enough reward to bolster participation rates, in combination with a large enough response cost to enhance motivation and commitment to adherence and maintenance of behavior change. Again, as noted on other topics in this chapter, the use of rewards and response costs is an area greatly in need of systematic and controlled investigations.

Several other issues associated with rewards and response costs need to be mentioned. One important issue concerns unintended consequences of rewards and response costs. If rewards are set too high, (a) employees may actually initiate the unhealthy behavior so they can participate in the program; (b) employees may lie about their status if self-report verification is used to determine receipt of the reward; and/or (c) employees not eligible for rewards may resent the rewards (e.g., that their company is willing to pay employees to stop smoking, but is not willing to reward employees who currently do not smoke).

A second issue has to do with the maintenance of behavior change once employees have met their goal and received reinforcement. According to Deci (1975), if a valued reward is contingent on a behavior and if this contingency is made salient, employees may attribute their behavior change to the presence of the extrinsic reward. When this happens the new behavior becomes dependent on the availability of that reward. The challenge is to transfer the behavior from being artificially tied to an extrinsic reinforcer (such as $250 for quitting smoking) and to tie it to naturally occurring reinforcers that may be both extrinsic and intrinsic (such as compliments from co-workers on "how good you look since you lost weight" coupled with feelings of increased energy and positive self-esteem).

Third, relapse and recycling behavior are common findings in health promotion (Brownell et al., 1986). Recycling behavior is different from relapse in that people who recycle go through several episodes of behavior-change attempts until they either achieve long-term behavior change or lose their motivation to try again. Relapse refers to an unsuccessful behavior-change attempt where the person stops trying to change. Rewards and incentives for behavior change but not for behavior maintenance may be ineffective for producing long-term behavior change and may even be dysfunctional by reinforcing the recycling episode.

Finally, there is the question of group versus individual rewards. Glasgow and Terborg (in press) discuss making rewards contingent on group goals when all people in the group are eligible. In a weight-loss program, for example, if a certain number of pounds are lost, including a specified amount of weight loss among those group members who are overweight, then the group might receive a common reward, such as a redecorated employee lounge. Individual rewards to members of the winning group could also be given.

In summary, companies in contrast with clinics and communities have strong financial incentives to promote healthy behaviors among their employees. Through regular payroll checks and periodic bonuses and incentives, companies also have built-in mechanisms for the distribution of financial rewards. Existing research suggests that reinforcement and response-cost manipulations are feasible at the worksite. More research is needed, however, to learn how to design and implement reward systems most effectively.

Environmental Facilitation

The third area in which worksites may have an advantage over clinic- and community-based health promotion programs with regard to participation, adherence, and long-term behavior change is in environmental manipulation. Many of the behaviors associated with health-risk factors may be thought of as habitual behaviors that are under stimulus control. Because employees spend a large part of the day at the worksite, environmental changes that cue and facilitate healthy behaviors may have substantial effects.

Earlier, several possible environmental changes were listed. Reductions in tobacco use and exposure to environmental tobacco smoke are areas that have received a considerable amount of attention. The health consequences of tobacco use are well documented, and evidence is accumulating that involuntary exposure to environmental tobacco smoke may also be hazardous (U.S. Department of Health and Human Services, 1986). This knowledge in combination with a growing public activism against smokers by nonsmokers has made smoking restrictions and smoking bans at the worksite increasingly common (Eriksen, 1986; Rigotti, 1986). Separating employees who smoke from those who do not smoke, providing "nonsmoking" company vehicles for employees who request them, and modifying air ventilation and circulation systems are a few of the ways that companies have tried to improve air quality and to control employee exposure to environmental tobacco smoke. However, very little systematic research has been done on smoking restrictions and bans. How should a company design and implement a smoking policy to ensure general compliance with a minimum of conflict? Do smoking restrictions and bans increase the likelihood that employees will quit smoking, or do they have the unintended effects of interfering with normal work activities and producing compensatory smoking during work breaks or while at home? Do smoking restrictions and bans affect employee recruitment and turnover? These are just a few of the questions that would benefit from systematic research.

Worksites can be designed to promote healthy behavior in several ways. Common design changes include (a) eliminating cigarette machines; (b) providing healthy foods and beverages in vending machines, the cafeteria, and at meetings; (c) labeling foods with nutritional information (e.g., the number of calories in the "lite lunch" special versus the other choices); (d) installing blood pressure and heart rate monitors, scales, and even exercise bikes and rowing machines in employee lounges; (e) adding or expanding shower and locker room facilities; (f) installing a basketball net and a volleyball net outside the building; (g) measuring and marking off distances for walking and jogging trails *inside* as well as outside the building; (h) building covered areas for storage of employee bicycles to encourage bicycling to work instead of driving; and (i) displaying signs that encourage healthy and safe behaviors (e.g., "Please fasten your seat belt" signs at parking lot exits). A company might decide to build a separate fitness facility, or it might remodel existing space to provide an exercise room. Such changes can easily cost $50,000 for remodeling and equipment costs for a small exercise room with shower facilities. But, as Scherer Brothers demonstrated, many changes can be made at little or no cost.

Environmental changes at the worksite can facilitate healthy behaviors, but in order to be successful, health promotion activities must be encouraged throughout the company and made a visible, high priority issue (Fielding, 1984). Top management must provide sufficient monetary and staff support so that a high quality program is offered. The budget for health promotion probably should be charged to corporate accounts rather than to the accounts of separate divisions or departments so that division and departmental managers are not penalized for program costs. Following Control Data's example, action teams can be formed with the task of proposing environmental changes that facilitate the adoption and maintenance of healthy life-styles. Action teams should meet on company time and can be given a limited budget to implement changes below a certain total cost. In this way, the action teams would function much like quality circles.

Because people spend so much time at work, and because a considerable amount of their behavior is under stimulus control, the worksite represents an excellent locale for planned intervention. This section has examined features and characteristics that make the worksite a particularly good context in which to enhance participation in health promotion programs, and in which to encourage workers' short-term adherence and long-term behavior change.

Evaluating the Effects of
Health Promotion Programs
at the Worksite

The federal government has set national goals for fitness and health (Harris, 1980), and research on health promotion has received substantial support from federal government agencies such as the National Heart, Lung, and Blood Institute and the National Cancer Institute (Matarazzo, 1982). Research has most often examined individuals as the unit of analysis. Families, schools, and communities also have been the focus of many studies, but very few studies have focused specifically on the worksite. The purpose of this section of the chapter is to discuss two important issues in health promotion research that pertain to the worksite. The first issue concerns research methodology, specifically the notions of program efficacy and program effectiveness, and questions about sample size and the appropriate unit of analysis. The second issue concerns cost-effectiveness and cost-benefit analyses.

Research Methodology

The dominant research method in health promotion research is the randomized clinical trial (RCT), also known as the randomized control trial. RCTs are preferred over quasi-experimental and nonexperimental trials because of the ability to make stronger causal inferences. In an RCT, enough cases to provide acceptable levels of statistical power are randomly assigned to treatment and control groups, and appropriate methodological design procedures are followed to minimize threats to validity. RCTs are especially well suited to pharmacological studies on the efficacy of a particular experimental drug. RCTs are also often used with psychosocial interventions that do not rely on drugs or medication, such as research investigating whether rapid smoking improves cessation rates in smoking-cessation programs.

Program efficacy. In health promotion research, distinctions are made between research on program efficacy, program effectiveness, and program evaluation (see Flay, 1986; and Wortman, 1983, for a thorough discussion of these issues). In studies of program efficacy, the question is whether the treatment does more good than harm *under ideal conditions of use.* According to Flay (1986), "ideal conditions of use" means that (a) a well-specified and standardized treatment or program exists; (b) the treatment or program is made available in a uniform fashion within a well-defined and standardized context to a specified target audience with known characteristics; and (c) the target audience completely accepts, participates in, complies with, or adheres to the treatment or program as delivered. The National Cancer Institute and the National Heart, Lung, and Blood Institute have defined various stages of research that usually are followed when a new treatment or program is introduced. Efficacy trials come first. If a treatment or program is not found to be efficacious, it will not be a candidate for further research. Although there are differing views as to the demonstrated efficacy of some pharmacological and psychosocial interventions for reducing premature morbidity and mortality (Becker, 1986; Kaplan, 1984), many health promotion programs have demonstrated reliable effects under ideal conditions of use and have advanced to later research stages.

Program effectiveness and program evaluation. Once program efficacy has been established, research moves to the next stage, which is program effectiveness. Program effectiveness examines whether the treatment does more good than harm *under typical conditions of use.* Flay (1986) distinguishes between two types of effectiveness research—treatment effectiveness and implementation effectiveness. In *treatment effectiveness* studies, an efficacious treatment or program is delivered in a standardized way to a specified target audience, but acceptance of and compliance with the treatment regimen may vary. In *implementation effectiveness* studies, an efficacious treatment or program is delivered in a standardized way, but *both* the target audience and acceptance of the treatment regimen may vary. In implementation effectiveness research, the actual implementation of the treatment or program can vary by design, or it can vary because it is left uncontrolled. When it varies by design, the study can be useful in determining whether different implementation strategies mediate outcomes.

Flay (1986) also distinguishes between program effectiveness studies and program evaluation studies. *Program evaluation* studies are different from effectiveness studies in that the treatment or program being evaluated has not been previously shown to be efficacious using the standards of an RCT.

Leverage Points to Enhance Effectiveness

The general notion is that RCTs represent the methodological ideal, and that the level of results obtained in efficacy trials will rarely if ever be attained in effectiveness trials or in evaluation studies. The use of quasi- or nonexperimental designs will even further diminish treatment effects because such studies are not conducted under ideal conditions of use. However, it is usually implied that as research advances from efficacy stages through effectiveness stages and finally to application stages, researchers should attempt to conduct rigorous research that is true to the ideals of RCTs that investigate treatment efficacy. Stated another way, researchers should attempt to control for such problems as history, testing, selection, compensatory rivalry and other threats to validity identified by Cook and Campbell (1979).

It is possible, however, that *some* of the emphasis on methodological control may be misguided and even detrimental to public health goals. This is not to say that RCTs no longer need to be done, or that sloppy research is acceptable in worksite studies of health promotion. Rather, the point here is that under certain circumstances, implementation effectiveness studies and program evaluation studies conducted at the worksite may actually produce stronger effects and ones having greater external validity than those previously demonstrated with program efficacy or treatment effectiveness trials.

The rationale for this statement is that most if not all of the health promotion programs that would be extended to the worksite have a substantial psychosocial aspect. It is argued here that *selective manipulation* of many of the variables Cook and Campbell (1979) list as threats to validity might actually *enhance treatment effects in a reliable way*. In other words, we should reconceptualize these variables as desirable implementation leverage points rather than as undesirable confounds. One of the reasons we can do this is because certain threats to validity have been shown to produce reliable outcomes. Therefore, it follows that these variables could be included as independent variables in implementation effectiveness studies, and that they also could be included as implementation techniques in program evaluation studies.

A good example of this approach is provided by research on expectation effects, for instance in the study by King (1974) on job enrichment. He manipulated core job dimensions to enrich the work employees were doing, and he also manipulated supervisor expectations. King found that the expectation manipulation actually had a greater effect than the job redesign manipulation. On one hand this study could be an embarrassment for advocates of job enrichment. But, on the other hand, it demonstrates that treatment effects may be enhanced when relevant people are made aware of expected outcomes. Depending on the purpose and design of the study, expectation effects can be desired outcomes rather than undesired artifacts.

A list of variables, taken from Cook and Campbell (1979), that could function as leverage points in implementation effectiveness trials is presented in Table 7.6 and they are discussed in the following pages. One variable that could be an effective leverage point is history. From a traditional design perspective, it would be unwise to implement a smoking-cessation intervention in a company in which the president, who was a heavy smoker, recently had a heart attack. The results would be open to an alternative explanation; that is, the president's heart attack temporarily increased employee awareness of the health consequences of smoking, and this may have inflated employee participation and adherence above and beyond the "true" effects of the intervention. However, anecdotal reports of why some companies started offering health promotion programs in the first place often include reference to some historical event that triggered action, such as the deaths of workers at Scherer Brothers Lumber Company. This fact leads to the hypothesis that health promotion programs at the worksite will be more effective when they are implemented soon after a critical historical event than if they are implemented in the absence of any attention-gathering event. A related hypothesis is that health promotion programs will be more effective if attention is deliberately focused on the critical historical event than if it is ignored or minimized.

A second variable that could enhance treatment effects is testing. When multiple waves of data are collected from the same individuals, one design concern is whether repeated assessment produces an independent effect. An alternative leverage-point strategy would be to build specifically in multiple waves of data collection. This could enhance employee interest, comprehension, and adherence, in addition to being a source of reinforcement. After all, one of the basic techniques of behavior modification is charting behavior.

A third variable that could be deliberately manipulated is self-selection. Recall that one of the findings in worksite health promotion studies is that people who are least at risk are those most likely to volunteer for the programs, while those most at risk are less likely to volunteer. One option is to give early preference to those most receptive to the program and to use this as a means for publicizing the program's effects throughout the company. Basically, that means using the early adopters as role models to motivate others to try the program. In marketing terminology, this is similar to a loss-leader—that is, advertising a particular product at a price below cost in an effort to draw more shoppers into the store, who then will spend money on other products that have regular profit margins.

A fourth variable is diffusion or imitation of treatments. This is a common problem when conducting experimental studies in organizations. Companies or groups within a company do not like being in the delayed treatment condition, especially if the early results are positive. But, from a public health perspective, the goal is to improve the health of all people in the company, not just those who participate in the program. This implies that early successes should be actively publicized throughout the company in order to encourage the diffusion and imitation of treatment.

Table 7.6
Potential Leverage Points in Implementation Effectiveness Trials

History — Time the intervention to follow an event that makes the organization more receptive to change.

Testing — Utilize repeated testing with feedback of scores to reinforce positive change and to enhance comprehension and compliance.

Selection — Encourage self-selection to better match employees to change programs and to identify those employees most motivated to change.

Diffusion or imitation of treatments — Active publication of a new behavior change program throughout the company may encourage the adoption of healthy practices among non-participating employees, thus producing a "spillover effect."

Compensatory rivalry — Competition between individuals or between departments can enhance treatment impact through higher participation rates and better compliance.

Evaluation apprehension — Health and lifestyle evaluations should be made salient so that employees want to present a "healthy" image.

Experimenter expectancies — Employees involved with behavior-change programs should expect to see positive change and should be encouraged to set "stretch" goals.

Selection × treatment interaction — Employees at different stages of readiness for change should be assigned to programs that best meet their needs.

Setting × treatment interaction — The implementation of a health promotion program should be continuously monitored and modified so as to maximize the use of all available leverage points in the organization at that point in time.

A fifth variable is compensatory rivalry. If a company or division finds out it is in the "control" group, it may attempt to achieve the same level of change as the group receiving the treatment. Compensatory rivalry is a special case of competition. Earlier it was noted that competition appears to be an effective social manipulation for enhancing participation in and adherence to a health promotion program. Because a company may not be able to offer a program to everyone who wants it, but must gradually funnel interested employees through the program, the operation of compensatory rivalry may be desirable because it can improve the health status of nonenrolled employees.

A sixth variable is evaluation apprehension. When people know that they are being evaluated and that their performance will be shared with relevant others, they may feel pressured to respond in ways that present themselves in a favorable manner. On college campuses you can frequently tell when a student is going for a job interview at the placement office because of the change in physical appearance and clothing. A similar effect may occur when employees complete a health-risk appraisal or undergo some type of physical fitness evaluation prior to participation in a health promotion program. Employees who have four or five beers every day after work may modify their behavior in anticipation of questions on alcohol use. Similarly, testing for body-fat percentage may elicit a crash diet in an attempt to lose a few extra pounds. There is generally nothing wrong with these behaviors. In fact, people should be encouraged to adopt healthy life-style habits. One application of evaluation apprehension effects is purposefully to increase the salience of life-style and physical fitness evaluation in order to produce short-term behavior change, and then to reinforce any change so that it is sustained.

A seventh variable is experimenter expectancies. An entire literature has developed around the social psychology of the experiment. One of the most often replicated findings is that experimenter (or teacher) expectations can be communicated to the participant, and these expectations produce valid change that can confound treatment effects. However, discussions with successful teachers or trainers or managers, typically reveal that they hold high expectations for their students and co-workers. These expectations influence those around them, so people should be encouraged to set "stretch" goals for themselves and others.

An eighth variable is selection by treatment interactions. The conventional research advice is that people may self-select themselves into treatments they think they will enjoy and this makes it difficult to determine the "true" effects of different treatments. But a long tradition of research in individual differences psychology indicates that proper classification prior to making assignments to treatment conditions can be more effective than simply putting everyone into the same condition. Brownell (1987) noted in his research on weight-loss programs that some people are "social" dieters and other people are "solo" dieters. Solo dieters might show low adherence and little weight loss if assigned to a weight-loss program that stresses social support and peer involvement. Hence Brownell et al. (1986) advocate screening as a method for enhancing treatment effects. Similarly, Prochaska and DiClemente (1983) demonstrated that people can be at various stages of readiness for change in the adoption of health promotion activities. Some people may be at the precontemplation stage, others at the contemplation stage, and still others in a maintenance stage or a lapse/recycle stage. The type of treatment should vary according to the stage of readiness.

Finally, there may be a setting by treatment interaction. This is a new leverage point—not one of the variables listed as a threat to validity by Cook and Campbell (1979). Specifically, a setting by treatment interaction refers to the fact that some techniques may work better in some settings while other techniques may work well in other settings. For example, Brownell et al. (1984) found that a weight-loss competition between different divisions of an organization was highly effective. However, in some companies, competition within the organization could be detrimental to morale and have serious aftereffects. Similarly, the use of prizes, certificates, and other awards might work especially well in a company that regularly and genuinely recognizes employee contributions. But in companies in which "Employee of the Month" awards are viewed as shams, recognition awards for participation in behavior-change programs might even be detrimental. The challenge is to tailor the implementation of the intervention to the relevant leverage points in a particular organization.

Another way to view a setting by treatment interaction is to see it as an implementation main effect. That is, the way the treatment is implemented may account for more variance in outcomes than does the actual treatment itself. Weiss (1987), in his presidential address to the Academy of Behavioral Medicine Research, specifically drew attention to this idea when he stated that the skill, knowledge, and expertise of the health counselor in providing feedback to a client on the results of a health-risk appraisal may be more important for behavior change than the particular health-risk appraisal instrument that was used. Similarly, the skill, knowledge, and expertise of the person(s) responsible for the implementation of a health promotion program at the worksite might be more important than the specifics of the program itself. For instance, the question that should be asked is not whether competition at the worksite increases participation and adherence. Rather, the question should be under what circumstances competition is appropriate, and how best to implement the form of competition most suitable to a given company.

Implementation Effectiveness Research

Conceptualized in this way, implementation effectiveness trials become very important for the scientific evaluation of health promotion programs at the worksite. The knowledge gained from this type of study would be extremely valuable for assisting companies with the implementation, and perhaps reimplementation, of health promotion activities. This type of research would tell us how to intervene successfully in organizations. Most of the existing research on health promotion at the worksite simply demonstrates that health promotion is feasible. It shows that in some instances procedures and techniques developed in clinical settings can be transferred to the worksite. While feasibility studies are still needed, more attention should focus on implementation effectiveness trials.

Unit of analysis and sample size as issues. Conducting good implementation effectiveness and program evaluation studies presents numerous problems. One problem that has received much attention concerns the proper unit of analysis. Health promotion studies at the worksite are legitimately viewed as dealing with individual employee change. These studies may seek to determine, for example, whether a bonus of $300 produces as much weight loss as does a response cost of the same amount. One tactic would be to find two companies willing to participate in the study and to assign them randomly to conditions. Perhaps data from a delayed-treatment control company also could be collected. The analysis would be one-way ANOVA or MANOVA with the sample size equal to the number of employees in the two, or three, companies. However, from a statistical perspective, this design is seriously deficient because it violates the assumption of independence. Because all employees in a given condition belong to the same company, they are *not* independent observations. This may decrease within-cell variability, resulting in an F statistic biased by an unknown amount in the direction of a false positive finding.

One solution to this problem is to set the unit of analysis equal to the unit of assignment. If, in our example, the bonus and response-cost manipulation is assigned to organizations, then organizations become the unit of analysis, and a sample of organizations must be randomly assigned to each condition. Because power levels off at around 15 cases per cell (Winer, 1971), a sample of about 15 organizations is needed for each condition. In a simple 2×2 factorial design, this translates to 60 organizations. Even someone not experienced in organizational research will quickly grasp the practical and methodological implications of trying to conduct research on 60 organizations in which treatments are randomly assigned to organizations. Some of the more obvious problems are (a) recruitment, (b) getting the organizations to wait "on hold" until funding is obtained, which often can take a year or longer, (c) matching organizations on relevant variables, (d) deciding what the relevant matching variables are in the first place, (e) coordinating data collection so that data from different organizations are synchronous, (f) deciding on a procedure for calculating organization means from individual level data when missing data exist for some individuals on some measures, (g) controlling for unplanned events that may seriously affect treatment, such as a company being taken over by a competitor, (h) preventing a company in the control group from initiating some form of treatment on their own, and (i) preventing nonparticipation or dropping out.

One good point concerning sample size computations is that when unit or organization means are used for analysis, the number of unit means can be reduced with no loss of statistical power. Barcikowski (1981), for example, calculated that with a population intraclass correlation of .05, alpha set at .05, power set at .80, and an effect size estimated at .25, a sample size of six organizations, with 40 employees per organization, randomly assigned to each cell in a one-factor two-treatment design (total $N = 12$ organizations) will produce the same power as would a total N of 62 individuals in an individual-assignment design. Also, Hopkins (1982) showed that the use of groups or organizations as the unit of analysis may be unnecessary when certain conditions are satisfied. Specifically, the following three conditions must exist: (a) individuals nested in organizations must be randomly selected for inclusion in the study, (b) organizations must be randomly assigned to treatments, and (c) sample sizes of both individuals and organizations must be equal or balanced. Unfortunately, however, Barcikowski's calculations still require relatively large numbers of organizations even for most simple designs, and Hopkins's recommendations are often impractical when dealing with organizations.

An argument that has been used to justify analysis of treatment effects at the individual level is the demonstrated lack of covariation among employees in the same organization. If intraclass correlations are low, by definition, the assumption of independence is *not* violated. Glasgow (personal communication, June, 1986), in a reanalysis of previously published data, found that the intraclass correlations in several of his studies on smoking cessation (see Klesges & Glasgow, 1986, for descriptions of the studies) rarely exceeded $r = .05$. It is inconsistent, however, to use the statistical argument of a low intraclass correlation as evidence that the assumption of independence has *not* been violated, and at the same time argue that one of the potential advantages of doing health promotion at the worksite is a deliberate spillover effect by which the treatment becomes a social phenomenon.

At the present time there is no widely accepted solution to the unit of analysis problem. Biostatisticians generally take on the conservative side, recommending that organizations be the unit of analysis, and that a substantial number of organizations be randomly assigned to treatments. This means that organizations are treated just like a well-defined population of individuals (for example, white adult males with blood pressure greater than 140/80 mm Hg) who are being randomly assigned to receive an experimental drug or a placebo. Psychologists and other behavioral scientists, however, are reluctant to comply with this recommendation for at least two reasons. First, applied psychologists in particular recognize the difficulty of doing true experiments in the field and often rely on statistical control as a substitute for experimental control, convenience samples as substitutes for random samples, and correlational studies as substitutes for experimental manipulation in honest attempts to "bootstrap" their theories. Research of this type is accepted in the best journals (for examples, see the *Journal of Applied Psychology, Academy of Management Journal*, and *Administrative Science Quarterly*). Second, statistics as practiced by most researchers with psychological training rarely require concern over violations of the assumption of independence. In sum, however, failure to resolve the unit of analysis problem will be a serious barrier to advancing research.

The action research model. One promising solution to the problem of doing implementation effectiveness research on health promotion at the worksite may be in the "action research" model. The action research model is widely used in studies of organizational change and development (French & Bell, 1984) and traces its beginnings to the Lewinian principles of experimentation and application.

To use the action research model, it is helpful to conceptualize health promotion activities at the worksite as techniques of planned organizational change. The question then becomes, not whether program A is more efficacious or effective than program B, but how existing scientific knowledge on health promotion activities can be implemented in a particular worksite to change attitudes, beliefs, values, and behaviors at the individual, group, and organizational levels. The usual assumption is that in order to produce meaningful and lasting change at the worksite, the core values and structures of the organization must be modified. This type of change requires that maximum attention be directed toward experimentation and documentation. Action research is the process of systematically collecting research data about an organization relative to some objective or goal, feeding those data back into the system, taking actions by altering selected variables within the system based both on the data and on theoretical hypotheses, and evaluating the results of these actions by collecting more data. It is an application of the scientific method of planning, manipulating, documenting, interpreting, evaluating, and planning. A key feature, however, is that the process involves the collaboration of the research team with organizational members.

At one level, action research can be meaningfully applied to a single unit or organization. The organization serves as its own control. This type of research is common in behavior modification studies and follows Sidman's (1960) notion of experimental control rather than controlled experiments. In order for findings to be valid, there must be careful and extensive documentation of the actions taken as well as the consequences of those actions, and there should be at least one attempt at treatment reversal as in an A-B-A design (see Komacki & Jensen, 1986).

At another level of action research, multiple organizations could be randomly assigned to different implementation conditions. For example, to learn if employee involvement is critical to the effective implementation and institutionalization of smoking policies, organizations could be randomly assigned to a high-intensity planned change intervention, a low-intensity planned change intervention, or a control group. Employees from each organization would be allowed to collaborate in the planning, manipulating, documenting, interpreting, evaluating, and planning cycle for their organization. In the high-intensity condition, they would receive considerable "hands-on" support from the research team, and in the low-intensity condition there would be minimal support from the research team. This type of manipulation is analogous to high-intensity, multifaceted treatment programs offered in clinical settings versus low-intensity, single-facet programs that are developed for self-study and individual use. The data from such a study could be analyzed in an ANOVA design using organizations as the unit of analysis. In addition, the data could be analyzed at the ideographic level, producing multiple in-depth analyses of the change process. Komacki and Jensen (1986) discuss within-group designs that collect multiple baseline data and use control groups and that are quite applicable to organizations. Their comments on the strengths and appropriate uses of such designs are highly relevant for health promotion research at the worksite.

The process of action research has its own set of problems and limitations, and the model is certain to have its critics. However, the strengths of the model are that it focuses on implementation and that it employs the scientific method. A valid conclusion from much of the research on health promotion at the worksite is that there is considerable variability in treatment effects across organizations. One explanation for this finding may have been based on differences in implementation. Implementation effectiveness trials that use the action research model merit further study at both the single-organization level and the multiple-organization level.

Cost-Effectiveness and Cost-Benefit Analyses

Another major issue in the evaluation of health promotion programs at the worksite has to do with cost-effectiveness analysis (CEA) and cost-benefit analysis (CBA). CEA and CBA have become important components of evaluation research as worksite health promotion programs have come under scrutiny by public and private sector organizations and by government funding agencies (Wortman, 1983). In fact, many granting agencies specifically request that CEA and CBA issues be addressed in research proposals. The worksite provides a particularly good context in which to do CEA and CBA calculations. This section of the chapter briefly reviews CEA and CBA and some of their unresolved issues. More detailed discussions can be found in Kristein (1982), Murphy, Gasparotto, and Opatz (1987); Warner and Luce (1982), and Weinstein and Stason (1977).

CEA examines the cost per unit of change when the outcome is measured in nonmonetary terms (e.g., the number of employees still abstinent from smoking after one year). CEA is useful when evaluating different programs that have similar objectives. Direct costs of the program, such as costs of equipment, materials, and facilitator salaries, are added to indirect costs, such as the dollar value of employee participation time; and this value is divided by the outcome index to form a ratio, such as $300 per abstinent smoker after one year. Existing data indicate that health promotion programs at the worksite are more cost-effective than are similar programs offered at clinics or community sites (Glasgow & Terborg, in press; Warner, in press). The results are particularly strong in dealing with hypertension (Alderman, 1984).

CBA examines the dollar value of program benefits. CBA can be done on a single program, on multiple programs with similar objectives (e.g., weight loss), or multiple programs with different objectives (e.g., weight loss versus smoking cessation). Typically, estimates of the dollar value associated with direct benefits (such as the actual dollar reduction in health-care costs) and indirect benefits (such as the avoidance of productivity losses resulting from poor employee health) are divided by the dollar value of direct and indirect program costs. Some worksite studies report a ratio of from \$1.54 to \$1.93 for every dollar invested (Browne, Russell, Morgan, Optenberg, & Clarke, 1984; Harris, 1986). It is also recommended, however, that the total dollar value of net savings be reported because the cost-benefit ratio, out of context, says nothing about the total number of dollars saved.

The logic and techniques of CEA and CBA appear straightforward, but there are several unresolved issues. There is considerable subjectivity in choosing the variables to include in the model, in estimating the dollar value of indirect costs and indirect benefits, in estimating the timing and duration of program effects, and in discounting the dollar value of costs and benefits that will occur in future time periods. Because of this subjectivity, it is crucial that sensitivity analyses be conducted in order to demonstrate the effects of varying particular assumptions on the resulting CEA and CBA ratios.

CEA and CBA analyses also may lead to decisions that are inconsistent with public health goals. One smoking-cessation program might be more cost-effective than another, but the more expensive and less efficient program might yield a higher number of successes. Similarly, an inexpensive program may produce a more favorable benefit-cost ratio than would a more expensive program, but, if the latter reaches more people when applied in the population, the total dollars saved can be greater even though the program has less efficient CEA and CBA ratios. It is important to understand the strengths and limitations of these techniques because CEA and CBA are used by decision makers when allocating scarce resources.

CEA and CBA analyses can be done at many levels. Health economists and policymakers responsible for shaping national health-care expenditures primarily take a national view. At this macrolevel, building models to do CEA, and CBA analyses becomes very complicated, and it is necessary to make numerous assumptions—for example, what is the dollar value of the lost contribution to society associated with the premature death of a 45-year-old male Caucasian with a college degree? Although CEA and CBA remain very complicated when conducted at the worksite level, and numerous assumptions still need to be made, for any given worksite it is possible to calculate highly accurate estimates of such things as operating costs associated with providing the health promotion program, medical expenses for employees with known risk factors, sick leave wages, costs of absenteeism and turnover, and even the dollar value of employee performance.

Terborg (1986b) developed such a model. The model examines the effects of a comprehensive health promotion program on the outcome variables of medical costs, lost productivity attributable to avoidable illness and injury, reduced employee turnover, and improved productivity resulting from a more alert, energetic, and motivated work force. This model builds on recent developments in techniques for estimating the dollar value associated with absenteeism, turnover, and productivity. For example, Hunter and Schmidt (1983) determined that the dollar value of the output produced by the average worker can be estimated as twice the person's salary. Thus, given an average salary of $20,000, the value of a person's output is $40,000 per year. A 1% decrement in performance due to poor health, which is a very conservative estimate, would translate into a cost of $400 per poor-health employee per year. Missed work because of illness and injury could account for an additional 1% decrease (Cascio, 1987) or another $400 per poor-health employee per year. This latter figure can be reduced by one-half if it is assumed that employees do not receive wages while they are sick. Increased medical costs can be estimated at an additional $600 per poor-health employee per year. Thus a conservative estimate of the incremental costs attributable to poor health is from $1,200 to $1,400 per employee per year. This figure does not include any savings that might result from a reduction in turnover as a result of a corporate health promotion program. And, with the cost of turnover for many entry-level jobs ranging from $2,000 to $15,000 per incident (Boudreau & Berger, 1985), even small reductions in turnover can translate into substantial savings.

These figures are crude estimates based on realistic but hypothetical data. A better approach would be to calculate more accurate figures using detailed procedures applied to data from a specific organization. Boudreau and Berger (1985), Cascio (1987), and Hunter and Schmidt (1983) present thorough discussions of these procedures. While problems with interpretation will never be totally solved, the techniques of CEA and CBA are accepted by economists and decision makers. Recent developments in the costing of employee behavior and performance and more detailed documentation of health-care costs make it possible to conduct meaningful CEA and CBA analyses for specific organizations. This is a distinct advantage over health promotion activities offered in clinical or community settings.

One final comment should be made about CEA and CBA as applied to health promotion programs at the worksite. Companies that adopt health promotion programs do not base that decision solely on the anticipated financial return on the investment. They also may adopt a health promotion program because their employees want it, because they think it is a worthwhile benefit to offer their employees, and/or because they think it may help reduce health-care costs and improve employee morale and productivity. Companies seem to be primarily concerned with whether a high quality program is being offered and whether employees enjoy and participate in the program. Cost becomes an issue in the context of these criteria. Companies do not want to be in a position of spending large sums of money on poor-quality programs that nobody uses. Warner (in press) has pointed out many of the problems with relying entirely on CBA as a rationale for health promotion at the worksite. He urges caution in the use of CBA, but supports the use of CEA. He believes that we should not have to sell the value of good health, but that an important issue is determining the most effective method for its delivery. One of the aims of this chapter has been to show why worksites are particularly good contexts for the delivery of health promotion programs.

Organizational Factors Associated with the Adoption and Institutionalization of Health Promotion Programs

The final section of this chapter takes a more macro view of health promotion at the worksite, particularly the question of how to facilitate the adoption and institutionalization of worksite health promotion programs.

Adoption of Health Promotion Programs

To begin, very little is known about how organizations adopt innovations in general (Kimberly & Evanisko, 1981), and even less is known about the adoption of health promotion programs in particular. In general, Kimberly and Evanisko (1981) state that the adoption of innovations seems to be a function of (a) the nature of the innovation (e.g., technical versus administrative innovations), (b) characteristics of individuals involved in making the decision (e.g., tenure with the organization, expertise, and involvement in organizational activities), (c) characteristics of the organization (e.g., size, degree of centralization and differentiation, availability of slack resources), and (d) characteristics of the organizational context (e.g., competitiveness of the industry). However, a summary of the available literature indicates that studies often produce noncomparable and occasionally contradictory results. About the only predictor that consistently relates to innovation is size—large organizations adopt more innovations more frequently than do small organizations.

Concerning the adoption of health promotion programs in particular, the most frequently cited work is the general theory of the diffusion of innovations as articulated by Rogers (1983). Orlandi (1986) discusses the theory as it applies to health promotion programs at the worksite. Briefly stated, the theory predicts that the rate of diffusion and adoption is a function of the following attributes: (a) perceived relative advantage of the innovation in dealing with a problem; (b) compatibility of the innovation with the value system of the organization; (c) simplicity and clarity, or lack of complexity, of the innovation; (d) flexibility or malleability of the innovation; (e) degree to which the innovation can be reversed or terminated without excessive cost; (f) relative degree of risk associated with adopting the innovation; (g) projected value of benefits compared to costs; and (h) long-term capacity to revise the innovation to meet future needs. Research investigating why organizations adopt health promotion programs, and research on the validity of Rogers's theory in general, is very much needed. This is an important topic for research.

Rogers's model (1983) also considers the stages of the innovation process. The first stage in the adoption of an innovation is acquiring knowledge about the innovation. The second stage, which Rogers calls persuasion, focuses on how the person (or organization) determines the potential advantages and disadvantages of adoption. The third stage involves the actual decision to adopt the innovation on a trial basis or to reject it. The fourth stage deals with implementation and it may include modifications of the original innovation so as to better fit the needs of the system. The final stage is confirmation, in which the decision maker either accepts the innovation or discontinues it. Other factors, such as salient characteristics of the decision maker, past experience, prior conditions, and availability of channels of communication and information also affect the innovation process. Bulow-Hube and Morisky (1987) present descriptive data concerning the stages in Rogers's theory as observed in worksite health promotion programs. Essentially, they found differences according to the size of the organization. Large organizations were more likely to have reached the implementation or confirmation stages, involved more people in the decision process, were more aware of the advantages and disadvantages of health promotion programs at the worksite, and perceived a greater responsibility for promoting employee health and safety. The study, however, used a cross-sectional design to examine a multistage process model. This design fails to rule out postdecision justification as an explanation for some of the results.

It is obvious that research is needed on the adoption of health promotion programs at the worksite, but given the general state of the literature on innovation, future studies will have to be conceptualized more carefully and conducted with greater methodological rigor if our knowledge is going to advance beyond the descriptive level.

Institutionalization of Health Promotion Programs

After an innovation is adopted, it may become institutionalized. For an innovation to become institutionalized means that it becomes an enduring and identifiable characteristic of the organization's social structure, one that is transmitted to new organizational members, and that shapes the behavior of the organization. Unfortunately, the research literature on the institutionalization of innovations is as disorganized and contradictory as the literature on innovation (see Goodman, Bazerman, & Conlon, 1980, for a review).

A few general points can be made, however. First, the innovation needs a sponsor who nurtures the innovation and protects it from critics. Second, the innovation must be consistent with the existing norms and values of the organization. Third, a critical mass of people must experience and use the innovation in a reinforcing way. Fourth, the formal organizational arrangements and structures must be compatible with and support the use of the innovation. Use of the action research model that was described earlier is recommended as a basis for the successful institutionalization of health promotion programs in organizations.

Conclusion

There has been a rapid expansion of health promotion activities at the worksite over the past 10 years (see Falkenberg, 1987; Fielding, 1984; Terborg, 1986a; and Wolfe, Ulrich, & Parker, in press, for reviews). This chapter has identified reasons why the worksite is a promising context for the delivery of health promotion programs, and it has identified areas for future research. Research is needed for at least two reasons. First, in contrast to the large number of literature reviews on the topic, there is in fact very little empirical research. Much of the published literature consists of descriptive studies or anecdotal reports. Second, the majority of research in the field has been done by occupational physicians, public health researchers, and clinical psychologists. The skills, methodologies, and theories of applied social psychologists, organizational psychologists, and organizational sociologists are required. Specifically needed are researchers who can build on the existing literature and conduct good social psychological research that is sensitive to organizational dynamics and program evaluation issues.

References

Alderman, M. H. (1984). Worksite treatment of hypertension. In J. Matarazzo, S. M. Weiss, J. A. Herd, N. E. Miller, & S. M. Weiss (Eds.), *Behavioral health: A handbook of health enhancement and disease prevention* (pp. 862-869). New York: John Wiley.

Allen, J. S., & Allen, R. F. (1986). Achieving health promotion objectives through cultural change systems. *American Journal of Health Promotion, 1,* 42-49.

Bandura, A. (1977). *Social learning theory.* Englewood Cliffs, NJ: Prentice-Hall.

Barcikowski, R. S. (1981). Statistical power with group mean as the unit of analysis. *Journal of Educational Statistics, 6,* 267-285.

Becker, M. H. (1986). The tyranny of health promotion. *Public Health Review, 14,* 15-25.

Bellingham, R., Johnson, D., McCauley, M., & Mendes, T. (1987). Projected cost savings from AT&T communications total life concept (TLC) process. In J. P. Opatz (Ed.), *Health promotion evaluation: Measuring the organizational impact* (pp. 35-42). Stevens Point, WI: National Wellness Association.

Belloc, N. B. (1973). Relationship of health practices and mortality. *Preventive Medicine, 2,* 67-81.

Boudreau, J. W., & Berger, L. J. (1985). Decision-theoretic utility analysis applied to employee separations and acquisitions. *Journal of Applied Psychology, 70,* 581-612.

Browne, D. W., Russell, M. L., Morgan, J. L., Optenberg, S. A., & Clarke, A. E. (1984). Reduced disability and health care costs in an industrial fitness program. *Journal of Occupational Medicine, 26,* 809-816.

Brownell, K. D. (1986). Weight control at the workplace: The power of social and behavioral factors. In M. F. Cataldo & T. J. Coates (Eds.), *Health promotion in industry: A behavioral medicine perspective* (pp. 143-161). New York: John Wiley.

Brownell, K. D. (1987, June). *Weight control.* Paper presented at the Annual Meeting of the Academy of Behavioral Medicine Research, Sebasco, Maine.

Brownell, K. D., Cohen, R. Y., Stunkard, A. J., Felix, M.R.J., & Cooley, N. B. (1984). Weight loss competitions at the worksite: Impact on weight, morale and cost-effectiveness. *American Journal of Public Health, 74,* 1283-1285.

Brownell, K. D., Glynn, T. J., Glasgow, R., Lando, H., Rand, C., Gottlieb, A., & Pinney, J. M. (1986). Task force 5: Interventions to prevent relapse. *Health Psychology, 5*(Suppl.), 53-68.

Bulow-Hube, S., & Morisky, D. E. (1987). The innovation-decision model and workplace health promotion programs. *Health Education Research: Theory and Practice, 2,* 15-25.

Cascio, W. E. (1987). *Costing human resources: The financial impact of behavior in organizations.* Boston: Kent.

Cook, T. D., & Campbell, D. T. (1979). *Quasi-experimentation: Design and analysis issues for field settings.* Chicago: Rand McNally.

Davis, M. F., Rosenberg, K., Iverson, D. C., Vernon, T. M., & Bauer, J. (1984). Worksite health promotion in Colorado. *Public Health Reports, 99,* 538-543.

Dawley, H. H., Jr., Fleischer, B. J., & Dawley, L. T. (1984). Smoking cessation with hospital employees: An example of worksite smoking cessation. *International Journal of the Addictions, 19,* 327-334.

Deci, E. L. (1975). *Intrinsic motivation.* New York: Plenum.

DiMatteo, M. R., & DiNicola, D. D. (1982). *Achieving patient compliance.* New York: Pergamon.

Dishman, R. K., Sallis, J. F., & Orenstein, D. R. (1985). The determinants of physical activity and exercise. *Public Health Reports, 100,* 158-171.

Eriksen, M. P. (1986). Workplace smoking control: Rationale and approaches. *Advances in Health Education and Promotion, 1,* 65-103.

Falkenberg, L. E. (1987). Employee fitness programs: Their impact on the employee and the organization. *Academy of Management Review, 12,* 511-522.

Fielding, J. E. (1984). Health promotion and disease prevention at the worksite. *Annual Review of Public Health, 5,* 237-265.

Fishbein, M., & Ajzen, I. (1975). *Belief, attitude, intention, and behavior.* Reading, MA: Addison-Wesley.

Flay, B. R. (1986). Efficacy and effectiveness trials (and other phases of research) in the development of health promotion programs. *Preventive Medicine, 15,* 451-474.

Follick, M. J., Fowler, J. L., & Browne, R. A. (1984). Attrition in worksite weight loss interventions: The effects of an incentive procedure. *Journal of Consulting and Clinical Psychology, 52,* 134-140.

Forster, J. L., Jeffery, R. W., Sullivan, S., & Snell, M. K. (1985). A work-site weight control program using financial incentives collected through payroll deduction. *Journal of Occupational Medicine, 27,* 804-808.

French, W. L., & Bell, C. H. (1984). *Organization development.* Englewood Cliffs, NJ: Prentice-Hall.

Glasgow, R. E., & Terborg, J. R. (in press). Occupational health promotion programs to reduce cardiovascular risk. *Journal of Consulting and Clinical Psychology.*

Goodman, P. S., Bazerman, M., & Conlon, E. (1980). Institutionalization of planned organizational change. *Research in Organizational Behavior, 2,* 215-246.

Green, L. W. (1984). Modifying and developing health behavior. *Annual Review of Public Health, 5,* 215-236.

Green, L. W., Wilson, A. L., & Lovato, C. Y. (1986). What changes can health promotion achieve and how long do these changes last? The trade-offs between expediency and durability. *Preventive Medicine, 15,* 508-521.

Harris, J. S. (1986). Northern Telecom: A million dollar medically based program in a rapidly changing high tech environment. *American Journal of Health Promotion, 1,* 50-59.

Harris, P. R. (1980). *Promoting health—preventing disease: Objectives for the nation.* Washington, DC: U.S. Government Printing Office.

Heiby, E. M., & Carlson, J. G. (1986). The health compliance model. *The Journal of Compliance in Health Care, 1,* 135-152.

Herzlinger, R. E., & Calkins, D. (1986). How companies tackle health care costs: Part III. *Harvard Business Review, 64,* 70-80.

Hopkins, K. D. (1982). The unit of analysis: Group means versus individual observations. *American Educational Research Journal, 19,* 5-18.

Hunter, J. E., & Schmidt, F. L. (1983). Quantifying the effects of psychological interventions on employee job performance and work-force productivity. *American Psychologist, 38,* 473-478.

Hyatt, J. (1986). Healthy returns. *Inc.,* Vol. 9, pp. 80-86.

Janis, I. L. (1983). The role of social support in adherence to stressful decisions. *American Psychologist, 38,* 143-160.

Jeffery, R. W., Gerber, W. M., Rosenthal, B. S., & Lindquist, R. A. (1983). Monetary contracts in weight control: Effectiveness of group and individual contracts of varying size. *Journal of Consulting and Clinical Psychology, 51,* 242-248.

Jose, W. S. II, Anderson, D. R., & Haight, S. A. (1987). The StayWell strategy for health care cost containment. In J. P. Opatz (Ed.), *Health promotion evaluation: Measuring the organizational impact* (pp. 15-34). Stevens Point, WI: National Wellness Association.

Kahneman, D., & Tversky, A. (1984). Choices, values, and frames. *American Psychologist, 39,* 341-350.

Kanouse, D. E., & Hanson, L. R. (1972). Negativity in evaluations. In E. E. Jones, D. E. Kanouse, H. H. Kelley, R. E. Nisbett, S. Valins, & B. Weiner (Eds.), *Attribution: Perceiving the causes of behavior.* Morristown, NJ: General Learning Press.

Kaplan, R. M. (1984). The connection between clinical health promotion and health status: A critical overview. *American Psychologist, 39,* 755-765.

Katz, D., Gutek, B. A., Kahn, R. L., & Barton, E. (1975). *Bureaucratic encounters.* Ann Arbor: Institute for Social Research.

Kazdin, A. E. (1980). *Behavior modification in applied settings.* Homewood, IL: Dorsey Press.

Kelly, P., & Kranzberg, M. (1978). *Technological innovation.* San Francisco: San Francisco Press.

Kelman, H. C. (1961). Processes of opinion change. *Public Opinion Quarterly, 25,* 57-78.

Kimberly, J. R., & Evanisko, M. J. (1981). Organizational innovation: The influence of individual, organizational, and contextual factors on hospital adoption of technological and administrative innovations. *Academy of Management Journal, 24,* 689-713.

King, A. S. (1974). Expectation effects on organizational change. *Administrative Science Quarterly, 19,* 221-230.

Klesges, R. C., & Glasgow, R. E. (1986). Smoking modification in the worksite. In M. F. Cataldo & T. J. Coates (Eds.), *Health and industry.* New York: John Wiley.

Komacki, J. L., & Jensen, M. (1986). Within-group designs: An alternative to traditional control group designs. In M. F. Cataldo & T. J. Coates (Eds.), *Health and industry.* New York: John Wiley.

Kondrasuk, J. N. (1984). Corporate physical fitness programs: The role of the personnel department. *Personnel Administrator, 29,* 75-80.

Kristein, M. M. (1982). The economics of health promotion at the worksite. *Health Education Quarterly, 9,* 27-36.

Lando, H. A. (1981). Effects of preparation, experimental contact, and a maintained reduction alternative on a broad spectrum program for eliminating smoking. *Addictive Behaviors, 6,* 123-133.

LaRosa, J. H., & Haines, C. M. (1986). *A guide to heart and lung health at the workplace: It's your business* (NIH Publication No. 86-2210). Washington, DC: U.S. Government Printing Office.

Levy, R. L. (1986). Social support and compliance: Salient methodological problems in compliance research. *The Journal of Compliance in Health Care, 1,* 189-198.

Lichtenstein, E., Glasgow, R. E., & Abrams, D. B. (1986). Social support in smoking cessation: In search of effective interventions. *Behavior Therapy, 17,* 607-619.

Matarazzo, J. D. (1982). Behavioral health's challenge to academic, scientific and professional psychology. *American Psychologist, 37,* 1-14.

Matarazzo, J. D. (1984). Behavioral health: A 1990 challenge for the health sciences professions. In J. D. Matarazzo, S. M. Weiss, J. A. Herd, N. E. Miller, & S. M. Weiss (Eds.), *Behavioral health: A handbook of health enhancement and disease prevention* (pp. 3-40). New York: John Wiley.

McDowell, J. J. (1982). The importance of Herrnstein's mathematical statement of the law of effect for behavior therapy. *American Psychologist, 37,* 771-779.

Murphy, R. J., Gasparotto, G., & Opatz, J. P. (1987). Current issues in the evaluation of worksite health promotion programs. In J. P. Opatz (Ed.), *Health promotion evaluation: Measuring the organizational impact* (pp. 1-14). Stevens Point, WI: National Wellness Association.

Naditch, M. P. (1986). STAYWELL: Evolution of a behavioral medicine program in industry. In M. F. Cataldo & T. J. Coates (Eds.), *Health and industry: A behavioral medicine perspective* (pp. 323-337). New York: John Wiley.

Orlandi, M. A. (1986). The diffusion and adoption of worksite health promotion innovations: An analysis of barriers. *Preventive Medicine, 15,* 522-536.

Paxton, R. (1981). Deposit contracts with smokers: Varying frequency and amount of repayments. *Behavior Research and Therapy, 19,* 117-123.

Pinder, C. (1984). *Work motivation: Theory, issues, and applications.* Glenview, IL: Scott, Foresman.

Prochaska, J. O., & DiClemente, C. C. (1983). Stages and processes of self-change of smoking: Toward an integrative model of change. *Journal of Consulting and Clinical Psychology, 51,* 390-395.

Rigotti, N. (1986). Policies restricting smoking in public places and the workplace. In Surgeon General's Report, *The health consequences of involuntary smoking* (DHHS Publication No. CDC 87-8398). Rockville, MD: U.S. Public Health Services.

Rogers, E. M. (1983). *Diffusion of innovations.* New York: Free Press.

Salancik, G. (1977). Commitment and the control of organizational behavior and belief. In B. Straw & G. Salancik (Eds.), *Directions in organizational behavior.* Chicago: St. Clair.

Shepard, D. S., & Pearlman, L. A. (1985). Health habits that pay off. *Business and Health, 2,* 37-41.

Shephard, R. J., Morgan, P., Finucane, R., & Schimmelfing, L. (1980). Factors influencing recruitment to an occupation fitness program. *Journal of Occupational Medicine, 22,* 389-398.

Sidman, M. (1960). *Tactics of scientific research.* New York: Basic Books.

Sorenson, G., Pechacek, T., & Pallonen, U. (1986). Occupational and worksite norms and attitudes about smoking cessation. *American Journal of Public Health, 76,* 544-549.

Syme, S. L. (1986). Strategies for health promotion. *Preventive Medicine, 15,* 492-507.

Terborg, J. R. (1986a). Health promotion at the worksite: A research challenge for personnel and human resources management. In K. H. Rowland & G. R. Ferris (Eds.), *Research in personnel and human management,* Vol. 4 (pp. 225-267). Greenwich, CT: JAI.

Terborg, J. R. (1986b, June). *A cost-benefit analysis of occupational health promotion programs.* Paper presented at the Conference on Strategic Human Resource Management, Duke University, Durham, North Carolina.

Triandis, H. C. (1980). Values, attitudes, and interpersonal behavior. In H. E. Howe & M. M. Page (Eds.), *1979 Nebraska symposium on motivation.* Lincoln: University of Nebraska Press.

Warner, K. E. (in press). Selling health promotion to corporate America: Uses and abuses of the economic argument. *Health Education Quarterly.*

Warner, K. E., & Luce, B. R. (1982). *Cost-benefit and cost-effectiveness analysis in health care.* Ann Arbor: Health Administration Press.

Weinstein, M., & Stason, W. (1977). Foundations of cost-effectiveness analysis for health and medical practices. *New England Journal of Medicine, 296,* 716-721.

Weiss, S. M. (1987, June). Presidential Address. Paper presented at the Annual Meeting of the Academy of Behavioral Medicine Research, Sebasco, Maine.

Winer, B. J. (1971). *Statistical principles in experimental design.* New York: McGraw-Hill.

Wolfe, R. A., Ulrich, D. O., & Parker, D. F. (in press). Employee health management: A review of the literature and a research agenda. *Journal of Management.*

Wortman, P. M. (1983). Evaluation research: A methodological perspective. *Annual Review of Psychology, 34,* 223-260.

U.S. Bureau of the Census. (1986). *Statistical abstract of the United States: 1986.* Washington, DC: U.S. Government Printing Office.

U.S. Department of Health and Human Services. (1985). *National Heart, Lung, and Blood Institute fiscal year 1985 fact book.* Bethesda, MD: National Institutes of Health.,

U.S. Department of Health and Human Services. (1986). *The health consequences of involuntary smoking: A report of the surgeon general* (DHHS Publication No. CDC 87-8398). Rockville, MD: U.S. Public Health Services.

8

The Community as a Focus
for Health Promotion

NATHAN MACCOBY

I first became interested in the applications of communication psychology to health in the early 1960s when I was recruited as a survey researcher to be a member of the Health Services Research Study Section of the National Institutes of Health. It became clear that a great many health problems had to do with people's knowledge, understanding, and attitudes concerning risk factors for disease.

In the winter of 1969-70, John Farquhar, professor of medicine at Stanford, visited the department of communication to seek help in research designed to teach people about the damages of heart disease. He pointed out that cardiovascular disease was the single greatest killer in our country and in the developed nations, and that the risk could be reduced by changes in people's behavior, such as not smoking cigarettes, exercising more, and

AUTHOR'S NOTE: The research reported in this chapter is being conducted by the Stanford Center for Research in Disease Prevention, John W. Farquhar, M.D., Director. The author is Associate Director of the Center. Additional researchers who have participated importantly in the conduct and reporting of this research include Stephen P. Fortmann, M.D., Peter Wood, Ph.D., D.Sc., William Haskell, Ph.D., June Flora, Ph.D., W. Barr Taylor, M.D., B. William Brown, Ph.D., Paul Williams, Ph.D., Douglas Solomon, Ph.D., and the late Janet K. Alexander, M.A.

changing dietary intake. He wanted to have a film made that would help in changing these behaviors.

I became especially interested because of the challenge these problems offered. My years of past work in tests and measurements, sample surveys, learning theory and application, and attitude formation and change via communication all were applicable to chronic disease prevention. My response to Farquhar's request to make a film was that I suspected it would turn out to be a much more complex problem, but I was eager to participate. We have worked together productively ever since.

This chapter reports the history of that effort. It begins with a bit of chronic disease epidemiology describing risk factors for cardiovascular disease and the role of behavior in these factors. It then describes briefly two major research efforts on community education, aimed at discovering how best to communicate and achieve the necessary changes in information, attitudes, and behavior, and thus in communitywide risk reduction. It describes the theoretical approaches, the methods, and the principal findings of the first study, the Three-Community Study (TCS), and the rationale and methods of the Five-City Project (FCP), which is still in progress.

Risk Factors in Chronic Diseases

Despite the advent of AIDS, chronic diseases have replaced infectious diseases as the principal causes of death in this and many other developed countries (National Heart, Lung, and Blood Institute, 1985, p. 25). The single biggest killer is cardiovascular and related diseases—those that take hold in the heart, arteries, and in cerebral blood vessels. Following cardiovascular diseases as the next largest cause of death is cancer, another major chronic disease. Next come accidents and chronic obstructive lung disease.

Two important facts are that some of the principal risk factors that contribute to cardiovascular disease are smoking cigarettes, high blood cholesterol, and elevated blood pressure, and that the risk of disease increases still more with a combination of these factors (Dawber, Kannel, & McNamara, 1964).

It is particularly relevant to psychologists that behavior is heavily implicated in all three of these risk factors. Smoking is obviously a behavior, and it is the single most important known threat to health. New evidence of its deadly consequences keeps coming to light. The recently publicized effects of passive smoking are one such example. It should also be noted that smoking is the principal source of lung cancer and of other lung diseases, such as chronic obstructive lung disease, one of the other leading causes of death.

Elevated blood cholesterol is the second risk factor. Certainly genetics plays an important role in the determination of levels of cholesterol. However, even people with good genes can be affected adversely by what they eat. The Japanese in Japan have very low blood cholesterol levels—so low that the upper tail of their distribution hardly overlaps the lower tail of the distribution of Americans. However, the Japanese in Hawaii have higher levels, and those in California are very much higher (Robertson et al., 1977). Both animal and human studies have shown that a diet high in fats, particularly saturated fats, without heavy and frequent exercise, typically results in high cholesterol levels—especially of the bad low-density variety—and that a diet lower in fats results in a more favorable picture.

High blood pressure presents a similar pattern. In our society, blood pressure tends to increase with age. In many societies, particularly less developed ones, it does not; and many individuals in our society do not display increasing blood pressure with age. Again, diet and lack of exercise are important contributors, and so is lack of adherence to a regimen of medication that can lower blood pressure and keep it under control (although medications may have adverse side effects as well).

If we look at the list of other chronic diseases, such as cancer and lung disease, and of accidents and injuries, in which alcohol consumption plays a major role, behavior is again at the root of the problem. Even in the growing scourge of AIDS, presently the worst uncontrolled infectious disease, preventive behavior is the only remedy currently available.

With respect to cardiovascular risk factors, it has been demonstrated that risk is a continuous function of rate. For instance, the more one smokes, the greater the risk; the higher the level of cholesterol, the greater the risk; and the higher the blood pressure, the greater the risk. However, there are terms in medical use that suggest a dichotomy, with values beyond a selected cut-point being pathological and values below that point being "normal." Such terms as *hypercholesterolemia, hyperlipidemia, hypertension,* and *obesity* are illustrative. I find the use of the term *hypertension* particularly misleading and unfortunate because it defines high blood pressure as based on arbitrary cut-points, variously set. It does not mean what it sounds like, that is, that people are tensed up psychologically. Yet, I feel that psychologists are among the slowest to give up the word *hypertension* in describing blood pressure values, perhaps because this current definitional confusion may be seen as promoting psychologists' roles in the prevention process. Such self-promotion is quite unnecessary because finding ways to control blood pressure in a population is an objective to which psychologists do have a great deal to contribute.

While it is possible for blood pressure, cholesterol, and weight to be too low, these are not typical problems for the overwhelming majority of Americans. For them, the lower the values the better, and the higher the values the greater is the risk of disease. While a blood pressure of 130/80 isn't bad, one of 110/68 would be less risky. A total cholesterol of 220 may be acceptable, but one of 175 is considerably less risky. Being 15% overweight is not usually regarded as being obese, but it entails greater risk than being 5% or 10% overweight.

From this perspective, it is clear that most Americans (and others) could benefit from reducing cholesterol, blood pressure, and smoking (in the latter case, to zero). The question then arises: How can we best accomplish these health-promotion objectives?

How Can We Change Health Behaviors?

At the Stanford Center for Research in Disease Prevention we have come to believe that community education is the most effective way to change health behavior. Two major reasons for that view are

(1) Risk is very widespread.
(2) Communities offer great potential for achieving widespread communication for change.

Community communication channels include the mass media, whose role in achieving behavior change is complex. Though a review of the evidence suggests that interpersonal sources of information are by nature more persuasive than are the media, some studies have yielded contrary findings (Chaffee, 1982). Furthermore, mass media interact in complex ways with other sources of communication. Media information may lead one to seek interpersonal confirmation, but the reverse is also true. For example, when people heard of President Kennedy's assassination from others, they checked the truth of the rumor by consulting radio, TV, and newspapers (Sheatsley & Feldman, 1965).

Diffusion of information and practices takes place partly via mass media,and partly through institutions and organized groups. Communities can take on major tasks, like health promotion, and use a myriad of facilities as means for organizing activities. Schools, worksites, churches, clubs, and families can all serve as agents of a communitywide effort to achieve reductions in health-risk behavior or to prevent such behavior from being learned and performed. The broadcast and news media can contribute, as can supermarkets, hospitals, recreation departments, schools and colleges, and worksites.

The community environment can also be altered in ways that are likely to reduce the incidence of risky activities. Important examples are cigarette machines kept away from minors or abolished; smoking banned in worksites and public places; cigarette advertising banned or heavily restricted; more healthful foods supplanting disease-promoting ones in schools, restaurants, fast food places, and food dispensing machines; and exercise opportunities made readily available to the public.

For these and other reasons, the Stanford Center for Research in Disease Prevention chose the community as its focus for experiments in health education.

The Three-Community Study

John W. Farquhar and his medical school colleagues, Peter D. Wood, Byron W. Brown, Jr., William Haskell, and Michael Stern, decided in 1970 to develop a research plan to explore efficient means of health risk reduction in the population at large and to test them in clinical trials. They saw the need for a broad interdisciplinary team of biomedical and social scientists to address the wide range of questions raised by the research problem, and so they consulted the school's department of communication and other behavioral scientists. This group began to assess how best to conduct a public education program in cardiovascular disease risk-reduction.

Since the primary risk factors of smoking, diet, and high blood pressure were distributed across large segments of the total adult population, techniques that would reach large numbers of people were called for. At this point, the idea of intervening in total communities via mass media was introduced. In view of the projected limitations in resources and personnel, the decision was made to limit the target population to all adults aged 35 to 59.

As a result of interaction with the behavioral scientists, the biomedical researchers made a basic change in the research plan. They turned the planning away from a medical model concerned with high-risk populations and key health-profession opinion leaders, to a more complex but potentially more effective community model, relying principally on communication as the basic intervention tool. Discussion then shifted to choosing a research design appropriate to the community model and a behavior-change strategy appropriate to the target population.

Since the media campaign was to be directed at entire communities, random assignment of individuals to the treatment or control condition was not feasible. An equally rigorous experimental method, treating a large number of geographically defined populations as single units and randomly assigning some of these communities to treatment conditions and some to control conditions, was not administratively possible. We concluded that the most realistic compromise between feasibility and rigor was a quasi-experimental research approach (Campbell & Stanley, 1966) on a small number of experimental units.

After considering the powerful cultural forces that reinforce and maintain the health habits that we wished to change, and remembering past failures of health education campaigns, we designed a heretofore untested combination of extensive mass media with a considerable amount of face-to-face instruction. We chose the latter method because it was a method that we judged most likely to succeed (Mendelsohn, 1973), and we planned to compare it with a more generally applicable treatment, though one not quite so promising of results. Therefore, another community was selected, where we administered treatments via mass media alone. We also chose to include three elements typically ignored in health campaigns: (1) the mass media materials were devised to teach specific behavioral skills, as well as perform the more usual tasks of offering information and affecting attitudes and motivation; (2) both the mass media and particularly the face-to-face instruction were designed to embody many previously validated self-control training principles and methods of achieving changes in behavior; and (3) the campaign design was based on careful analysis of the specific needs and the media consumption patterns of the intended audience. Our overall goal was to create and evaluate methods for effecting changes in smoking, exercise, and diet that would be both cost-effective and applicable to large population groups.

Research Design

Three roughly comparable communities in northern California were selected. Tracy was chosen as a control because it was relatively distant and isolated from the media in other communities. Gilroy and Watsonville, the other two communities, share some media channels (television and radio), but each town has its own newspaper. These two cities received different strategies of health education over a period of two years. Both received health education through the mass media, and in Watsonville we also carried out a randomized experiment with a sample of persons at higher levels of risk for cardiovascular disease, employing intensive face-to-face instruction for two-thirds of this group and exposing the other one-third only to health education through the media, as a control against intensive instruction under a mass media umbrella.

To assess the effects of these interventions, we gathered baseline and yearly follow-up data from surveys composed of interviews and medical examinations of a representative (multistage probability) sample of 35- to 59-year-old men and women from each of the three communities. The schedule of surveys and educational campaigns is presented in Table 8.1. Since the measurement process itself could have effects, surveys were withheld from an additional sample (the "after-only" sample) in each community until the end of the first year of study, so that effects of the measurement process itself could be judged.

Survey and Medical Examinations

Our annual interviews in the three communities were designed to measure both knowledge about heart disease and individual behavior related to cardiovascular risk. The assessment covered several variables. Knowledge of risk factors was measured with a test of knowledge about dietary and other risk factors associated with coronary heart disease. Of the 25 multiple-choice items in the test, 3 were concerned with the role of smoking in heart disease, 14 with eating habits and heart disease, 4 with physical activity, 2 with body weight, and 2 with general information about heart disease. Eating habits were assessed in an interview, which allowed us to estimate daily intake of cholesterol, saturated and polyunsaturated fats, sugar, and alcohol, based on estimates of food composition (Stern, Farquhar, Maccoby, & Russell, 1976). Participants were also asked to

Table 8.1
Three-Community Study Design

City	1972	1973		1974		1975	
Watsonville (W)	Baseline survey (S1)	Media campaign. Intensive instruction (II) for 2/3 of high-risk participants	Second survey (S2)	Media campaign. Intensive instruction (II) for 2/3 of high-risk participants	Third survey (S3)	Maintenance (low-level) media campaign. II: Summer follow-up	Fourth survey (S4)
Gilroy (G)	Baseline survey (S1)	Media campaign	Second survey (S2)	Media campaign	Third survey (S3)	Maintenance (low-level) media campaign	Fourth survey (S4)
Tracy (T)	Baseline survey (S1)		Second survey (S2)		Third survey (S3)		Fourth survey (S4)

SOURCE: Maccoby (1980, p. 201). Reprinted by permission.

report their smoking behavior: whether they smoked cigarettes, pipes, or cigars, and their daily rate of smoking. Self-reports of smoking status were validated through an assay of plasma thiocyanate concentration, which indicated that only about 4% of those reporting abstinence may have given inaccurate reports (Butts, Kuehneman, & Widdowson, 1974).

Coincident with the interview, we also collected physiological data from participants at baseline and after one, two, and three years. These data included values of plasma total cholesterol and triglyceride concentrations, systolic and diastolic blood pressure, and relative weight (percent of ideal weight according to Metropolitan Life Insurance tables). Data were gathered in a survey center set up in each of the three communities, and results were sent to participants and their physicians.

The overall risk of coronary heart disease for each of the participants was estimated from a multiple logistic function of risk factors predicting the probability of developing coronary heart disease within 12 years, based on the person's age, sex, weight, smoking rate, and electrocardiographic findings (Truett, Cornfield, & Kannel, 1967). This calculation allowed us to identify the high-risk study groups just mentioned and to monitor the estimated risk of coronary heart disease for participants in all 12 surveys over the course of the study period (four measures from each of the three communities).

Mass Media Campaign

The experimental design involved development and application of both mass media and face-to-face instruction campaigns. These communication efforts were designed to overcome deficiencies in previous unsuccessful campaigns to change behavior. Each campaign was intended to produce awareness of the probable causes of coronary disease and of the specific behaviors that may reduce risk. The campaigns also aimed to provide the knowledge and skills necessary to accomplish recommended behavior changes. Lastly, the campaigns were designed to help the individual become self-sufficient in maintaining new health habits and skills. Dietary habits recommended for all participants were those that, if followed, would lead to a reduced intake of saturated fat, cholesterol, salt, sugar, and alcohol. We also urged reduction in body weight through caloric reduction and increased physical activity. Cigarette smokers were educated on the need and methods for ceasing or at least reducing their daily rate of cigarette consumption.

For the mass media campaign, a coordinated set of messages was prepared for the lay audiences in Gilroy and Watsonville. Over time, these basic messages were transformed into a variety of media (e.g., TV spots, bus cards) and released to the target audience through a variety of the most generally available media channels. A broad range of materials was produced: about 50 television spots, several hours of radio programming, weekly newspaper columns, newspaper advertisements and stories, billboards, printed material sent via direct mail to participants, posters, and other materials. Because of the sizable Spanish-speaking population in the communities, the campaign was presented in both Spanish and English. The media campaign began two months after the initial survey and continued for nine months in 1973, stopped during the second survey, and then continued for nine more months in 1974, and on a very reduced basis in 1975 (Farquhar, 1977; Maccoby, Farquhar, Wood, & Alexander, 1977).

The dominant characteristic of the mass media campaign structure was its organization as a total integrated information system such that its primary functions (creative transformation of the medical risk-reduction messages into media events, formative evaluation of those events, their distribution in coordinated packages over time, and their cumulative effectiveness in promoting change) could all interact to improve and refine decisions on how best to allocate the remaining available resources. This system was managed by continuous monitoring of the target audience's existing knowledge, beliefs, attitudes, risk-related behavior, and media use. At the onset of the campaign, decisions were based primarily on data gathered at the initial survey, from the pretesting on local audiences of various media productions, and on practical considerations arising from the likely availability for our purposes of privately owned mass media. While the campaign was under way, further guidance was obtained from the second annual survey and from a series of systematic but informal small-scale information-gathering efforts designed to provide media planners with immediate feedback on the public's awareness and acceptance of specified sets of media events, as well as to gauge the progress to date. Thus the total campaign could be seen as a set of phased media events in which the information obtained from monitoring was used to refocus priorities, reset directions, and modulate the course of the campaign in the desired direction.

Intensive Instruction

The intensive face-to-face instruction program was directed at a randomly selected two-thirds of the Watsonville participants whom we had identified as being in the top quartile of risk of coronary heart disease, according to the multiple logistic formula. These individuals and their physicians were informed by letter of their relatively high-risk status, and this notification was considered part of the treatment for the group. Their spouses were also invited to participate. The educational effort was launched six months after the first baseline survey and was conducted intensively over a 10-week period. A less intense effort was conducted during the second year. A total of 107 of 113 participants originally assigned to receive intensive instruction were successfully recruited for treatment, and 67 high-risk individuals (and 34 spouses) completed all four interviews and examinations.

The intensive instruction program was composed of education and persuasion in the context of social learning and self-control training procedures designed to achieve the same changes in cholesterol and fat consumption, body weight, cigarette smoking, and physical exercise that were advocated in the media campaign (Meyer, Maccoby, & Farquhar, 1977). It was conducted by a team of graduate students in communication, physicians, and health educators specially trained in behavior modification techniques. The protocols were pretested in a controlled setting before being applied in the field. The basic sequential strategy was as follows: to present information about behavior that influences risk of coronary heart disease, stimulate personal analysis of existing behavior, demonstrate desired skills (e.g., food selection and preparation), guide the individual through tentative practice of those skills, and gradually withdraw instructor participation. The expectation was that the behavior would be maintained in the group setting without the instructor. During the initial stage, intensive instruction was conducted in group classes and home counseling sessions. During the second year, the frequency and amount of contact was successively reduced. A less intensive educational campaign was conducted in the summer months of the third year. It consisted primarily of individual counseling in difficult problem areas—for example, smoking and weight loss—and social activities, such as parties, picnics, and hikes, which were intended primarily to encourage participants to maintain changes that had been produced during the first stage of instruction.

Main Results

First of all, we investigated whether our audiences were paying any attention to us. One indication of this came from the measure of logo recognition. We used a musical theme to open and close all TV and radio programs and spots. In our TV spots and programs, as well as in all our printed materials, we showed a conventional heart shape with electro-cardiographic curves inside it. We found that recognition of our logo increased ultimately to include almost all of the population of the two communities in which we carried out a media program.

The results of the education programs may be characterized in terms of knowledge gained, and changes in behavior, in physiology, and in overall risk. For each of these sets of results, we compared the control community (Tracy) to the mass-media-only community (Gilroy) and the mass-media-plus-intensive-instruction community (Watsonville), for both the total and high-risk samples. In order to have an additional mass-media-only community for comparison purposes, we added an analysis of the Watsonville sample, omitting the intensive instruction and weighting the remainder proportionately. This sample we termed *Watsonville recon-stituted* (see tables). Significance tests on all comparisons were based on net change—that is, change in the intervention community minus the change in the control community. The number of cases (n) shown in the tables is the number of participants completing all four measures.

Knowledge. The 25-item test on risk factors in cardiovascular disease was given as part of the basic interview with our sample in all three communities. Clearly, there were knowledge gains over time everywhere. Even in Tracy, where we did not use the education approach, the general health education program (independent of ours) had an effect on public knowledge. However, the two communities in which we did campaign showed markedly greater improvements in knowledge, both as compared with their baseline scores and as compared to Tracy, the control community (see Tables 8.2 and 8.3).

Behavior. Important among the behavior changes that we hoped to help people achieve were those involving cigarette smoking and various aspects of food intake. We assisted people who smoked in learning how to cease smoking, and those who did not yet smoke in learning how to avoid the habit. In diet, we tried to educate people to adopt healthier eating habits, particularly to eat foods lower in saturated fats and in cholesterol, and to eat less salt and fewer calories. Tables 8.4 and 8.5 show some of the findings on smoking.

Although some reduction in the number of smokers took place in the communities with only the mass media campaign (Gilroy and "Watsonville reconstituted"), the only substantial reductions in the percentage of cigarette smokers occurred in Watsonville, and primarily among the Watsonville persons who received intensive instruction (see Table 8.5). The mass-media-only education program did not display much efficacy in helping people learn to cease smoking, though the secular trend was such that the nonintervention community, Tracy, showed a drop in the number of smokers. However, those who received intensive instruction showed a dramatic change: Half of the original smokers were nonsmokers three years after the education program began, and this despite very little added instruction during the third year.

Dietary cholesterol. Table 8.6 presents our best estimates of changes in the consumption of cholesterol in participants' diets, in terms of milligrams ingested per day. Diet intake was measured by a shortened dietary history designed to characterize the usual dietary behavior of participants concerning particular foods (Fortmann et al., 1981). Although small, nonsignificant changes may have been taking place in the noneducation

Table 8.2
Knowledge of Risk Factors and Changes in Knowledge, in Total Community Samples

Measure	Tracy n = 364	Gilroy n = 363	Watsonville reconstituted n = 384	Watsonville n = 384
Baseline mean no. correct	11.4	11.2	11.2	11.2
% change, end of year 1	1.7	18.1**	30.9**	36.3**
% change, end of year 2	6.3	26.5**	36.0**	40.8**
% change, end of year 3	12.8	35.0**	38.2**	43.4**

**p < .01

Table 8.3
Knowledge of Risk Factors and Changes in Knowledge, in High-Risk Samples

Measure	Tracy n = 89	Gilroy n = 85	Watsonville control n = 37	Watsonville intensive instruction n = 67
Baseline mean no. correct	10.8	11.1	11.3	10.9
% change, end of year 1	1.9	16.4**	29.8**	54.2**
% change, end of year 2	5.2	27.7**	30.4**	54.2**
% change, end of year 3	14.0	33.9**	27.9**	57.0**

**p < .01

community (Tracy), the magnitude and stability of the reductions of dietary cholesterol reported in the two education towns were impressive (all ps were $< .01$).

Similar findings appeared for the high-risk subsamples (Table 8.7). Again, while small, nonsignificant reductions may have been taking place in Tracy, substantial and highly significant reductions in dietary cholesterol took place in the mass media communities. That was particularly the case among those high-risk, intensively instructed people in Watsonville, whose initial level of cholesterol ingestion was already lower than others' at baseline.

Physiology. Recall that the main object of this study was to discover generally usable ways of helping whole communities to reduce their risk of cardiovascular disease. That risk is best assessed through smoking, blood

Table 8.4
Changes in Percentage of Cigarette Smokers:
Total Community Samples

Measure	Tracy n = 364	Gilroy n = 363	Watsonville reconstituted n = 384	Watsonville n = 384
Baseline (% of smokers)	29.8	36.0	31.6	34.8
% change, end of year 1	1.8	–7.7*	–4.2	–15.0*
% change, end of year 2	0.9	–4.9	1.7	–17.0*
% change, end of year 3	–2.5	–7.1*	–8.0**	–23.4*

*$p < .05$; **$p < .01$

Table 8.5
Changes in Percentage of Cigarette Smokers:
High-Risk Samples

Measure	Tracy n = 89	Gilroy n = 85	Watsonville control n = 37	Watsonville intensive instruction n = 67
Baseline (% of smokers)	52.0	62.4	52.5	62.3
% change, end of year 1	–8.2	–14.8	0	–31.3**
% change, end of year 2	–12.2	–13.1	0	–43.6**
% change, end of year 3	–14.9	–11.3	0	–50.0**

**$p < .01$

pressure, and serum cholesterol. Systolic blood pressure has been found to be a very important precursor of cardiovascular events. In the important longitudinal study conducted at Framingham, Massachusetts, the predictive value of systolic blood pressure was found to be superior to that of diastolic blood pressure, and the measure was therefore incorporated in their multiple logistic prediction of risk (Truett et al., 1967).

In the present study, both intervention communities showed statistically significant mean reductions in systolic blood pressure (Table 8.8). Although this reduction would be clinically insignificant in amount for any given individual when it is remembered that most participants showed moderate or low readings at baseline, the mean reductions are important.

Again, among high-risk participants (many of whom qualified for this classification to a considerable extent because of their relatively high systolic blood pressures), the scores were initially higher, and they showed larger changes in the mass media communities. Unlike many of our other

Table 8.6
Changes in Dietary Cholesterol in Total Community Samples

Measure	Tracy n = 364	Gilroy n = 363	Watsonville reconstituted n = 384	Watsonville n = 384
Baseline (mg/day)	493.7	546.4	521.5	514.4
% change, end of year 1	–10.2	–24.6**	–26.3**	–29.7**
% change, end of year 2	–6.7	–28.0**	–28.7**	–31.4**
% change, end of year 3	–9.2	–31.5**	31.5**	–33.7**

**$p < .01$

Table 8.7
Changes in Dietary Cholesterol in High-Risk Samples

Measure	Tracy n = 89	Gilroy n = 85	Watsonville control n = 37	Watsonville intensive instruction n = 67
Baseline (mg/day)	518.1	595.8	498.8	480.5
% change, end of year 1	–10.3	–29.0**	–28.2*	–41.7**
% change, end of year 2	– 7.9	–31.2**	–25.2*	–37.3**
% change, end of year 3	–13.4	–38.6**	–27.2*	–42.3**

*$p < .05$; **$p < .01$

findings, however, the reductions among those receiving intensive instruction were not greater than for their mass-media-only controls (Table 8.9).

Overall risk. Finally, the best overall indicator of risk is a single, combined measure—an adaptation of the Framingham multiple logistic function of risk. There were substantial and gratifying reductions in overall risk in the communities in which we conducted our educational campaigns (Tables 8.10 and 8.11). Interestingly, the mass-media-only conditions showed as much change as the community where the high-risk subsample was given intensive instruction. However, some retrogression occurred during the third year in the mass-media-only town (Gilroy) when educational programming was sharply curtailed, but it did not occur in the mass media town that included those receiving intensive instruction (Watsonville). Apparently the supplemental use of face-to-face instruction gives behavior changes more staying power.

Table 8.8
Changes in Systolic Blood Pressure in Total Community Samples

Measure	Tracy n = 364	Gilroy n = 363	Watsonville reconstituted n = 384	Watsonville n = 384
Baseline (mm/Hg)	128.6	131.8	133.0	133.4
% change, end of year 1	3.2	-2.2**	-0.5	-1.3**
% change, end of year 2	1.3	-7.3**	-4.6**	-4.6**
% change, end of year 3	0.9	-4.3**	-4.4**	-3.8**

**p < .01

Table 8.9
Changes in Systolic Blood Pressure in High-Risk Samples

Measure	Tracy n = 89	Gilroy n = 85	Watsonville control n = 37	Watsonville intensive instruction n = 67
Baseline (mm Hg)	138.2	148.0	147.8	150.3
% change, end of year 1	1.1	-4.3**	-2.6**	-6.4**
% change, end of year 2	-1.9	-10.7**	-8.3**	-7.7**
% change, end of year 3	-2.0	-8.7**	-8.9**	-6.6**

*p < .05; **p < .01

Discussion

In previous studies of weight loss, blood pressure detection and control, smoking cessation, and dietary composition changes, selected persons have served as subjects. In this study entire communities were the targets of education for change. The data just reported were from probability samples of those communities. However, loss of sample subjects in successive waves of measurement may somewhat limit the unbiased nature of the findings. In addition, there were some notable lacks of success. Sustained weight loss did not occur. However, average weight did not increase in the intervention towns, but it did in the control community. Also, cessation of smoking occurred primarily among those receiving intensive instruction.

In spite of these limitations, the changes that did take place were impressive. In general, the changes in knowledge, behavior, and—most

Table 8.10
Changes in Multiple Logistic Function of Risk for
Total Community Samples

Measure	Tracy $n = 364$	Gilroy $n = 363$	Watsonville reconstituted $n = 384$	Watsonville $n = 384$
Baseline	0.081	0.076	0.093	0.920
% change, end of year 1	7.7	−4.7**	−4.3**	−12.9**
% change, end of year 2	6.5	−17.3**	−16.2**	−18.4**
% change, end of year 3	3.3	−8.8**	−12.8**	−15.2**

**$p < .01$

Table 8.11
Changes in Multiple Logistic Function of Risk for
High-Risk Samples

Measure	Tracy $n = 89$	Gilroy $n = 85$	Watsonville control $n = 37$	Watsonville intensive instruction $n = 67$
Baseline	0.172	0.160	0.199	0.183
% change, end of year 1	4.4	−10.7**	−7.8**	−29.0**
% change, end of year 2	−2.0	−24.0**	−24.7**	−30.3**
% change, end of year 3	−8.0	−16.1**	−23.1**	−29.0**

*$p < .05$; **$p < .01$.

important—physiological measures achieved in the first year were maintained and actually improved in the second year of education. Even during the third year, when educational efforts all but ceased, most changes were maintained, especially in the community containing persons who received intensive instruction.

This study demonstrates that mass media, when appropriately used, can increase knowledge and help people to adopt improved health habits. The results led us to believe, however, that the power of this method could be considerably enhanced if we could devise ways of employing the media to stimulate and coordinate face-to-face instructional programs in natural settings, such as schools, places of work, and community groups. This study led, therefore, to a further investigation designed to test these ideas.

The Five-City Project (FCP)

This project differs from the Three-Community Study (TCS) in several ways:

(1) The two communities selected for education are much larger and more socially complex than are those in the previous study, and the health education campaign is aimed at benefiting the entire population.

(2) Three moderate-sized cities were selected as controls, rather than the one town of the TCS, resulting in a total population size of 350,000 in five cities, as compared to 43,000 in the TCS.

(3) The project is running for nine years, and a community organization method (discussed in a later section) is being used to create a cost-effective and lasting program of community health promotion.

(4) People selected from a broader age range (12-74) are taking part in the surveys. In contrast to the longitudinal cohort design of the TCS, repeated independent samples as well as longitudinal cohorts have been drawn every two years, in order to monitor communitywide changes independent of survey effects.

(5) With the cooperation of local health officials, the FCP is monitoring the annual rates of fatal and nonfatal cardiovascular events in the five cities.

Research Design

The major aim of the FCP is to test the hypothesis that a significant decrease in the multiple logistic function of risk for the experimentally educated communities will lead to a decline in morbidity and mortality from cardiovascular disease beyond any that is attributable to the secular trend. A six-year education program is designed to stimulate and maintain the changes in life-style that will result in a communitywide reduction in risk of cardiovascular disease. Population surveys, epidemiologic surveillance, and other assessment methods are combined to evaluate the effects of the education program. The overall design is illustrated in Table 8.12.

Communitywide changes in knowledge, behavior, and cardiovascular

Table 8.12
Stanford Five-City Project Design

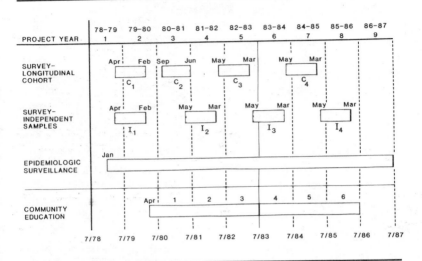

SOURCE: Farquhar et al. (1985). Reprinted by permission.

risk—independent of survey effects—are being determined through comparison of the four biennial cross-sectional sample surveys conducted in the two education cities and two of the three reference communities. Each survey in each city has approximately 650 cases. Studies of the process of change in individuals are possible by comparing the successive surveys of the longitudinal cohort, which was drawn from the first independent sample.

A major goal of the FCP is to use the survey and surveillance data to analyze the secular trends in cardiovascular risk factors, morbidity, and mortality during a time of generally declining mortality, the cause of which is uncertain. This will add important epidemiological information on the causes of cardiovascular disease. The survey data will also be used to explore hypotheses about knowledge, behavior, attitudes, and risk, in order to add basic information on health behavior.

This research design is a compromise between the desirable and the feasible. We would have preferred a larger number of cities, randomly assigned to treatment and control conditions. However, this would have increased the expense and the need to isolate the cities from undue influence by each other, thus making randomization impossible (Farquhar, 1978).

Risk Factors and Health Behaviors

The major cardiovascular risk factors selected for attention in the FCP are cigarette use, arterial blood pressure (BP), plasma low-density lipoprotein (LDL) cholesterol, and plasma high-density lipoprotein (HDL) cholesterol. These risk factors have been linked with several health behaviors or conditions that therefore become major areas for the intervention: smoking, nutrition, exercise, high blood pressure, and obesity. Nutrition behavior is known to affect BP (through salt intake and weight control), LDL cholesterol (through dietary saturated fat, cholesterol, and fiber, and weight control), and HDL cholesterol (through weight control). Exercise affects BP (through weight control), LDL cholesterol (through weight control), and HDL cholesterol (through weight control, and perhaps also directly). High blood pressure treatment will affect that portion of the BP distribution appropriate for drug therapy. The other factors are identified to enable specific treatment plans to be made when appropriate.

Although it is convenient to consider each risk factor and health behavior separately, there is a danger of implying a fragmentation that is not present. In fact, the educational program in the FCP is a highly unified one. People who attend a smoking cessation class, for example, are encouraged to begin exercise, to substitute healthy foods for the smoking habit, and so forth. We are presenting a single life-style that is most likely to be healthy. It involves being vigorous, active, and self-confident, eating a wide variety of enjoyable foods, and not smoking. It is this basically healthy and happy image that binds together the various elements of the intervention and makes the educational programs and materials coherent and, to an extent, indivisible.

Education Program

The education program has three goals. The first is to generate an increase in the knowledge and skills of individuals and in the educational practices of community organizations such that risk-factor reduction and decreased morbidity and mortality are achieved. This education program aims to stimulate and to maintain life-style changes within the study population so that at least a 10% reduction in overall risk status will be achieved after two years of intervention. It was estimated that a greater than 20% reduction in overall risk would be achieved if the following mean changes of magnitude occurred in individual risk factors: (a) smoking—a 9% net decrease in the proportion of smokers, (b) weight—a 2% net reduction in relative weight, (c) blood pressure—a 7% net drop in systolic blood pressure, and (d) blood cholesterol—a 4% net reduction. The education program was planned to run for a total of six years in order to create changes of approximately this magnitude, which are needed to detect related changes in morbidity and mortality (Fortmann et al., 1986).

A second goal is to carry out the education program in a way that creates a self-sustaining health-promotion structure, embedded within the organizational fabric of the communities, that will continue to function after the project ends. This transfer process is currently taking place.

The third goal is to derive a model for cost-effective community health promotion from the experience and data accumulated in the TCS and in this study, the broad features of which would have general applicability in many other American communities. The current Kaiser Family Foundation community support program is aimed at demonstrating and extending this applicability.[1]

Theoretical Perspectives

A variety of perspectives and theoretical formulations had to be blended in order successfully to design and carry out the educational program described here. In addition to the clearly relevant field of community organization, which creates a receptive environment for our educational materials and programs, we have also found it necessary to borrow from the communication-behavior-change framework and the social marketing framework. The communication-behavior-change framework is based on a social-psychological perspective concerning the individual and group learning that is needed within the overall community organization method. This perspective is particularly germane to the content of the educational materials. The social marketing framework, based on marketing principles, is especially relevant to the practical issues of how to design and distribute the educational products.

Communication-behavior-change framework. This perspective indicates how individuals and groups change knowledge, attitudes, and behavior. Our picture of the change process draws on the prior work of others: the social learning theory of Bandura (1979); the hierarchy of learning model of Ray et al. (1973); the communication-persuasion approach of McGuire (1969); the attitude change formulation of Ajzen and Fishbein (1980); and the innovation-diffusion model of Rogers and Shoemaker (1971). The communication-behavior-change approach emphasizes the following features, which are relevant to community-based education and health promotion.

(1) Become aware (gain attention). The agenda-setting function (McCombs & Shaw, 1972; Shaw & McCombs, 1977) is to gain the public's attention and focus it on certain specific issues and problems. The existence of the problem must be established in the public's mind, and an awareness of potential solutions must be promoted. In our society, the mass media generally play an important agenda-setting role in moving issues from the periphery of attention to the focus.

(2) Increase knowledge (provide information). Once a particular topic or subject matter is on the public agenda, an educational program must present information, in layman's terms, that makes the issue interesting and understandable. Messages should be designed to make the issue personally meaningful and to set the stage for action. The messages must be retained in a form that predisposes individuals to act in a different way in the future.

(3) Increase motivation (provide incentives). Change is more likely when individuals clearly perceive the personal and social benefits of change, and these benefits can be emphasized by appropriate communication.

(4) Learn skills (provide training). When changes in complex habits of long standing are involved, it may be necessary to provide skills training in how to start making changes, both by providing step-by-step instruction and by promoting the availability of self-help and professional resources.

(5) Take action (model). Ideally, this phase of an overall behavior-change strategy would provide educational inputs that act as cues to trigger specific actions. Messages would indicate clear action paths and attempt to stimulate the trial adoption of new behaviors.

(6) Maintain changes (provide support and guidance). At this stage, inputs should provide a sense of social support and approval and serve as reminders for performing the learned (more healthy) acts. Gaining self-efficacy and learning self-management methods are important aspects of the maintenance phase.

In health promotion programs with multiple objectives, not everything can be done all at once for everyone. Planners must have a rational basis for making selections from among competing interventions or messages and for sequencing their actions over time. The communication-behavior-change framework can be a general guide, suggesting how to break down the large community-health-promotion task into manageable pieces.

Social marketing framework. The concept of social marketing (Kotler & Levy, 1983) is that marketing principles and techniques can be usefully applied to social change programs to improve their effectiveness.

The design and implementation of the FCP education program in general, and the media campaign in particular, can therefore be viewed as an application of social marketing to community health promotion. In social marketing, the focus is on the transaction, in which something of value is exchanged among parties. The marketing process begins with an understanding of the consumer. That understanding directs the creation of products or services with price, promotion, and distribution organized to attract the customer.

The techniques of social marketing are divided by McCarthy (1968) into four elements—the "four P's" of marketing management: "the right PRODUCT backed by the right PROMOTION and put in the right PLACE at the right PRICE."

The *product* element is concerned with designing appropriate educational products in "packages" that target audiences find desirable and are willing to accept or purchase and use. Health promotion products may take a tangible form (such as a low-cholesterol cookbook) or may be quite intangible (a message to reduce blood pressure).

The *promotion* element is concerned with how to make the product familiar, acceptable, and even desirable, usually through some form of communication, such as advertising, personal selling, publicity, or sales promotion.

The *place* element involves the provision of adequate and compatible distribution and response channels. Motivated persons should know where the product can be obtained, and this aspect of marketing involves arranging for accessible outlets that permit the translation of motivations into actions through well-established patterns of distributioi..

The *price* element represents the costs that the buyer must accept in order to obtain the product. Price includes money costs, opportunity costs, energy costs, and psychic costs, and thus the notion of "transaction" is included in this formulation of social marketing. The marketer's approach to selling a social product is to consider how the rewards for buying the product can be increased relative to the costs, or the costs reduced relative to the rewards.

Although semantic analogies can be drawn between social marketing elements and the communication-behavior-change elements previously described, it is clear that the social marketing framework adds to our theory and practice by guiding us to deal more effectively with the practical realities of marketing our products in the complex urban environments of modern America.

The application of social marketing to community health promotion rests on the health promoter's ability to control or arrange the elements of product, promotion, price, and place. It assumes that the social marketer has a clear understanding of consumer attributes and consumer needs and has the requisite flexibility to design and produce needed commodities or services. It further assumes that adequate distribution systems exist, providing a place where consumers can intersect with the product. A marketing model also assumes that a transaction is possible within the circumstances of people's lives, and that they can afford and will pay the price of the product. Finally, it requires knowledge of results of prior actions (the equivalent of sales data) as the basis for product design and system management.

Community organization framework. We have assumed that a process of community organization would play a significant role in both the initial success and the durability of our program. In accord with this assumption, our educational program has been conducted in a manner that encourages involvement from the outset by local community groups and is designed to lead to local ownership and control. The following assumptions have been made:

(1) Mass media education alone is powerful, but its effects may be augmented by community organization.

(2) Interpersonal influence can be enhanced inexpensively through community organization, and this can produce a multiplier effect that will increase behavior change.

(3) Organizations can expand an educational program's delivery system in ways that are important for achieving communitywide health education.

(4) Organizations can help the process of community adoption of risk-reduction programs by sponsoring them as their own, thus increasing the likelihood of continuing health education programs and long-term behavior change in their communities.

(5) Formation of new organizations can be catalyzed by researchers' external efforts, thus increasing the array of groups concerned with health education and health promotion.

Our use of community organizing affects all phases of our education program development (see Rothman, 1979). Following the early phases of program development, the major function of community organization is to provide a receptive environment for the educational products to be used effectively. In contrast, we rely most heavily on the communication-behavior-change framework to guide our choice of content, and on social marketing to improve design and distribution. Finally, community organization has the task of inducing community groups to create their own educational products.

Formative Evaluation

Formative research, as distinct from summative research, is intended to provide data for use in designing educational strategies, to help in designing programs and materials for meeting specific objectives for the target audiences, and to monitor the progress of the educational program. A general criticism of health communication campaigns in the literature (Atkin, 1979) involves their lack of formative research, which often results in design of materials and programs that are not able to meet the objectives of the overall effort. In our health promotion programs, a core element has always been our ability to conduct and use formative research.

There are numerous areas in which formative research is undertaken to assist the design, development, production, and distribution of the education program. Audience segmentation and needs analysis, for example, ask who the appropriate audience is for a given topic and what they need (e.g., more information, skills, or motivation). Program design and testing evaluate the best place and time for a given program and evaluate an early version to determine what is working and what needs changing. Message design and testing answer analogous questions for media products, such as television spots. Finally, the effectiveness of individual programs and messages is evaluated to the extent possible when they are introduced into general use.

Broadcast Media Programs

Our media programs have been designed using the communication-behavior-change and social marketing frameworks, and refined through formative evaluation. The overriding goal of the use of broadcast media in the FCP is the encouragement of lasting behavior change that results in cardiovascular risk-factor modification and, ultimately, in reductions in morbidity and mortality. Underlying this major goal are two subgoals: broadcast media programs must encourage direct behavior change and also indirect change through support of community events. Some products are designed to support community programs (particularly by encouraging recruitment), whereas others are designed to create direct changes in knowledge, attitudes, and behavior on the part of the target audience. Some products are hybrids: for example, a smoking cessation television show could encourage cessation as well as recruit individuals into smoking cessation programs available in the community.

A variety of factors determine the format, content, and time sequence of broadcast media products. Certain products are essential to support programs requested by community groups, and some media products are requested by the mass media outlets themselves. The decision-making process for most of the media productions, however, is highly related to our particular risk-factor goals during a certain period of time. For example, such planning is based on a careful understanding of risk-factor goals; on the knowledge, attitudes, behaviors, and desires for change among the majority of adult smokers; and on estimates of the efficacy of various approaches to smoking cessation and maintenance of nonsmoking. A major function of the broadcast media is to reduce the threshold for exposure to communications in greater depth, such as in print media.

Print Media Programs

Print media are able to provide higher information-density messages on a particular topic than are broadcast media, which are most capable of presenting relatively low information-density messages. Print messages can be read and reread at the user's own pace. Therefore, they provide a large amount of information in a user-oriented format. With this in mind, the FCP has invested a substantial amount of effort in print media, particularly in topic areas that require more than the superficial amount of information that can be provided in typical broadcast media programs. To this end, formative research efforts of various kinds have been used to design, modify, and distribute printed material. The FCP has conceptualized four types of printed materials: big print, media promotion print, support print, and local print.

Big print is designed to meet the objective of developing effective prototype media products. Big print pieces are developed, written, designed, and produced by the professional staff at Stanford. They are intended to carry a major message of the project and to have a relatively long time span. There is a reciprocal relationship between big print and community organization; each supports and magnifies the impact of the other. Big print functions largely as an exogenous medium within our previously mentioned classification scheme, but it also plays a role in some collaborative education programs when it is used as a text for various groups.

Media promotion print is any print piece whose primary objective is to motivate individuals to attend to the FCP's media events. This form of print is subjected to the same process of formative research as big print, and follow-up evaluation also takes place to assess its effectiveness.

Educational *support print* includes any piece whose purpose is to support classes or workshops. Its goals include reinforcing the knowledge and skills being taught in an educational program and providing additional information not presented by the instructor or leader.

Local print is used to meet the project's objective of developing endogenous print materials. Local print includes any piece needed in the communities where fast turnaround is a central priority, such as print needed for promoting and recruiting for local activities, classes, and groups.

Evaluation Through Health Surveys

Each health survey includes both physiological and behavioral measures. The physiological measures are as follows:

(1) Body height and weight.
(2) Blood pressure by two methods (mercury manometer and semi-automated machine).
(3) Nonfasting venous blood sample analyzed for plasma thiocyanate (as a measure of amount of smoking), total cholesterol, triglycerides, and cholesterol content of lipoprotein subfractions.
(4) Expired air carbon monoxide.
(5) Urinary sodium, potassium, and creatinine (as an index of prior sodium chloride intake).

(6) A low-level bicycle exercise test (as a measure of fitness).

Blood pressure is obtained as indirect brachial artery pressure (systolic and fifth-phase diastolic) on participants sitting at rest for two minutes before the first measurement. Pressures are obtained twice using a Sphygmetrics Infrasonic Automatic Blood Pressure Recorder (SR-2), and this is followed by dual measurements using a standard mercury sphygmomanometer and auscultation.

Lipid analyses follow long-established methods of the Lipid Research Clinic's Program (U.S. Department of Health, Education and Welfare, 1974). Plasma thiocyanate determination follows the procedure of Butts, Kuehneman, and Widdowson (1974), as used in the Multiple Risk Factor Intervention Trial. Expired air carbon monoxide is measured on the Ecolyzer apparatus. Urine samples are frozen after collection and shipped to Stanford twice monthly. Standard laboratory procedures are used for determination of urinary sodium and potassium (flame photometry) and creatinine.

The low-level exercise test, using a Schwinn electric-brake stationary cycle ergometer, is performed following blood pressure measurement and blood sampling. Measurements of pulse rate are made using a Quinton Instrument Cardiotachometer. A small number of participants are excluded from the test according to very conservative criteria. The test is designed to obtain a pulse rate index of relative fitness after a standard work load that is estimated to be 70% of maximum aerobic capacity.

The behavioral measures of the health survey include a broad range of attitude and knowledge assessments, behavioral intention measures, self-reported behavior, and dietary and physical activity recalls. In addition, questions are asked for use in formative evaluation, such as attitudes toward different types of educational materials. Of course, standard demographic and medication-use data are collected.

A final method of data collection is community epidemiological surveillance, to allow calculation of comparable, city-specific rates for total mortality, cardiovascular mortality, fatal myocardial infarction, nonfatal myocardial infarction, fatal stroke, and nonfatal stroke. The mortality rates mentioned are obtainable from vital statistics, but these are problematic because they rely on the unaided interpretation of death certificate diagnoses. A common method for obtaining morbidity rates is to identify a cohort of individuals and follow them through time with repeated, thorough examinations that discover the occurrence of new events; however, such cohort studies are large and expensive. Thus the needed mortality statistics are available inexpensively, but their accuracy is suspect, and the morbidity data are unobtainable except at great expense. Community surveillance is designed, therefore, to obtain accurate mortality statistics and to obtain morbidity statistics at an acceptable cost (Gillum, 1978).

Potential fatal events are identified from death certificates and nonfatal events from hospital discharge records. Nonclinical or "silent" infarctions are not identified. All potential events are investigated by hospital chart review or family interview. The resulting data are reviewed at Stanford by trained analysts, using standard criteria for each type of event (Fortmann et al., 1986). The analysts are unaware of the community of origin, and they review the cases independently. A final end point is assigned by a computer algorithm applied to the analysts' digest of each case. If the analysts disagree on a case, it is reviewed by a physician.

Five-City Project Preliminary Results

The final results of the Five-City Project are not yet in. There will be one more independent sample (I5) and one more cohort sample (C5) taken at the end of 1989. The surveillance of morbidity and mortality, which are expected to lag behind changes in risk, will be carried on for several more years.

Main interim results from the cohort sample (comparing C4 with C1) indicate significant improvements in knowledge of cardiovascular risk factors, reductions in blood pressure (both systolic and diastolic), and reduction in pulse rate. Total risk—that is, the multiple logistic function used as a predictor of a cardiovascular event within 12 years—has also decreased significantly.

Summary

Our research shows that, by using an interdisciplinary staff of cardiologists, epidemiologists, behavioral scientists, biostatisticians, and communication specialists, it is possible to mount community-based studies aimed at reducing the incidence and prevalence of chronic disease, especially cardiovascular disease. Methodologically, quasi-experimental designs involving collection of a variety of demographic, physiological, and behavioral data can both furnish baselines for prospective intervention studies and assist in the design and creation of such interventions.

The Three-Community Study has provided substantial indications that risk factors in cardiovascular disease can be reduced through community education. The Five-City Project is an attempt to replicate and extend these findings by additional means of intervention, including communication-behavior-change, social marketing, and community organization approaches. Through these, it is hoped that desired changes can be not only accomplished but also institutionalized—that is, maintained with sufficient magnitude and duration to reduce significantly the long-term morbidity and mortality due to cardiovascular disease.

Note

1. In 1986, the Henry J. Kaiser Family Foundation launched a national community-health-promotion grant program designed to assist communities in using existing knowledge about disease prevention and health promotion. In addition to direct grants to community groups, the Foundation will sponsor and fund four Health Promotion Resource Centers (HPRCs) to provide training, materials, and evaluation to individuals and organizations in participating communities. The first such center was established at Stanford in 1986 to cover the 13 western states. The HPRC, directed by John W. Farquhar, M.D., is an integral part of the Center for Research in Disease Prevention.

References

Ajzen, I., & Fishbein, M. (1980). *Understanding attitudes and predicting social behavior.* Englewood Cliffs, NJ: Prentice-Hall.

Atkin, C. K. (1979). Research evidence on mass mediated health communication campaigns. In D. Nimmo (Ed.), *Communication yearbook 3.* New Brunswick, NJ: Transaction Books.

Bandura, A. (1979). *Social learning theory.* Englewood Cliffs, NJ: Prentice Hall.

Butts, W. C., Kuehneman, M., & Widdowson, G. M. (1974). Automated method for determining serum thiocyanate to distinguish smokers from nonsmokers. *Clinical Chemistry, 20,* 1344-1348.

Campbell, D. T., & Stanley, J. C. (1966). *Experimental and quasi-experimental designs for research.* Chicago: Rand McNally.

Chaffee, S. H. (1982). Mass media and interpersonal channels: Competitive, convergent or complementary? In G. Gumpert & R. Cathcard (Eds.), *Inter/media: Interpersonal communication in a media world* (pp. 57-77). New York: Oxford University Press.

Dawber, T. R., Kannel, W. B., & McNamara, P. M. (1964). The prediction of coronary heart disease. *Transactions of the Association of Life Insurance Medical Directors of America, 47*, 70-105.

Farquhar, J. W. (1978). The community-based model of life-style intervention trials. *American Journal of Epidemiology, 108*, 103-111.

Farquhar, J. W., Fortmann, S. P., Maccoby, N., Haskell, W. L. et al. (1985). The Stanford Five-City Project: Design and methods. *American Journal of Epidemiology, 122*, 323-334.

Farquhar, J. W., Maccoby, N., Wood, P. D., Breitrose, H., Haskell, W. L., Meyer, A. J., Alexander, J. K., Brown, B. W., McAlister, A. L., Nash, J. D., & Stern, M. P. (1977). Communication education for cardiovascular health. *Lancet, 1*, 1192-1195.

Fortmann, S. P., Haskell, W. L., Williams, P. T. et al. (1986). Community surveillance of cardiovascular diseases in the Stanford Five-City Project: Methods and initial experience. *American Journal of Epidemiology, 123*, 656-669.

Fortmann, S. P., Williams, P. T., Hulley, S. B., Haskell, W. L., & Farquhar, J. W. (1981). Effect of health education on dietary behavior: The Stanford Three Community Study. *American Journal of Clinical Nutrition, 34*, 2030-2038.

Gillum, R. F. (1978). Community surveillance for cardiovascular disease: Methods, problems, applications—A review. *Journal of Chronic Diseases, 311*, 87-94.

Kotler, P., & Levy, S. J. (1983). Broadening the concept of marketing. In P. Kotler, O. C. Ferrel, & C. Lamb (Eds.), *Cases and readings for marketing for nonprofit organizations* (pp. 3-40). Englewood Cliffs, NJ: Prentice-Hall.

Maccoby, N. (1980). Promoting positive health behaviors in adults. In L. A. Bond & J. C. Rosen (Eds.), *Competence and coping during adulthood.* Hanover, NH: University Press of New England.

Maccoby, N., Farquhar, J. W., Wood, P. F., & Alexander, J. K. (1977). Reducing the risk of cardiovascular disease: Effects of a community-based campaign on knowledge and behavior. *Journal of Community Health, 3*, 100-114.

McCarthy, E. J. (1968). *Basic marketing: A management approach* (3rd ed.). Homewood, IL: Irwin.

McCombs, M. E., & Shaw, D. L. (1972). The agenda setting function of mass media. *Public Opinion Quarterly, 36*, 176-187.

McGuire, W. J. (1969). The nature of attitudes and attitude change. In G. Lindsey & E. Aronson (Eds.), *The handbook of social psychology* (2nd ed., Vol. 3). Reading, MA: Addison-Wesley.

Mendelsohn, H. (1973). Some reasons why information campaigns can succeed. *Public Opinion Quarterly, 37*, 50-61.

Meyer, A. J., Maccoby, N., & Farquhar, J. W. (1977). The role of opinion leadership and the diffusion of innovations in a cardiovascular health education campaign. In D. Nimmo (Ed.), *Communication yearbook I.* New Brunswick, NJ: Transaction Books.

National Heart, Lung, and Blood Institute. (1985). *NHLBI fact book.* Washington, DC: U.S. Department of Health and Human Services.

Ray, M. L., Sawyer, A. G., Rothschild, M. L., Heeler, R. M., Strong, E. C., & Reed, J. B. (1973). Marketing communication and the hierarchy of effects. In P. Clarke (Ed.), *New models for mass communication research.* Beverly Hills, CA: Sage.

Robertson, T. L., Kato, H., Rhoads, G. G. et al. (1977). Epidemiologic studies of coronary heart disease and stroke in Japanese men living in Japan, Hawaii, and California: Incidence of myocardial infarction and death from coronary heart disease. *American Journal of Cardiology, 39,* 239-243.

Rogers, E. M., & Shoemaker, F. F. (1971). *Communication of innovations: A cross-cultural approach.* New York: Free Press.

Rothman, J. (1979). Three models of community organization practice, their mixing and phasing. In F. M. Cox, J. L. Erlich, J. Rothman et al. (Eds.), *Strategies of community organization* (3rd ed., pp. 25-44). Chicago: Peacock.

Shaw, D. L., & McCombs, M. E. (1977). *The emergence of American political issues.* St. Paul, MN: West.

Sheatsley, P. B., & Feldman, J. J. (1965). A national survey on public reactions and behavior. In B. S. Greenberg & R. B. Parker (Eds.), *The Kennedy assassination and the American public* (pp. 149-177). Stanford, CA: Stanford University Press.

Stern, M. P., Farquhar, J. W., Maccoby, N., & Russell, S. H. (1976). Results of a two-year health education campaign on dietary behavior: The Stanford Three Community Study. *Circulation, 54,* 826-833.

Truett, J., Cornfield, J., & Kannel, W. (1967). A multivariate analysis of the risk of coronary heart disease in Framingham. *Journal of Chronic Diseases, 20,* 511-524

U.S. Department of Health, Education and Welfare (1974). *Lipid Research Clinics manual of laboratory operations: Vol. 1. Lipid and lipoprotein analysis* (DHEW Pub. No. NIH-75-628). Washington, DC: U.S. Government Printing Office.

9

The Value Dimension in Studies of Health Promotion

ROBERT M. KAPLAN

Health promotion efforts have become a major force in American health care. Health promotion is the effort to ensure a healthier population through disease prevention and the promotion of healthy lifestyles. To help promote health, many new providers have entered the health care system. The focus of this chapter is on the rapid development of the new health care specialty. Several themes are considered, including the definition of health, the definition of health promotion, and assumptions relevant to the provision of health promotion. These assumptions include the strength of epidemiologic evidence supporting current interventions and the probability that health promotion interventions will alter health outcomes.

I became interested in health status measurement when I moved to the University of California, San Diego, nearly 15 years ago. At that time, a group of investigators headed by J. W. Bush, a physician, began to explore the multidimensional nature of health status. Over the years, we expanded our investigations from basic methodologic studies to applications in policy analysis, clinical trials, and program evaluation. In 1981, I received a Research Career Development Award from the National Institutes of Health, allowing me a five-year leave from teaching in order to develop new lines of research. I spent much of the first two years attending the basic science courses in medical school, and I then became intensely interested in epidemiologic methods and findings. Epidemiology is the basic science that focuses on the distribution and determinants of disease. Many of the methods used by epidemiologists are similar to those used in applied social psychology. On the basis of my studies, I began thinking more about the rationale that underlies many health promotion interventions. Health outcomes, like many behavioral variables, are probabilistically determined, and risk factors are related to health outcomes by probabilistic models. Some of these associations between risks and outcomes are strong and others are weak, yet we have come to think of risks in all-or-none terms. These interests are the basis for most of my current work, which focuses on the quantification of health risks and the relationship of these risks to health outcomes.

Any evaluation of health promotion necessarily depends on the definition of health outcome. Thus it is appropriate to begin with the outcome variable—the definition of health status.

Health Status

The conceptualization and measurement of health are rarely discussed in the health promotion literature. Yet, there is an extensive literature on health outcome measurement that is represented in several published volumes and specialty journals. The National Center for Health Statistics even has a well-established Clearinghouse on Health Status Indexes, which has provided regular summaries of recent advances over the course of the last 15 years.

Health status is the only reasonable focal point for clinical health promotion activities. All participants in the health care system have the goal of making people live longer and improving the quality of life in the years prior to death. These concepts are operationalized in several measures (Bergner, Bobbitt, & Pollard, 1976; Bush, Chen, & Patrick, 1973; Kaplan, Bush, & Berry, 1976, 1978; Kaplan, 1985c, 1986). Many variables often studied by health educators are important primarily in relation to health status. For example, stress is important because it may affect health. Similarly, lack of exercise, cigarette smoking, high-sodium diets, and red meat consumption have been shown to be risk factors for poor health outcomes. However, risk factors should not be confused with the outcomes. The importance of risk factors is that they have probabilistic relationships to undesirable events. However, illnesses, such as heart disease, are far from being perfectly predicted as a result of known risk factors. This is illustrated rather dramatically in the pooling project, a major effort that pools results from six large prospective studies on the prediction of heart disease. Within a 10-year period, only about 10% of men with two or more risk factors developed coronary heart disease; fully 90% of men who had two or more risk factors did not develop problems. Of those who developed heart disease, 58% had only one risk factor or no risk factors at all (Inter-Society Commission for Heart Disease Resources, 1970). Thus risk factors provide probabilistic information that accounts for only a limited proportion of the variance in predicting health outcomes.

Risk factors are often assessed by measuring blood chemistry or blood pressure. The trend toward focusing on these risk factors is important to evaluate. Several papers published in the health promotion literature emphasize that blood triglycerides can be moderately changed by dietary interventions. Yet, with the exception of extremely high triglyceride values, triglycerides are uncorrelated with health outcomes (Luepker, 1985). In other words, we may be successfully modifying a component of blood chemistry that is not ordinarily related to health outcomes. Also, there has been disparagement of behavioral and functional outcomes by some behavioral scientists, but I have argued that it is actually the functional outcomes, including death, that should be the major focus. These outcomes have become commonly used in major clinical trials evaluating new pharmaceutical products (Bombardier et al., 1986) as well as in major medical studies and health surveys (Kaplan, in press).

Many different indicators have been used as general health outcome measures (Kaplan, 1985c; Stewart, Ware, Brook, & Davies-Avery, 1978; Torrance, 1976). The most useful ones are those capable of combining mortality and morbidity. Morbidity (illness) can best be addressed through its effects on quality of life (Kaplan & Anderson, 1987). Comprehensive measures should combine different types of morbidity so that benefits and consequences can be assessed simultaneously (Sullivan, 1966). As Mosteller noted in his presidential address to the American Association for the Advancement of Science, death rates (mortality) are too crude to measure the efficacy of surgery because many surgical benefits are aimed at improving the quality of life. These quality-of-life effects should also be quantified. Surgery also poses risks to health that are reflected in quality of life and in mortality. Several measures have been proposed to provide comprehensive summaries of treatment benefits and side effects upon mortality, morbidity, and the quality of life (Mosteller, 1981).

Once health status is defined, we can progress to examining its mediators. Mediators of health status include cognitive and social variables, such as coping and social support, environmental factors, such as pollution, noise, and exposure (Cohen, Evans, Krantz, & Stokols, 1980), and aspects of the immune system (Biondi & Pancheri, 1985). In addition, disease states may be conceptualized as mediators of health status. Diseases are important because they affect the quality of life and mortality. Heart disease, for example, is a concern because it affects current quality of life and the probability that future quality of life will be affected or premature death will occur. If heart disease had no effect on quality or duration of life, it would be of little concern.

There may be considerable variability in the way the same disease affects functioning or quality of life. For many chronic diseases, there is no medical or surgical cure, and the major function of health care is to improve or maintain functioning (often through alleviating symptoms). A remedy for a disease would be of little value if remediating the disease did not improve quality of life or change the probability that quality of life would be affected in the future.

In summary, extending life duration and improving life quality in years prior to death are the two most important objectives of health care. If this premise is accepted, the next major challenge is to quantify these constructs.

Values in Health Outcome

Over the course of the last decade, our group has attempted to quantify health outcome. Our approach is to express the benefits of medical care, behavioral interventions, or preventive programs in terms of well-years. Well-years, or as they are sometimes called, Quality Adjusted Life Years (QALYs), integrate morbidity and mortality to express health status in terms of equivalents of well-years of life. For example, if a cigarette smoker died of heart disease at age 50, and we would have expected him to live to age 75, it would be concluded that the disease caused him to lose 25 life-years. If 100 cigarette smokers died at age 50 (and also had life expectancies of 75 years), we might conclude that 2,500 life-years (100 people X 25 years) had been lost. Yet, death is not the only outcome of concern in heart disease. Many adults suffer myocardial infarctions that leave them somewhat disabled over a longer period of time. Although they are still alive, the quality of their lives has diminished. Our model permits various degrees of disability to be compared to one another. A disease that reduces the quality of life by one-half will subtract .5 well-years over the course of one year. If it affects two people, it will subtract 1.0 well-years (= 2 X .5) over a one-year period. A medical treatment that improves quality of life by .2 for each of five individuals will result in a production of one well-year if the benefit is maintained over a one-year period. Using this system, it is possible to express the benefits of various programs by showing how many equivalents of well-years they produce.

An important consideration is that not all health programs have equivalent costs. In periods of scarce resources, it is necessary to find the most efficient use of limited funds. Our approach provides a framework within which to make policy decisions that require selection between competing alternatives. Preventive services may compete with traditional medical services for the scarce health care dollar, and we believe preventive services can be competitive in such analyses. Performing such comparisons requires the use of a General Health Policy Model, which we have described in several publications (Kaplan & Bush, 1982; Kaplan, 1985a, 1985b; Kaplan, Atkins, & Timms, 1984; Kaplan & Anderson, 1987).

The details of the General Health Policy Model are beyond the scope of the present chapter. Suffice it to say that the model contains three components. First, individuals are classified according to their ability to function on scales of mobility (e.g., able to travel around the community, or limited to house, bed, or hospital), physical activity (e.g., walking with various degrees of limitation), and social activity (e.g., ability to perform social roles and self-care). These are objective, observable health states. The observable health states are then weighted by preferences or utilities, which represent the perceived desirability of the various states. This preference, or value, component is discussed in more detail in this chapter. The third component is prognosis, or the expected duration of an individual's stay in each observable state.

Table 9.1 gives a simple example of the concept of well-years. Suppose that a group of individuals was in a well state for 65.2 years, in a state of nonbed disability for 4.5 years, and in a state of bed disability for 1.9 years before their deaths at the average age of 71.6 calendar years. In order to make adjustments for the diminished quality of life they suffered in the disability states, the duration of stay in each state (Y_k) is multiplied by the preference associated with the state (W_k). For instance, the 4.5 years of nonbed disability become 2.7 equivalents of well-years when we adjust for the preferences associated with inhabiting that state. Overall, the well-life expectancy for this group is 68.5 years. In other words, their disability has reduced the quality of their lives by an estimated 3.1 years.

The preference weighting of the observable health states is crucial to this system. In order to obtain these weights, sample case descriptions were created, using factorial designs that varied mobility, physical activity, social activity, symptoms, and age. Using concepts from Anderson's (1981) functional measurement methodology, we obtained preferences that, we believe, represent an interval response scale (Kaplan, 1982; Kaplan, Bush, & Berry, 1979). In addition, a model representing these preferences has been cross-validated for other case descriptions and has been shown to be stable over a one-year period (Kaplan & Anderson, 1987). Using this standardized set of weights, obtained from a random sample of the population, we can begin to make comprehensive evaluations of health programs.

Examples from Medical Care

We conceptualize health interventions, including health promotion, as a series of trade-offs between risks and benefits. Most often, the risks and benefits are quantified in completely different units. Therefore, benefits of treatment are often emphasized, while the side effects may be discounted because they are conceptualized differently. It is instructive to consider two examples representing medical approaches to prevention.

The first case involves insulin-dependent diabetes mellitus. Patients with this condition are at increased risk for complications in a variety of organ systems because of persistent unregulated blood sugar. In insulin-dependent diabetes, cells in the pancreas fail to produce insulin, a hormone essential for carbohydrate metabolism. Without supplemental injections of insulin, life expectancy is less than two years. Correlational evidence suggests that the degree of high blood sugar is associated with the long-term risks of diabetic complications (Tchobroutsky, 1978). The most common serious complication of diabetes is retinopathy, or pathology of the retina. It has been suggested that very aggressive medical management of high blood sugar may result in a reduction of such complications (Job, Eschwege,

Table 9.1
Illustrative Computation of the Well-Life Expectancy

State	k	Y_k	W_k	$W_k Y_k$
Well	A	65.2	1.00	65.2
Nonbed disability	B	4.5	.59	2.7
Bed disability	C	1.9	.34	.6
Current life expectancy................. 71.6 life-years				
Well-life expectancy .... 68.5 well-years				

Source: Kaplan & Bush (1982)

Guyot-Argenton, Audry, & Tchobroutsky, 1976), but other studies fail to find these benefits (Ballugooie et al., 1984). For the sake of argument, let us assume that the probability a diabetic patient will develop retinopathy over the course of 25 years is approximately .5. In other words, approximately half of the people will develop some vision disturbances some years into the future. Aggressive treatment of diabetes might reduce this probability to .35. Often not discussed, however, is that the aggressive treatment might have negative consequences. For example, clinical studies suggest that half of the patients undergoing aggressive treatment experience symptoms of shakiness, sweating, or upset stomachs on half of the days. Consequently, the question is: What would patients be willing to trade for a reduction of 15% in the probability they would develop a vision disturbance within 25 years? Would they be willing to experience minor symptoms on half of the days starting immediately? There is no simple answer to this question, although we are currently trying to analyze it formally. The point, however, is that the ultimate evaluation is heavily dependent on values or preferences for different objectively measured levels of health status.

A similar issue concerns the treatment of high blood pressure. Substantial epidemiologic evidence suggests that elevated blood pressure is a significant risk factor for heart disease and stroke (Dawber, 1980). In addition, clinical trials, such as the Hypertension Detection and Follow-up Program (1979) reveal that reduction of blood pressure results in reduced risks of poor health outcomes. However, many people are unaware that they have high blood pressure, and many of those who are aware of it are unwilling to take the necessary actions to control the condition. One reason for lack of awareness is that high blood pressure is often unaccompanied by symptoms. Furthermore, initiation of treatment may cause symptoms that did not exist before, including headache, fatigue, depression, and, in males, impotence. The task of analysis is to consider the health benefits of treatment minus its negative health consequences. This again involves weighting of these benefits and side effects by both their probabilities and their desirabilities. After careful analysis, Weinstein and Stason (1976) demonstrated that the benefits of treatment outweigh the side effects and that programs to screen and treat high blood pressure were very effective relative to their cost. All things considered, this analysis suggests a greater value for the potential benefit of blood pressure reduction than for the offsetting potential consequences and side effects of treatment. Further, the costs associated with this net benefit are lower than those required to achieve the same effect through other programs.

Examples from Health Promotion

Our group believes that a general conceptualization of health status may help direct future efforts in medical care and health promotion. All providers in the health care system have the common objectives of making life longer and making life better. Surgery produces well-years of life either by extending life duration or by improving functioning in years prior to death. Similarly, health promotion is designed to prevent early death or to improve quality of life. Some treatments, such as surgery, might produce a large benefit for a small number of people. Conversely, programs in health promotion may produce a small benefit for a large number of people. Considering the comparative cost to produce a well-year of life may help guide public policy in this arena.

Not all efforts in health promotion have the same potential. In the following sections, examples that have shaped our thinking are described. In some areas, such as smoking prevention, the health benefits are substantial. In other areas, such as heart disease prevention, the benefits are a matter of some debate. In still other areas, such as exercise programs in the worksite, the evidence may be totally lacking. Each of these three efforts toward health promotion is discussed in turn below.

Smoking Prevention

Cigarette smoking may cause as many as 485,000 deaths per year in the United States from cancer, heart disease, and other maladies (Ravenholt,

1985). In addition, cigarette smoking is a major cause of disability. For example, smoking is the major risk factor for chronic obstructive pulmonary disease (National Institutes of Health, 1979). These diseases, which include emphysema, asthma, and chronic bronchitis, are, together, the fifth leading cause of death in the United States and account for approximately 34 days of restricted activity per 100 persons per year (Brashear, 1980). Recent reports suggest that well over a million potential years of life are lost to chronic lung diseases each year in the United States (Kaplan, Reis, & Atkins, 1985).

Smoking is a prevalent habit in the United States. It is estimated that 34.8% of males older than 20 years smoke cigarettes. Although this is a decrease from 52.1% in 1965, cigarette smoking is still the major potentially modifiable behavior associated with a variety of serious health outcomes. In addition, cigarette smoking among minority groups is not declining (National Center for Health Statistics, 1983). Cigarette use among women peaked in 1965 and has declined only slightly since then. The 1983 data show that approximately 30% of adult women use cigarettes. Cigarette smoking during pregnancy has significant adverse effects upon unborn children. Epidemiologic data suggest that cigarette use may be related to spontaneous abortion, premature birth, and death of infants during the first days of life (U.S. Department of Health, Education, and Welfare, 1979).

Although there is some debate (Flay, 1987), there is reasonably satisfactory evidence that social-psychologically based programs emphasizing peer resistance can substantially reduce the chances that adolescents will develop the smoking habit (Killen, 1985). By a variety of different calculations, it is clear that these programs may produce a substantial number of well-years at a relatively low cost.

A wide variety of smoking cessation methods have been evaluated (Schwartz, 1987). These approaches range from self-help, to nicotine chewing gum, to complex behavior modification programs. Recent trends suggest that a variety of interventions may be successful. Physician-assisted interventions may be particularly helpful. In addition, behavioral intervention techniques using nicotine fading and smoke holding have produced some encouraging results. However, after reviewing literally hundreds of studies, Schwartz (1987) suggested that the most important trend is the developing negative attitude toward tobacco products.

Smoking cessation programs are designed to produce health benefits. Ultimately, smoking-prevention programs and smoking-cessation programs should be evaluated in terms of the well-years or quality adjusted life years that they produce. Then, interventions designed to prevent or decrease smoking can be compared directly to other interventions in health care.

Heart Disease Prevention Through Dietary Change

In previous papers and comments, I have critically reviewed the assumptions underlying health promotion for the prevention of heart disease (Kaplan, 1984, 1985a, 1986). Most health promotion efforts are based on a series of assumptions. The first assumption is that behavior is a risk factor for serious illness. This assumption has considerable support, as suggested in Table 9.2. The table describes behaviors that have been identified in epidemiologic studies as relevant to the five most common causes of death.

In efforts directed toward the prevention of heart disease, the major focus has been on serum cholesterol. Studies have consistently shown that serum cholesterol concentrations predict a small but significant percentage of the mortality from coronary heart disease. For example, Stamler, Wentworth, and Neaton (1986) recently summarized mortality data from over 350,000 men whose cholesterol had been measured some years earlier. These analyses confirmed earlier reports indicating a systematic relationship between serum cholesterol and mortality from heart disease.

Food may contain cholesterol and saturated fat. Early studies by Keys and Anderson (1955) revealed that dietary cholesterol was not associated with serum cholesterol, but that "luxury" diets containing a high percentage of calories from animal fat increased the risk of death from heart disease. The health promotion literature, as well as popular literature and product advertisements, all emphasize the link between diet and detrimental health outcomes. However, the direct relationship between dietary factors and serum cholesterol has been unclear. Some studies (Keys & Anderson, 1955) have shown that the mean serum cholesterol level is higher in countries where, on the average, high levels of fat are consumed than it is in countries where lower levels of fat are consumed. Yet, correlational studies within each of these cultures fail to show significant associations between cholesterol consumption and serum cholesterol. Most variability in serum cholesterol is unrelated to diet because most cholesterol is produced endogenously (Steinberg, 1979).

One of the most interesting analyses of the diet / heart disease relationship

Table 9.2
Top Five Causes of Death, Life-Years Lost, and Associated Behavioral Variables

Rank as Cause of Death	Cause [a]	1985 Cause— Specific Mortality (rate/100,000) [b]	Years of Potential Life Lost [b, c]	Behavioral Correlates	Reference
1	diseases of the heart	325.0	1,600,265	smoking, high-fat diet, sedentary lifestyle	Anderson, Castelli, & Levy (1987)
2	malignant neoplasms	191.7	1,813,245	smoking, high-fat/low-fiber diet	Willett & MacMahon (1984)
3	cerebrovascular disease	64.0	253,044	smoking, high-fat diet, high-sodium diet	Dawber (1980)
4	unintentional injuries	38.6	2,235,064	alcohol use, failure to use seatbelts	Sleet (1987)
5	chronic obstructive pulmonary disease	31.2	129,815	smoking	Kaplan, Reis, & Atkins (1985)

a. According to the ICD ninth revision codes.
b. Data from *Mortality and Morbidity Weekly Report*, 36(15), Table V, April 24, 1987, p. 235.
c. Based on assumed 65-year life expectancy; excludes death prior to 1 year of age.

217

was performed by Stallones (1983). Using data from six prospective American epidemiologic studies and one British study, Stallones compared those who eventually died of heart disease with those who did not die of heart disease. Within each of these populations, those who developed heart disease did not consume more calories, more fat, or more cholesterol than did those who remained well (see Figure 9.1). In fact, small (but nonsignificant) differences in the opposite direction were observed for dietary cholesterol.

The failure to find an association between dietary habits and serum cholesterol has been frustrating. There is evidence from metabolic wards that serum cholesterol can be manipulated through diet. Yet, we have essentially no evidence from free-living populations that dietary habits make a difference. Jacobs, Anderson, and Blackburn (1979) explain this difference away because of measurement error in the assessment of dietary habits. They argue that attenuation caused by this measurement error obscures a potentially true correlation. However, this possible explanation for a nonsignificant correlation does not mean that a significant correlation does indeed exist.

A second assumption in health promotion efforts is that risk reduction will result in disease reduction. If certain behaviors and poor habits cause disease, then modified risk-related behaviors should reduce the incidence of the disease. This assumption has now been evaluated in several experiments, but evidence for it is inconclusive. At least nine prospective studies relevant to reducing the risk of heart disease through cholesterol reduction have been reported in the literature. These studies are summarized in Table 9.3. Positive results were obtained in studies of the New York anticoronary club (Christakis et al., 1966), a Norwegian sample of volunteers (Leren, 1966), a group of VA patients in Los Angeles (Dayton & Pearce, 1964), and groups of Finnish mental patients (Miettinen, Turnpeinen, Elosuo, Paavilainen, & Karvonen, 1972). The most convincing evidence for dietary effects was obtained in a study of 1,200 Norwegian men, half assigned to a special intervention focusing on dietary change and smoking control (Hjermann, Byre, Holme, & Leren, 1981). Men in these special treatments had significantly lower rates of death from coronary disease in comparison to men assigned to a control group. All five of these studies suggest that dietary or behavior changes may result in reductions of deaths from heart disease. However, in each of these studies there was an unexpected finding for total deaths: Mortality averaged over all causes was not affected by the experimental dietary interventions. Reductions in deaths from heart disease were associated with increases in deaths from other causes, in most cases cancer.

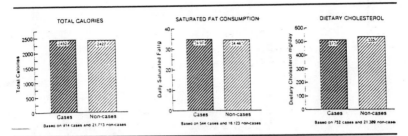

Figure 9.1 Differences in consumption of total calories, saturated fat, and dietary cholesterol for adults who did or did not die of heart disease in seven major epidemiologic studies. Source: Kaplan (1985a).

Four of the studies summarized in Table 9.3 failed to find significant benefits of the dietary interventions. For example, the Multiple Risk Factors Intervention Trial (MRFIT) compared groups given or not given counseling to reduce a variety of coronary risk factors. Although the experimental group showed some modest reduction in risk scores, so did the control group (Multiple Risk Factors Intervention Trial Research Group, 1982). Upon long-term follow-up, heart disease mortality in the two groups did not differ significantly. Because of the inconsistent picture that emerged from the studies, the National Heart, Lung, and Blood Institute decided to conduct the long-term Coronary Primary Prevention Trial, which was completed in 1984 (Lipid Research Clinic's Program, 1984a, 1984b). This randomized experimental trial assigned high-risk men to either a placebo or cholestyramine, a drug that is known to reduce serum cholesterol levels significantly. Long-term follow-up was conducted over a 10-year period to determine differential mortalities from heart disease in the two groups. Cholestyramine was successful in lowering cholesterol by an average of 8.5% in the treatment group. Those in the treatment group experienced 24% fewer heart disease deaths and 19% fewer heart attacks than did the placebo group. As in other studies, differences between the groups in total mortality were not statistically significant.

Although the results of the Coronary Primary Prevention Trial are very impressive, it is important to consider them in light of most health promotion efforts. Upon publication of the trial results, many magazines and newspapers attributed the results to diet. In fact, the program did not use diet to control cholesterol levels, because both treatment and placebo groups received the same diet. In the planning stages of the trial, diet, rather than medicine, had been considered as the intervention, but preliminary analyses failed to reveal the expected effect of diet. Plans for the diet trial

Table 9.3
Summary of Selected Experimental Trials on Risk Reduction Through Cholesterol Change

Study	Sample	Intervention	Duration (years)	Outcome	Comment
New York anti-coronary club (Christakis et al., 1966)	814 diet	prudent diet	5	decrease in CHD	control group not randomly assigned
Oslo I (Leren, 1966)	206 diet, 206 control (post-MI)	diet high in polyunsaturated fat	5	decrease in MI, decrease in CHD, NS trend for CHD mortality	
Los Angeles VA (Dayton & Pearce, 1964)	424 diet, 422 control	diet low in saturated fat	8	reduction in ischemic heart disease	subjects very old at entry (66 years)
Finnish mental hospital (Miettinen et al., 1972)	10,612 in cross-over design	diet low in saturated fat and high in polyunsaturated fat	6	trend toward reduction in CHD	effect only apparent in some subgroups
Oslo II (Hjermann et al., 1981)	604 special intervention, 628 control	smoking control and diet high in polyunsaturated fat	5	reduction in MI and sudden death	best evidence for dietary effects
Coronary Primary Prevention Trial (CPPT) (Lipid Research Clinic's Program, 1984a, b)	1,906 drug group, 1,900 placebo group (high-risk)	cholestyramine resin	10	decrease in MI, decrease in CHD mortality	best evidence for effects of cholesterol lowering
Medical Research Council (1975)	199 diet, 194 control (post-MI)	diet and soy oil	2-7	no effect	
Coronary Drug Project (1970)	1,103 clofibrate, 1,119 niacin, 2,789 placebo (post-MI)	clofibrate or niacin	5	no effect for either drug	possible toxic effect of clofibrate
Multiple Risk Factors Intervention Trial (MRFIT) (1982)	special intervention, usual care (high-risk)	counseling for several CHD risk factors and antihypertensive medication	8	no effect	possible toxic side effect of antihypertensive medication for men with ECG abnormalities

NOTE: MI—myocardial infarction; CHD—coronary heart disease; NS—nonsignificant
SOURCE: Kaplan (1985a).

had to be discontinued because the required sample size would have required resources even beyond the $150 million used for the trial.

Most health promotion efforts are directed toward those who are currently well. The CPPT included only those above the 95th percentile in serum cholesterol. The results tell us very little about benefits of diet or cholestyramine for those who do not already have significantly elevated cholesterol. Even for those at high risk, the results may be difficult to understand. Although there was a 24% reduction in mortality in the treated group, the actual percentage of patients who died was similar in the two groups. In the placebo group, there were 38 deaths among 1,900 participants (2%). In the cholestyramine group, there were 30 deaths among 1,906 participants (1.6%). Cholestyramine costs about $150 per month (Kolata, 1984). It is a grainy substance with an unpleasant taste that is taken with liquid several times each day. Those with high cholesterol levels must ask themselves whether they would be willing to pay $150 each month over the course of 7-10 years for an unpleasant medication that would reduce their chances of dying from heart disease from 2% to 1.6%. Even with a sample size of over 3,800, this difference was not statistically significant using a two-tailed test. More importantly, it must be reemphasized that this difference was the probability of dying from heart disease. There was no difference whatsoever in total deaths: 3.7% of those in the placebo group died while 3.6% in the cholestyramine group died. The successful intervention in this study and in other studies showed changes only in the *cause* of death. It seems rather unsatisfactory to leave life-expectancy unaffected while influencing only the reason listed on a death certificate.

Another, perhaps naive, assumption made by health promotion specialists is that behavior is easily changed. As noted in an earlier review (Kaplan, 1984), longstanding health behaviors are often very resistant to modification. Weight loss, for example, is produced by many programs in the short-run. However, those few studies including longer-term follow-up rarely demonstrate lasting benefits (Foreyt et al., 1982). Lasting dietary modification, attributed exclusively to intervention, has also been difficult to document (Jeffery, 1987).

Exercise

It is widely believed that regular exercise may prevent coronary heart disease. However, the epidemiologic literature does not clearly confirm or disconfirm this belief. Studies of San Francisco longshoremen (Paffen-barger & Hale, 1975), British civil servants (Morris, Pollard, Everitt, & Chave, 1980), and Harvard alumni (Paffenbarger, Wing, Hyde, & Jung, 1983) have all demonstrated that men who engage in vigorous physical activity over the course of years experience lower rates of heart disease mortality and morbidity than do men who are habitually less active. However, none of these studies involved random assignment of men to various activity levels. Thus it is not clear whether the results reflect "selection" or "protection." In other words, it may be that healthier men prefer to be more physically active rather than that physical activity protects health. Advocacy of exercise also implies that its protective effects relevant to heart disease are not offset by damaging effects that are reflected in other diseases (Paffenbarger, Hyde, Wing, & Hirsh, 1986). Whether or not significant side effects are associated with exercise has not been clearly established.

The study of Harvard alumni has been particularly influential because recent data demonstrate that exercise is associated with lower death rates from all causes—not only heart disease (Paffenbarger, Hyde, Wing, & Hirsh, 1986). On the other hand, a Seattle study of men and women suggested that the rate of heart attack during exercise is significantly higher than the rate for sedentary people during the same length of time, though the same study demonstrated that the protective effects of exercise outweigh the risks of having a heart attack during an exercise session (Siscovick, Weiss, Fletcher, & Lasky, 1984). Van Camp and Peterson (1986) reported that serious complications in supervised exercise programs for heart disease patients are rare. They observed only one fatality per 750,000 patient hours of supervised exercise and about nine cardiac arrests per million patient hours of exercise. These outcomes are not greatly different than would be expected without exercise for patients in this age group.

Although exercise may not cause heart attacks, various studies have suggested that regular exercise is associated with muscle strains, cramps, torn ligaments, and blisters. Among the over 2,000 entrants to the London Marathon, it was noted that 26 participants were sent to the hospital and four remained under care overnight (Nicholl & Williams, 1983). A follow-up study of participants in an Atlanta recreational run revealed that during the year following the race more than one-third of these regular runners suffered some temporary setback because of an injury. In all, 15% had consulted a doctor about their injuries, and a remarkable 7% had had collisions with bicycles or cars or were bitten by dogs (Koplan, Powell,

Sikes, Shirley, & Campbell, 1982). In summary, neither the risks nor the benefits of exercise have been fully or clearly documented.

In her analysis of exercise, Russell (1986) questions whether the costs of exercise programs have been thoroughly considered. For example, adults beginning an exercise program accrue a variety of expenses, including medical expenses. The American Heart Association (1972) recommended that a physician thoroughly evaluate adults considering an exercise program. In England, where the existence of socialized medicine may influence such policies, the Royal College of Physicians (1983) suggested that most people do not need a medical exam before starting an exercise program. Instead, they recommended that people begin their programs slowly and seek medical advice if they have unexpected symptoms.

Worksite health promotion programs have also gained considerable attention. However, Russell (1986) suggests that the costs of these programs are often not well estimated. A company may need to pay for training facilities, exercise supervisors, locker rooms, and so on. The exercisers may need to spend money on running shoes, extra soap and water for additional showers, additional medical evaluations, medical costs for the care of injuries, and other expenses. Given data currently available, Russell was unable to estimate either the costs or benefits of an exercise program.

In considering an exercise program, we must recognize that benefits come at a cost. The value we place on time, and the trade-off of the benefits of fitness and the pain of activity must be considered. In order to evaluate health programs thoroughly, we should estimate their costs, risks, and benefits. In this section, some of the difficulties in estimating the costs and benefits of health promotion have been considered. The next section discusses the possibility that health promotion may create risks.

Can Health Promotion Be Dangerous?

In the preceding examples, we have considered situations in which health promotion efforts are highly likely to produce health status benefits (cigarette smoking), are possibly linked to health status benefits (heart disease prevention), and are unknown (exercise). It is also possible that some health promotion efforts distract from real medical concerns or may even promote behaviors that are damaging. Two examples are considered below. One focuses on the growth consequences of dietary fat restriction and the other on carcinogenic effects of toxic wastes and foods.

Growth Consequences of Dietary Fat Restriction

There are probably few risks associated with dietary fat restriction. In fact, consumption of a prudent diet is recommended by virtually all groups that have studied it. Yet, some people assume that if reduction in dietary fat is good, then complete elimination is better. Some groups have gone toward the extremes in cholesterol and fat deprivation. For example, "vegans" are people who follow a vegetarian diet characterized by the Zen macrobiotic regimen. This diet completely eliminates animal products (Dwyer, Dietz, Andrews, & Suskind, 1982).

Cholesterol is essential for life. Since it serves as the basis for many other hormones, a debate has developed as to whether there should be fat and cholesterol restriction for children. Some evidence suggests that cholesterol plaque in blood vessels begins to develop in childhood, and therefore, intervention should occur early in life. On the other hand, there has been concern about the side effects of fat and cholesterol reduction for children. As a result, some pediatricians (Barness, 1986) suggest that restriction of dietary cholesterol is not warranted for children at this time. The American Academy of Pediatrics Committee on Nutrition (1986), upon review of the question, ultimately advocated a prudent diet, but concluded that the major dietary variations recommended for adults should not be prescribed for children.

This is clearly a very complex issue. Berwick, Cretin, and Keeler (1980) thoroughly reviewed the issue and concluded that dietary modification for children would increase life-years at a relatively low cost. On the other hand, there is some concern about extreme variations in diet because during the adolescent growth years, cholesterol is metabolized rapidly. This is exemplified by a relatively simple study by Boyer and Kaplan (1978). In it, 2,074 students in the San Diego City Schools had blood samples taken as part of an epidemiologic investigation. The cross-sectional data are shown in Figure 9.2, which demonstrates that there was a very substantial reduction in serum cholesterol between the ages of 13 and 15. Then, as growth slowed, the mean serum cholesterol returned to its former dangerously high level.

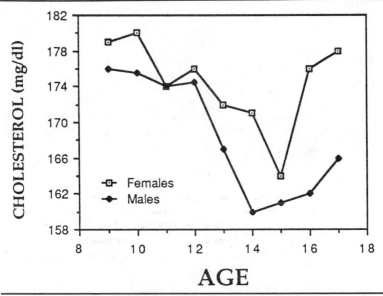

Figure 9.2 Relationship between serum cholesterol and age in San Diego adolescents.
SOURCE: Boyer & Kaplan (1978).

It is interesting to consider cultures in which there has been more restriction of dietary fats. For example, the city of Sendai in Japan has measured the heights and weights of children every spring and autumn since 1936, including during the troubled times of the Second World War. The secular trends in height and weight of sixth-grade Japanese children are shown in Figure 9.3. Their average height and weight dropped during the Second World War, but since then they have steadily risen each year through the late 1970s (Kondo, Takahashi, Kato, Takahashi, & Ikeda, 1978). Corresponding to these increases in growth are increases in the consumption of fats and proteins in the diet. The point of decrement during the Second World War also corresponds to a period in which fats were less available to Japanese.

Related evidence relevant to the growth of American children has been presented by Pugliese, Lifshitz, Grad, Fort, and Marks-Katz (1983). They studied 14 adolescents who had undergone severe caloric restriction because of their fear of obesity. These youths were not diagnosed as having anorexia nervosa, but they consumed a small percentage of the calories recommended for their age. Figure 9.4 provides an example of the growth

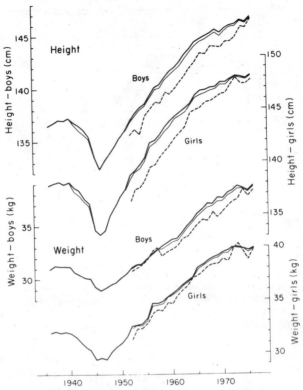

——, the old city area of Sendai; ----, the new city area of Sendai; ——, Sendai City.

Figure 9.3 Height and weight of the 6th-year grade pupils in primary schools as measured in October. SOURCE: Kondo et al. (1978).

pattern for one of these children. The figure suggests that the child was growing normally until age 9, when very restrictive dieting began. Within a few years, growth was interrupted. The arrow in the figure shows the point at age 17 when there was intervention and growth was resumed. Still, at age 18, the child was below the 5th percentile in height and weight. Other evidence suggests that diet believed to reduce the risk of heart disease for adults may result in decreased linear growth for children. This has led some

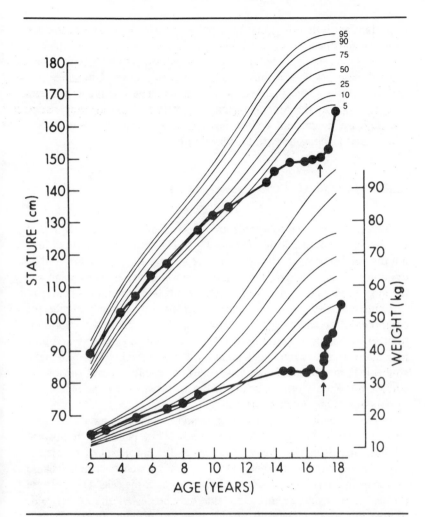

Figure 9.4 Growth description with severe dietary restriction. The scales represent percentile standards for height and weight, while the plotted values are for the clinical case.
SOURCE: Pugliese et al. (1983).

investigators to suggest that parental misconceptions and health beliefs concerning diet may cause failure to thrive in their children (Pugliese, Weyman-Daum, Moses, & Lifshitz, 1987).

What interpretation can we make of these data? Perhaps the most important one is that there may be a trade-off between ultimate protection from coronary heart disease and childhood growth. In other words, placing children on a very restricted diet may reduce their serum cholesterol and heart disease risk, but it may also reduce their stature. Ultimately, the choice involves social preferences and values. The middle-ground diet recommended by the American Academy of Pediatrics may not provide the ultimate protection against heart disease. However, it may also contribute to average growth for the culture.

Carcinogenic Effects of Toxic Wastes and Foods

Environmental health hazards are of major public concern. In recent California elections, both Democrats and Republicans accused one another of being weak in their stand regarding toxic polluters. Public opinion polls demonstrated that fear of carcinogens in the environment was the most important political concern for a substantial number of citizens.

Epidemiologists have been able to screen only a small number of compounds for carcinogenicity. The major problem is the enormous number of chemical compounds. Each evaluation is expensive and may take many years to complete. Ultimately, the best test involves systematic studies in human beings. Lower levels of evidence might come from animal studies, although there are many instances in which compounds cause tumors in rats but not in humans.

In recent years, molecular biologists and biochemists have developed new tests for screening many compounds. They believe in multistage models, suggesting that cancer develops as the end result of a series of genetic changes in specific cells. In the early stages, a chemical might cause problems in the copying of genetic information in the cells' DNA. These problems, or errors, are mutations that may be passed on to other cells. Simple mutations can result in alterations in proteins that ultimately produce cancer. Chemical tests are now available to screen large numbers of compounds to determine if they produce this initial stage of amino acid alteration. Ames (1983) has developed a bacterial assay that produces derived estimates of carcinogenic potency from quantitative mutagenicity observations.

Early results using the Ames Test have produced some rather surprising results. According to this work, there is substantial carcinogenic potential in many fresh foods advocated by health promotion specialists. According to Ames (1986), exposure to chemicals accounts for only a very small percentage of the total number of carcinogens we ingest. He estimates that 99.99% of all carcinogens come from natural foods and other products we voluntarily consume, including cigarettes and alcohol. He argues that man-made pesticides in our food are present in concentrations of about 100 parts per billion (ppb), and most of these residues are not carcinogenic. Yet, coffee contains natural carcinogens such as hydrogen peroxide in concentrations of about 4,000 ppb. In other words, carcinogenic exposure in coffee consumption is more than 40 times greater than that from DDT on garden crops. Cola drinks, which contain the carcinogen formaldehyde, have a concentration of about 7,900 ppb. Beer also contains formaldehyde at about 700 ppb.

Ames has also tested a wide variety of fruits and vegetables. He argues that plants contain natural pesticides that may be 10,000 times greater in concentration than man-made pesticides. These natural pesticides have been found in all plants tested, and they make up 5% to 10% of the plant's weight. These naturally occurring compounds are a natural adaptation to attacks by fungi, insects, and predators. Substantial mutagenetic potential has been identified in parsley, celery, mushrooms, and basil. Ames suggests that alfalfa sprouts, a major staple in vegetarian sandwiches, have remarkable mutagenetic potential. Animal studies confirm the carcinogenic potential for each of these substances. Ames further argues that the carcinogens found in water supplies have remarkably trivial concentrations compared to the exposure we have in ordinary food substances. Some of the most potent carcinogens identified to date, such as aflatoxin, are found in peanut butter, corn products, and apple juice.

Carcinogens are common, not rare. Yet, in the policy arena, we have focused on some while ignoring others. For instance, the compound ethylene dibromide (EDB), often found in muffins, was singled out for elimination by the Food and Drug Administration. Yet, aflatoxin found in peanut butter is 1,000 times more potent a carcinogen in rats than is EDB. The risks associated with eating a peanut butter sandwich far outweigh those of consuming a muffin severely contaminated with EDB (Ames, 1983). I must emphasize that the Ames analyses are controversial. Some reviewers distrust risk assessments altogether (Hattis & Kennedy, 1986); others contend that Ames has failed to consider the bioaccumulation of these substances (Epstein & Swartz, 1984). Yet, all observers seem to agree that the effects of various substances should be monitored and quantified.

Our General Health Policy Model can help direct us toward elimination of the most severe threats. Ames's work, and other epidemiologic studies, suggest that there are few serious carcinogenic consequences of most dietary habits (Ames, 1986, says he has no fear even of peanut butter sandwiches). Yet, not all carcinogens are of equal potency. Cigarettes have enormous potency and may cause 400,000 deaths per year. Alcohol, in pure concentration, may have concentrations of formaldehyde at 50 million ppb, or 5% of its content. Heavy alcohol use is believed to cause 100,000 deaths per year and approximately 3% of all cancers.

Health promotion efforts designed to motivate avoidance of any carcinogen may result in confusion and anxiety. As more tests are performed, more substances will be found to be carcinogenic. Yet death rates from most cancers are declining rather than increasing. Only lung cancer, which is highly correlated with cigarette use, is on the increase. Consideration of how consumption of various substances ultimately results in well-years of life could help direct our efforts toward elimination of the most potent substances and toward peaceful coexistence with others.

Conclusions

Several conclusions may be drawn from our review. First, epidemiology is a very immature science. Measurement of outcomes is crude, and most major questions remain unanswered. Epidemiology borrows its methods from the social sciences, and so there are tremendous opportunities for transferring methodological skills to this developing science.

The application of social psychology to health promotion has primarily emphasized persuasion. We have accepted information provided by other sciences and used it to persuade people to modify risky behaviors. Yet social psychologists have not always critically analyzed the validity of the messages they transmit. There is more room to contribute to deciding what information should be disseminated. It seems premature to modify children's diets, for example, when we are uncertain what diets are good for them.

A major theme in our work has been the recognition that health status includes a value or preference dimension. All health endeavors seek to either extend the duration of life or improve quality of life. To some extent, quality is a value. Maximizing life expectancy or quality of life can sometimes be complicated. Treatments that have potential benefits often have negative side effects. As yet, we understand little about the complex processes that underlie individual preferences for various courses of action. Human information processing relevant to these complex health decisions is only now beginning to be studied.

To date there have been very few attempts to compare different health promotion interventions in terms of the health benefits they produce. However, such approaches may help us understand how best to use our health care resources. One recent analysis, for example, used computer simulation techniques to estimate the benefits of lowering cholesterol, reducing blood pressure, or reducing cigarette smoking. For men, it was estimated that reducing cholesterol by 6.7%, which was the amount obtained in clinical trials of cholesterol reduction, added only about four months to the life expectancy for 20-year-old men and two months for 60-year-old men. Simulation of blood pressure reduction by 14.3% increased the anticipated life expectancy by 24 months for men in both the 20- and 60-year-old categories. In comparison, discontinuance of cigarette use would produce increases of 70 months for a 20-year-old and 32 months for a 60-year-old (Taylor, Pass, Shepard, & Komaroff, 1987). The elimination of all risk factors is theoretically desirable. However, changes in some risk factors may produce greater benefits than would changes in others.

In conclusion, I hope not to be interpreted as negative with regard to health promotion efforts. However, the actual data are quite complex and deserve continuing critical evaluation. A scientific perspective will help identify risk factors, potential mechanisms for risk reduction, and efficiency in service delivery. Considering a General Health Policy Model would help direct health promotion efforts toward the most effective and efficient use of resources.

References

American Academy of Pediatrics Committee on Nutrition. (1986). Prudent lifestyle for children: Dietary fat and cholesterol. *Pediatrics, 78,* 521-525.

American Heart Association. (1972). *Committee on exercise, exercise testing, and training of apparently healthy individuals: A handbook for physicians.* New York: Author.

Ames, B. N. (1983). Dietary carcinogens and anticarcinogens. Oxygen radicals and degenerative diseases. *Science, 221,* 1256-1264.

Ames, B. N. (1986, May 15). Cancer scares over trivia. *Los Angeles Times,* Part II, p. 7.

Anderson, K. M., Castelli, W. P., & Levy, D. (1987). Cholesterol and mortality: 30 years of follow-up from the Framingham study. *Journal of the American Medical Association,* *257,* 2176-2184.

Anderson, N. H. (1981). *Information integration theory.* New York: Academic Press.

Ballugooie, E., Hooymans, J.M.M., Timmerman, Z., Reitsma, W. D., Sluiter, W. J., Schweitzer, N., & Doorenbos, H. (1984). Rapid deterioration of diabetic retinopathy during treatment with continuous subcutaneous insulin infusion. *Diabetes Care, 7,* 236-242.

Barness, L. A. (1986). Cholesterol and children. *Journal of the American Medical Association, 256,* 2871-2872.

Bergner, N., Bobbitt, R. A., & Pollard, W. E. (1976). Sickness impact profile: Validation of a health status measure. *Medical Care, 14,* 57-61.

Berwick, D., Cretin, S., & Keeler, E. (1980). *Cholesterol, children and heart disease: An analysis of alternatives.* New York: Oxford University Press.

Biondi, M., & Pancheri, P. (1985). Stress, personality, immunity, and cancer: A challenge for psychosomatic medicine. In R. M. Kaplan & M. H. Criqui (Eds.), *Behavioral epidemiology and disease prevention* (pp. 127-142). New York: Plenum.

Blackburn, H. (1983). Diet and atherosclerosis. Epidemiologic evidence and public health implications. *Preventive Medicine, 12,* 2.

Bombardier, C., Ware, J., Russell, I. J., Larson, M., Chalmers, A., & Read, J. L. (1986). Auranofic therapy in quality of life for patients with rheumatoid arthritis: Results of a multi-center trial. *American Journal of Medicine, 81,* 565-578.

Boyer, J., & Kaplan, R. M. (1978). *Coronary risk factors: Early detection in a school population.* Unpublished manuscript, San Diego.

Brashear, R. E. (1980). Chronic obstructive pulmonary disease. In D. H. Simmons (Ed.), *Current pulmonology* (Vol. 2, pp. 1-39). Boston: Houghton-Mifflin.

Bush, J. W., Chen, M. M., & Patrick, D. L. (1973). A cost-effectiveness analysis using a health status index: Analysis of the New York State PKU screening program. In R. Berg (Ed.), *Health status indexes* (pp. 172-208). Chicago: Hospital Research and Educational Trust.

Cambien, F., Ducimetiere, P., & Richard, J. (1980). Total serum cholesterol and cancer mortality in a middle-age male population. *American Journal of Epidemiology, 112,* 388-394.

Christakis, G., Ringles, S. H., Archer, M., Winslow, G., Jampel, S., Stevenson, J., Friedman, G., Fein, H., Kraus, A., & James, G. (1966). The anti-coronary club: A dietary approach to the prevention of coronary heart disease. A seven year report. *American Journal of Public Health, 56,* 299-314.

Cohen, S., Evans, G. W., Krantz, D. S., & Stokols, D. (1980). Physiological, motivational, and cognitive effects of aircraft noise on children: Moving from the laboratory to the field. *American Psychologist, 35,* 231-243.

Coronary Drug Project Research Group. (1970). The coronary drug project: Initial findings leading to modification of its research protocol. *Journal of the American Medical Association, 214,* 1303-1313.

Dawber, T. R. (1980). *The Framingham study: The epidemiology of atherosclerotic disease.* Cambridge, MA: Harvard University Press.

Dayton, S., & Pearce, M. L. (1964). Prevention of coronary heart disease and other complications of atherosclerosis by modified diet. *American Journal of Medicine, 46,* 751-762.

Dwyer, J. T., Dietz, W. H., Andrews, E. M., & Suskind, R. M. (1982). Nutritional status of vegetarian children. *American Journal of Clinical Nutrition, 35,* 204-216.

Epstein, S. S., & Swartz, J. B. (1984). Comment on Ames. *Science, 224,* 660-668.

Flay, B. R. (1987). Mass media and smoking cessation: A critical review. *American Journal of Public Health, 77,* 153-160.

Foreyt, J. P., Mitchell, R. E., Garner, D. T., Gee, M., Scott, L. W., & Gotto, A. M. (1982). Behavioral treatment of obesity: Results and limitations. *Behavior Therapy, 13,* 153-161.

Hattis, D., & Kennedy, D. (1986, May-June). Assessing risks from health hazards: An imperfect science. *Technological Review,* pp. 60-81.

Hjermann, I., Byre, K. V., Holme, I., & Leren, P. (1981). Effect of diet and smoking intervention on the incidence of coronary heart disease: Report from the Oslo Study Group of a randomized trial in healthy men. *Lancet, 2,* 1303-1310.

Hypertension Detection and Follow-up Program Cooperative Group. (1979). Five-year findings of the hypertension detection and follow-up program: Reduction in mortality of persons with high blood pressure, including mild hypertension. *Journal of the American Medical Association, 242,* 2562-2571.

Inter-Society Commission for Heart Disease Resources. (1970). Primary prevention of atherosclerotic diseases. *Circulation, 42,* A55-A95.

Jacobs, D. R., Anderson, J. T., & Blackburn, H. (1979). Diet and serum cholesterol: Do zero correlations negate the relationship? *American Journal of Epidemiology, 110,* 77-87.

Jeffery, R. W. (1987). Behavioral treatment of obesity. *Annals of Behavioral Medicine, 9,* 20-24.

Job, D., Eschwege, B., Guyot-Argenton, C., Audry, J. P., & Tchobroutsky, G. (1976). Effect of multiple daily injections on the course of diabetic retinopathy. *Diabetes, 25,* 463-469.

Kaplan, R. M. (1982). Human preference measurement for health decisions and evaluation of long-term care. In R. L. Kane & R. A. Kane (Eds.), *Values in long-term care* (pp. 157-189). Lexington, MA: Heath.

Kaplan, R. M. (1984). The connection between clinical health promotion and health status: A critical review. *American Psychologist, 39,* 755-765.

Kaplan, R. M. (1985a). Behavioral epidemiology, health promotion, and health services. *Medical Care, 23,* 564-583.

Kaplan, R. M. (1985b). Quality-of-life measurement. In P. Karoly (Ed.), *Measurement strategies in health psychology* (pp. 115-146). New York: Wiley-Interscience.

Kaplan, R. M. (1985c). Quantification of health outcomes for policy studies in behavioral epidemiology. In R. M. Kaplan & M. H. Criqui (Eds.), *Behavioral epidemiology and disease prevention* (pp. 29-47). New York: Plenum.

Kaplan, R. M. (1986). Health promotion and coronary heart disease: A rejoinder. *American Psychologist, 41,* 98-99.

Kaplan, R. M. (in press). Health-related quality of life assessment in cardiovascular disease. *Journal of Consulting and Clinical Psychology.*

Kaplan, R. M., & Anderson, J. P. (1987). The quality of well-being scale: Rationale for a single quality of life index. In S. Walker (Ed.), *Quality of life assessment.* London: Ciba Geigy.

Kaplan, R. M., & Atkins, C. J. (1985). Behavioral management of type II diabetes mellitus. In R. M. Kaplan & M. H. Criqui (Eds.), *Behavioral epidemiology and disease prevention.* New York: Plenum.

Kaplan, R. M., Atkins, C. J., & Timms, R. M. (1984). Validity of a quality of well-being scale as an outcome measure in chronic obstructive pulmonary disease. *Journal of Chronic Diseases, 37,* 85-95.

Kaplan, R. M., & Bush, J. W. (1982). Health-related quality of life measurement for evaluation research and policy analysis. *Health Psychology, 1,* 61-80.

Kaplan, R. M., Bush, J. W., & Berry, C. C. (1976). Health status: Types of validity for an index of well-being. *Health Services Research, 11,* 478-507.

Kaplan, R. M., Bush, J. W., & Berry, C. C. (1978). The reliability, stability, and generalizability of a health status index. *American Statistical Association, Proceedings of the Social Statistics Section,* 704-709.

Kaplan, R. M., Bush, J. W., & Berry, C. C. (1979). Health status index: Category rating versus magnitude estimation for measuring levels of well-being. *Medical Care, 17,* 501-525.

Kaplan, R. M., Reis, A., & Atkins, C. J. (1985). Behavioral management of chronic obstructive pulmonary disease. *Annals of Behavioral Medicine, 7,* 5-10.

Keys, A., & Anderson, J. T. (1955). *The relationship of diet to the development of atherosclerosis in man* (National Research Council Publication No. 388, pp. 181-196). Washington, DC: National Academy of Sciences.

Killen, J. D. (1985). Prevention of adolescent tobacco smoking: The social pressure resistance training approach. *Journal of Child Psychology and Psychiatry, 26,* 7-15.

Kolata, G. (1984). Lowered cholesterol decreases heart disease. *Science, 223,* 381-382.

Kondo, D., Takahashi, E., Kato, A., Takahashi, S., & Ikeda, M. (1978). Secular trends in height and weight of Japanese peoples. *Tohoku Journal of Experimental Medicine, 26,* 203-213.

Koplan, J. P., Powell, K. E., Sikes, R. K., Shirley, R. W., & Campbell, C. C. (1982). An epidemiologic study of the benefits and risks of running. *Journal of the American Medical Association, 248,* 3118-3121.

Leren, P. (1966). The effect of plasma lowering diet in male survivors of myocardial infarction. *Acta Medicine Scandinavia, 46* (Suppl. 466), 1-92.

Lipid Research Clinic's Program. (1984a). The lipid research clinic's coronary primary prevention trial results: I. Reduction in the incidence of coronary heart disease. *Journal of the American Medical Association, 253,* 351-364.

Lipid Research Clinic's Program (1984b). The lipid research clinic's coronary primary prevention trial results: II. The relationship of reduction in incidence of coronary heart disease to cholesterol lowering. *Journal of the American Medical Association, 251,* 365-374.

Luepker, R. V. (1985). Diet and coronary heart disease: The role of lipids and obesity. In R. G. Hutchinson (Ed.), *Coronary prevention* (pp. 91-123). Chicago: Yearbook Medical.

Medical Research Council. (1975). Coronary drug research group: Clofibrate and niacin in coronary heart disease. *Journal of the American Medical Association, 231,* 360-428.

Miettinen, M., Turnpeinen, O., Elosuo, R., Paavilainen, E., & Karvonen, M. J. (1972). Effect of cholesterol lowering diet on mortality from coronary heart disease and other causes: A 12-year clinical trial in men and women. *Lancet, 2,* 835-838.

Morris, J. N., Pollard, R., Everitt, M. G., & Chave, S.P.W. (1980). Vigorous exercise in leisure-time protection against coronary heart disease. *Lancet, 2,* 1207-1210.

Mosteller, F. (1981). Innovation and evaluation. *Science, 211,* 881-886.

Multiple Risk Factors Intervention Trial Research Group. (1982). Multiple risk factors intervention trial. *Journal of the American Medical Association, 248,* 1, 1465-1477.

National Center for Health Statistics. (1983). *Health and prevention profile, United States, 1983* (HHS Publication, PHS 84-1232). Washington, DC: U.S. Government Printing Office.

National Institutes of Health. (1979). *Epidemiology of respiratory diseases: Task force report on state of knowledge, problems, needs* (NIH Publication No. 81-2019). Washington, DC: U.S. Government Printing Office.

Nicholl, J. P., & Williams, B. T. (1983). Injuries sustained by runners during a popular marathon. *British Journal of Sports Medicine, 17,* 10-15.

Paffenbarger, R. S., & Hale, W. E. (1975). Work activity and coronary heart mortality. *New England Journal of Medicine, 292,* 545-550.

Paffenbarger, R. S., Hyde, R. T., Wing, A. L., & Hirsh, C. (1986). Physical activity, all-cause mortality and longevity of college alumni. *New England Journal of Medicine, 314,* 605-613.

Paffenbarger, R. S., Wing, A. L., Hyde, R. T., & Jung, D. L. (1983). Physical activity and incidence of hypertension in college alumni. *American Journal of Epidemiology, 117,* 245-256.

Pugliese, M. T., Lifshitz, F., Grad, G., Fort, P., & Marks-Katz, M. (1983). Fear of obesity: A cause of short stature and delayed puberty. *New England Journal of Medicine, 309,* 513-518.

Pugliese, M. T., Weyman-Daum, M., Moses, N., & Lifshitz, F. (1987). Parental health beliefs as a cause of non-organic failure to thrive. *Pediatrics, 80,* 175-182.

Rahimtoola, S. H. (1985). Cholesterol and coronary heart disease: A perspective. *Journal of the American Medical Association, 253,* 2094-2095.

Ravenholt, R. T. (1985). Tobacco's impact on 20th century U.S. mortality patterns. *American Journal of Preventive Medicine, 1,* 4-17.

Royal College of Physicians. (1983). Symposium: Exercise, health, and medicine. *Lancet, 1,* 1171.

Russell, L. B. (1986). *Is prevention better than cure?* Washington, DC: Brookings Institution.

Schwartz, A. L. (1987). *Review and evaluation of smoking cessation methods: The United States and Canada 1978-1985* (NIH Publication No. 87-2940). Washington, DC: U.S. Department of Health and Human Services, National Cancer Institution.

Siscovick, D. S., Weiss, N. S., Fletcher, R. H., & Lasky, T. (1984). The incidence of primary cardiac arrest during vigorous exercise. *New England Journal of Medicine, 311,* 874-877.

Sleet, D. A. (1987). Murder vehicle trauma and safety belt use in the context of public health priorities. *Journal of Trauma, 27,* 695-702.

Stallones, R. A. (1983). Ischemic heart disease and lipids in blood and diet. *Annual Review of Nutrition, 3,* 155-185.

Stamler, J., Wentworth, D., & Neaton, J. D. (1986). Is the relationship between serum cholesterol and risk of premature death from coronary heart disease continuous and graded? *Journal of the American Medical Association, 256,* 2823-2828.

Steinberg, D. (1979). Metabolism of lipoprotein at the cellular level in relation to atherogenesis. In N. E. Miller & B. Lewis (Eds.), *Lipoproteins, atherosclerosis and coronary heart disease* (pp. 31-48). Amsterdam: Elsevier.

Stewart, A. L., Ware, J. E., Brook, R. H., & Davies-Avery, A. (1978). *Conceptualization and measurement of health for adults: Vol. 2. Physical health in terms of functioning.* Santa Monica, CA: Rand Corporation.

Sullivan, D. F. (1966). *Conceptual problems in developing an index of health.* Washington, DC: National Center for Health Statistics.

Taylor, W. C., Pass, T. M., Shepard, D. S., & Komaroff, A. L. (1987). Cholesterol reduction in life expectancy: A model incorporating multiple risk factors. *Annuals of Internal Medicine, 106,* 605-614.

Tchobroutsky, G. (1978). Relation of diabetic control to development of microvascular complications. *Diabetologia, 15,* 143-152.

Torrance, G. W. (1976). Toward a utility theory foundation for health status index models. *Health Services Research, 11,* 439-469.

U.S. Department of Health, Education, Welfare. (1979). *Smoking and health: A report of the Surgeon General* (DHEW Publication No. (PHS)79-50066). Washington, DC: U.S. Government Printing Office.

Van Camp, S. P., & Peterson, R. A. (1986). Cardiovascular complications of outpatient cardiac rehabilitation programs. *Journal of the American Medical Association, 256,* 1160-1163.

Weinstein, N. C., & Stason, W. B. (1976). *Hypertension: A policy perspective.* Cambridge, MA: Harvard University Press.

Willett, W. C., & MacMahon, B. (1984). Diet and cancer: An overview. *New England Journal of Medicine, 310,* 697.

Wolfgang, M. (1958). *Patterns in criminal homicide.* Philadelphia: University of Pennsylvania Press.

Author Index

Subject Index

About the Authors

PAUL R. CHEEK graduated from Lewis and Clark College and pursued graduate work at Claremont Graduate School. His research interests include attributional models of health-related behaviors and models of helping and coping in relation to social and health psychology. He is currently designing computer graphics for a variety of art forms including silk-screening, video character generation and animation, and wall art.

SHELDON COHEN received his Ph.D. from New York University in 1973. He was on the faculty of the University of Oregon for nine years and has been Professor of Psychology at Carnegie-Mellon University since 1982. His recent books include *Behavior, Health, and Environmental Stress* (1986, with several coauthors) and *Social Support and Health* (1985, with S. L. Syme). He is currently investigating the roles of psychosocial factors in smoking cessation and relapse and in susceptibility to infectious diseases.

GAYLE A. DAKOF received her Ph.D. in psychology from the University of California, Berkeley, and is an American Cancer Society Post-Doctoral Fellow at UCLA. Her primary research interest is in individual and family adaptation to family disease.

MELODY A. GRAHAM is a doctoral student in applied social psychology at Claremont Graduate School, having received an M.A. degree from Claremont in 1986. She is conducting research in the field of health psychology on coping with stressful life events, and she recently published an article in the *American Journal of Obstetrics and Gynecology* on psychological factors affecting coping with fetal death.

ROBERT M. KAPLAN is Professor of Psychology and Director of the Center for Behavioral Medicine at San Diego State University, as well as

Professor of Community and Family Medicine at the University of California, San Diego. He received his Ph.D. from the University of California, Riverside, and he has also taught there, as well as for NATO, the National Center for Health Statistics, and the Public Health Service. In addition to being a principal investigator on more than 20 health-related research projects, he has published over 100 articles and books related to applied psychology.

NATHAN MACCOBY took his B.A., M.A., and Ph.D. degrees from Reed College, the University of Washington, and the University of Michigan, respectively. In World War II he was a communication psychologist in the U.S. Army, and later taught communications and chaired the Psychology Department at Boston University. In 1958, he moved to the Communication Department at Stanford University, where he has served as chairman, Director of the Institute of Communication Research, and most recently Associate Director of the Stanford Center for Research in Disease Prevention. He is a past president of the International Communication Association and has published over 50 articles on attitude change, communication, and health psychology.

STUART OSKAMP is Professor of Psychology at Claremont Graduate School. He received his Ph.D. from Stanford University and has had visiting appointments at the University of Michigan, University of Bristol, London School of Economics and Political Science, and University of New South Wales. His main research interests are in the areas of attitudes and attitude change, behavioral aspects of energy and resource conservation, and social issues and public policy. His books include *Attitudes and Opinions* and *Applied Social Psychology*. He is a past president of the APA Division of Population and Environmental Psychology and is editor of the *Journal of Social Issues*.

SHIRLYNN SPACAPAN is Assistant Professor of Psychology at Harvey Mudd College, one of the Claremont Colleges. She received her Ph.D. from the University of Oregon in 1982, where she taught for two years before moving to Claremont. Her research has focused on both environmental stressors and organizational turnover. She is currently studying topics at the interface of environmental psychology and organizational behavior, such as perceived control in the workplace and workplace design.

SHELLEY E. TAYLOR received her Ph.D. in social psychology from Yale University. She is Professor of Psychology at UCLA and codirector of the Health Psychology program there. Her research interests include social cognition and adjustment to victimizing circumstances such as chronic disease. She is author of *Health Psychology* and *Social Cognition* (with S. T. Fiske) and has published over 100 papers on health, social cognition, social support, and related topics.

JAMES R. TERBORG is Professor of Management and Head of the Department of Management at the University of Oregon. He received his Ph.D. in organizational psychology from Purdue University in 1975, subsequently taught in the psychology department at the University of Illinois and the University of Houston, and has been a Visiting Research Scientist at Oregon Research Institute. He is a Fellow in APA Division 14 and chairs the Organizational Behavior Division in the Academy of Management. He has published many articles in leading psychology and management journals, serves on the editorial boards of several journals, and is a frequent contributor to edited books.

SUZANNE C. THOMPSON earned her Ph.D. in psychology from UCLA and is an Assistant Professor of Psychology at Pomona College and at Claremont Graduate School. Her publications include articles on the effects of perceived control, coping with stressful life experiences, the role of meaning in the adjustment process, and attributions for negative events. She is currently studying adjustment among stroke patients and their families, and investigating ways to increase patient question-asking in physician office visits.

GAIL M. WILLIAMSON is a graduate student in the Ph.D. program in Social/Health Psychology at Carnegie-Mellon University, having received her M.S. in 1986. Her research interests center on examining the determinants of stress among providers of social support. She is currently examining the effects of providing aid in communal and exchange relationships on the helper's affective and transient self-evaluative responses.

NOTES

NOTES

NOTES

NOTES

NOTES